OWEN PRODUCTIONS

1 August 77

Bob Merlis
Warner Bros. Records
3300 Warner Blvd.
Burbank, Calf. 91510

Dear Bob,

    Enclosed please find all the available information I have on Prince at this time. I'll send you more as it accumulates. Call me if you have any ideas. When referring to Prince in any correspondence please use the name "Prince" only. Don't refer to him as "Prince Nelson", "Prince Rogers Nelson" or "The Prince". Looking forward to working with you.

Sincerely,

Owen R. Husney

P.S. Please address further correspondence to American Artists, 430 Oak Grove, Suite 110, Mpls., Mn. 55403. Thank you.

Loring Park Office Bldg. • 430 Oak Grove • Minneapolis, Minnesota 55403 • 612/871-6200

FAMOUS PEOPLE WHO'VE MET ME

FAMOUS PEOPLE WHO'VE MET ME

by Owen Husney

"The Man Who Discovered Prince"

ROTHCO PRESS • LOS ANGELES, CALIFORNIA

Published by
ROTHCO PRESS
8033 West Sunset Blvd., Suite 1022
Los Angeles, CA 90046

COVER DESIGN: NICOLE GINELLI
COVER CONCEPT: EVAN HUSNEY

Rothco Press is a division of Over Easy Media Inc.

Trade Paperback ISBN: 978-1-945436-20-8

FOR:

Lauren Schneider

Jordan and Evan

Irving and Georgette

Norton

Lauren Siegel

Thank You

Chris Moon — for your foresight and persistence

Shirley Rivkin — for being my "other mother" and giving the world:
David "Z" Rivkin
Stephen Rivkin
Bobby "Z" Rivkin

Britt — for being the "away from home mother" to Prince and Andre and turning Prince on to Joni Mitchell

Peter Himmelman — for being the original BIG MUSE

Rob and Christine for your encouragement and telling me: "It's ready when it's ready."

John Skipp — for putting my book in order and jamming to "Spoonful of Love" while doing it

Fred Rubin — for pointing out my run-on sentences and teaching me how one word can change the flavor of an entire chapter

All the people, famous and otherwise, who've met me

Special thank you to my wife, Lauren Schneider, for your unending encouragement, spell checks, and grammar suggestions — and especially for minimal complaints at seeing the back of my head for over three years as I typed away. This is your book too.

Kitcat: (1999-2017) my daytime companion and creative muse (mews)

Thank you to Prince for being the most intelligent, creative, and compelling person I have ever allowed into my life.

I've relied on memory for what I've written going back sixty plus years. In a few instances I've combined events for expediency. What you are about to read is 98% true. If I've made an error, and you are in the 2%, please notify me immediately. I'll make the correction in the next printing. I've changed a few names to protect the guilty.

Introduction

I was sitting near the front row of Prince and The Revolution's first public performance in the fall of 1979, at the Capri Theater in North Minneapolis. I was 17, an up and coming musician, and in my estimation, a pretty damn good one. While I thought I was getting some altitude with my own music career — flying, maybe, twenty or thirty feet straight into the air, what I saw that night was Prince, ascending twenty or thirty thousand feet — and then some. I had been schooled... no, make that humbled, by his astounding musicianship.

That was the second time I'd seen Prince perform. The first time, I was playing rhythm guitar with Alexander O'Neal & The Black Market Band, which featured R&B great, Alexander O'Neal on vocals. We were the ostensible "headliners" at legendary KMOJ DJ, Pharaoh Black's, Soul To Sunday New Years Eve Party at the Holiday Inn, in downtown Minneapolis. In fact, however, The Black Market Band was only last on the bill. Unfortunately for us, (and only a music-biz insider would know this) when you go on stage last, at say, 2:00 AM on New Year's Eve, when nearly every person has left the venue, you're not headlining any show at all. The band that goes on just before the stroke of midnight is the real headliner. That night, that coveted position belonged to Champagne, a local band featuring none other than the kings of the North side: Morris Day, Andre Simone, and this little dude with a huge afro who called himself Prince.

I watched these guys with a mix of awe and envy. Andre Cymone had a device at his feet called a Mutron Funk Box that made his bass sound as if each note were being processed through some insanely good Wah-Wah pedal. His playing had a degree of finesses and rhythmic sophistication that I could only marvel at. Morris Day was kickin' it on the drums; tight, crisp, unlike anything I'd ever heard live. Soon Alexander O'Neal was motioning to me, pointing towards Prince. "You see how he's choppin out that rhythm with his right hand? You see the way his rhythm don't stop? His name is Prince. They say he's got a record deal on Warner Brothers."

Warner Bothers? Record deal? Hold up! This was Minneapolis, not New York or LA. This was the sticks, the prairie —the frozen boondocks for god's sake. Who'd ever even dreamed of scoring a major recording deal from outta this place? Well, a guy named Owen Husney did. Soon, I started hearing his name all around Minneapolis. People didn't dare speak it too loud; Husney was a name uttered in hushed, reverential tones: "Look. Over there! That's Owen Husney. He's the one that went out to LA and got Prince a massive recording deal!"

Two years out of high school, Sussman Lawrence, the new wave rock band I'd formed with four of my friends, won first place in a contest sponsored by KQRS, Minneapolis's classic rock station. The prize was the opportunity to record one of our songs at Owen's, American Artists Studios. I spotted him there, coming out of the bathroom and heading for the coffee machine. I was rarely at a loss for words, but there was so much mystery (at least in my mind) surrounding Owen I was completely tongue-tied.

Owen is, in some sense, even more of a mystery today than he was back then. But it's a different kind of mystery, a more potent, more spiritual sort than you'd expect from someone who'd accomplished so much in the often, callous (and sometimes depraved) business of music. Owen's great gift, as you'll soon read in these pages, is his unfettered ability to love. He loves people first and foremost; he loves nurturing them, loves seeing their dreams grow to fruition. He is at heart a teacher —a first rate facilitator who spots possibilities that others fail to see. But don't get me wrong; he's no monk. He has at times, throughout his long career, been exceedingly, if not ruthlessly, tenacious in his pursuit of those possibilities; and he's not a bit shy about depicting that tenacity with self-effacing humor and great élan in the stories you're about to encounter.

I ascribe at least some of Owen's tenacity to his Syrian, Sephardic Jewish ancestry. His father is Syrian, a dyed-in-the-wool Aleppine; his grandfather, Eli Husney, the patriarch of the Husney clan, was a noted Rabbi and scholar. The Syrian Jews are well known in the diaspora, and in particular, the American diaspora, for being stubbornly attached to their cultural roots, whether it's their food, their language, or their spiritual values. There is, within that ancient community, a strong sense that they are carrying something of great value through time and space. Owen's anecdotes all seem to pulse with that same urgency.

Whether you're a baby boomer, a gen-xer, or a millennial, prepare to laugh your ass off as you get a true insider's perspective on the sheer insanity of the music business. You will learn much from this mysterious, tenacious, raconteur —just as I have. Perhaps most of all, you'll learn that dreams are best achieved when the desire to make them real is commensurate with the nerve it takes to make them so. And let me tell you, Owen Husney rarely fails on either count.

—*Peter Himmelman, Minneapolis, Minnesota. January 2018*

Aunt Frances

In the winter of 1953, my Aunt Frances took an extended vacation to Los Angeles. She stepped inside a booth at a five & dime, put a quarter in the slot, and made a 78-rpm acetate recording.

A week later the little souvenir recording arrived in the mail at our house in Minneapolis. My mother, sister and I stood silent as my father yanked open the phonograph side of our Admiral Combo TV. He placed the tone arm, with its crude metal stylus down on the stiff rotating disk. The tiny grilled speaker initially offered only hisses and pops. Then, over the din, we heard someone clear their throat and a familiar voice came to life, "Hi everybody. It's Aunt Frances from California! Today, we took a bus to the ocean in Santa Monica. Uncle Julius carried a picnic basket and we dined on fresh fruit and sandwiches as we listened to the waves and watched sailboats on the horizon. Right now we're in Hollywood, and the sky is so clear and blue that I can see a snow-capped mountain in the distance. Everyone's front yard has orange and grapefruit trees, and people are wearing shorts in January! Time's up, gotta go, see you in a few weeks. Love, Aunt Frances."

I was just six years old when that window to the world showed up at my doorstep. I played it over and over, though each time the hisses and pops grew louder. But that weak recording had a profound influence on my life. First, was the recognition that somewhere there was a warm alternative to winter's cold and ice. Second, was that sound recordings could be made in an instant, shipped cross-country, and affect people's lives — not just once, but again and again.

I never got the chance to say this, so I'll say it now: Thank you Aunt Frances.

Prologue

J anis Joplin sat alone in a dim makeshift dressing room on the second floor of the old Minneapolis Armory. Shards of glass were splayed everywhere; across the floor, into her wardrobe case, and deep within the spread of food I prepared for her.

"I'm so sorry Janis." I said, stunned and embarrassed.

"It's okay Owen, I've witnessed much worse. Ya ever been to the Fillmore?"

It was hard to imagine anything worse. Kids, hoping to gain free admittance to the show scaled the wall of the old Armory and broke into her dressing room by smashing the window and climbing in.

The Armory was a bad decision from the start. My client, Howard Stein, was intent on locating an alternative to the expensive Metropolitan Sports Center and Minneapolis Auditorium. I suggested the dormant Minneapolis Armory. It had been shuttered for years. The city agreed to rent it to us but in the long run it proved to be a cesspool of a venue.

Janis was gracious, accepted my apology, and even offered a quick smile. But I was taken aback by her looks. In person she was squat and frumpy, and the long greasy hair that streamed down her face did little to cover what I assumed to be pockmarks.

"Thank you, Janis. I'm sending up some fresh drinks and food, and someone is on the way to clean up this fucking mess. You go on in forty-five minutes. I'm so sorry."

I returned to the stage to check out the progress of the set up when her road manager approached me.

"Janis was quite impressed with you."

"That's great, I'm so sorry about what happened."

"Well, she asked if you'd like to meet up with her in her room tonight."

I knew what that meant and I had no interest — so I lied.

"My fiancé will be at the show. She'll be expecting me to go home with her tonight. Please let Janis know."

Janis took the stage, larger than life, and gave one of the most intense and brilliant performances I'd ever witnessed. Once on stage she was transformed. She worked the stage from side to side belting out her hits with a vocal range of pure soul. And she was so fucking sexy as she threw her whole body, hips and breasts, into the performance. I was standing on the side of the stage and could not take my eyes off of her. I not only wanted Janis, I needed her. After the show I ran up to the road manager and asked for her.

"I'm sorry man. She went back to her hotel room with someone from the crew."

* * * *

I was charged with organizing the security force, planning the backstage food, and all logistics for the Rolling Stones' appearance at Minneapolis's Met Center in 1972. The event, featuring Stevie Wonder as the opening act, was so monumental that I wound up on the front page of the *Minneapolis Star/Tribune* for being the local dude-in-charge. Strict adherence to the group's equipment rider was a must. One of the items on the list was downright impossible. It called for a new Steinway grand piano to be provided at the promoter's expense. The grand piano was to be used by legendary keyboardist, Nicky Hopkins, who played with the Stones on many of their recording sessions.

The piano was such a large expense that renting it was the only option. But no one in Minneapolis would rent it to a bunch of musician hippies no matter how internationally known they were. In desperation I phoned Schmitt Music in downtown Minneapolis. "Are you crazy?" Came the salesman's response. "You could buy three Cadillac's for what that piano is worth. Why would we rent it to you? One tiny scratch and the instrument is worthless!" "Because you can't buy that kind of publicity!" I shot back with authority. "You'll dwarf the competition by being associated with the Stones. I'll even get some pictures for your walls. This is historic — you'll be a hero!" The salesman talked to his boss and they agreed to rent it to us for one night providing they personally drop it off at sound check and pick it up immediately after the show. "You've got a deal." Backstage before the show, Mick thanked me directly for doing the impossible and making the piano happen. "Most blokes can't even get the food right let alone a Steinway grand," he said. I was beaming.

After the show I went upstairs to help settle the box office and went home. The next morning my phone rang at 6 A.M. "You little asshole, you ruined me!" Shocked, I stayed silent. "I was fired this morning." He screamed. "What happened?" "Well, I guess the stage was a little too wobbly for your motherfucking Stones so they sawed off the legs about a quarter of the way up to make the piano stable. Now, the piano is useless and I'm out of a job." With that he hung up and I never heard from him again. To be honest, I never even knew his name.

* * * *

Sly Stone was the greatest of 'em all. Almost singlehandedly he forged and changed the nature of pop and R&B music with his group, The Family Stone. A true genius, Sly combined elements of each genre into a new art form by changing the rules, breaking the color barrier, and giving us some of the biggest hits of the period. But showing up for concerts and being on time was not one of his strong suits.

Dick Shapiro and I were now the go-to guys for all concert promoters who brought shows into the five-state Midwest area. Almost every promoter used our services for security, backstage food, advertising, and hotel arrangements. One of those concerts was Sly and the Family Stone in Milwaukee, Wisconsin. But Sly was a no-show at the last minute, leaving the promoter with major losses. Fearing a major lawsuit, his booking agency scheduled a makeup date in Minneapolis at the Met Sports Center for a reduced price.

The night of the show we sat with our fingers crossed waiting for Sly to arrive at the venue. The clock ticked on past the start time. The sold out audience grew anxious after an hour of waiting and began stomping their feet and chanting, "Sly, Sly, Sly!" Then they started to scream, "We want our money back!" This was going to be a shit storm of huge proportions. Then, it was decided that I would go out and announce to the audience that Sly was delayed at the airport and that he was on his way. A howl of approval went up from the audience. But I was lying my ass off. As I stepped off stage a man approached me and pulled out a gun. "If he doesn't show things are going to get fucked up — get it!" "But I'm just the MC," I said, thinking quickly. "I'll get the promoter." I ran backstage like a scared bunny in a forest fire. Just then, someone shouted, "He's here!" I ran back to Sly's dressing room, but on the way I noticed something odd. Sly had instructed the limo driver to drive him to his dressing room! The limo was literally driving down the hallways of the Met Center!

When the driver dropped Sly at his dressing room I read him the riot act. "You almost got me killed. Get your ass on stage!" My idol only smirked at me as his band members climbed on stage to a huge cheer from the audience. Sly sauntered on to the stage and took his place as the crowd went wild. His first song was the hit, "Thank You (Falettinme Be Mice Elf Agin)." But this time, as I stood on the side of the stage, Sly stared directly at me and started singing, "*Fuck* You (Falettinme Be Mice Elf Agin)."

* * * *

When Joe Cocker played the Met Sports Center the food rider expressly requested a case of Dom Perignon champagne — properly chilled, and placed in Mr. Cocker's dressing room out of view. At that time, a bottle of Dom Perignon was one of the most expensive champagnes in the world.

Backstage, Joe thanked me profusely for adhering to the food rider and gave me a bottle of the champagne as a thank you (I still have that bottle to this day; undrinkable, but a prized souvenir). His road manager then asked if I'd like to be the MC for the evening and introduce the opening act, Dr. Hook and the Medicine show, as well as Joe Cocker. I jumped at the opportunity to walk out in front of fifteen thousand people and get them riled up. Dr. Hook had a huge hit at the time with, "Cover of the Rolling Stone," and Joe Cocker's career was on fire. I walked out on stage and screamed, "Are you ready to rock and roll!" The audience responded with a deafening, YES! I felt the power. "Ladies and gentlemen, directly from the cover of the Rolling Stone, Dr. Hook and the Medicine show!" The crowd roared as Dr. Hook took the stage. After one song, Dr. Hook, said, "What do you want to hear?" Fifteen thousand people roared back in unison: "JOE COCKER!!"

* * * *

The Labor Temple was the Minneapolis equivalent of Bill Graham's Fillmore West in San Francisco. Built in the early twenties, it was the perfect hippie heaven, complete with a light show and tons of illicit drugs. Almost every psychedelic act that played the Fillmore also played the Labor Temple. Dave Wachter, promoted most of the legendary shows there and was a well known fixture in town. How Dick Shapiro and I muscled our way in to promoting at the old wooden concert hall escapes me. I think we bought off the manager.

Johnny Winter was one of the first acts we booked. I was charged with driving Johnny around and getting him to the hotel. Rick Derringer was playing with him at the time. As a guitar player I was a big fan of Rick's going back to his days with The McCoys and their hit, "Hang on Sloopy." And I idolized Johnny.

We hung out in their hotel room and later on I drove them to the gig. Backstage, someone was passing around a joint. I took a hit and proceeded to stage right in case anyone needed me. Once

I was in position I realized that the pot I just smoked was by far the most potent shit I'd *ever* had. Not knowing if I was going to pass out, I spread my legs to try to stabilize myself. *In my stupor* I was oblivious to the fact that the electrical had failed on Johnny's side of the stage and his amp was out. Johnny was trying to get my attention, but I was concentrating on staying upright.

While the rest of the band played on I didn't notice Johnny coming up behind me. Hearing someone scream I turned towards the direction of the noise. "Fuuuuccccckkkkkk!!" He screamed at the top of his well-trained lungs an inch from my face. "THE FUCKING POWER IS OUT!!" It's well known that Johnny was born with Albinism, the complete lack of any pigmentation that normally gives color to skin, hair, or eyes. What I saw was a stone white face, white eyebrows, white disheveled hair and beady bright red eyes contorted in devil anger. I fell to the ground. People said I was in a fetal position when they revived me.

* * * *

Prince and I returned to our home in the Hollywood Hills from the Guitar Center down on Sunset Boulevard. He had taken a rare break from mixing his first album. I'm sure Prince would have been content to work endlessly but the recording engineer demanded a break. After all, it was Sunday, and they had been working for two weeks straight. So did Prince want to go to the ocean and relax in the sun, or shop on Melrose? No. He wanted to checkout the latest instruments at Guitar Center.

When we returned, my wife Britt was vacuuming in the living room. We were telling her about our day when Prince let out a huge gasp. "Oh, no! You just vacuumed up my new ring! I dropped it and the vacuum cleaner sucked it up!" Everything and everyone stopped cold. Calmly, without hesitation, Britt took out the bag on the vacuum, opened it, and began to carefully sift through its nasty innards'. After a minute or two she let out a blood-curdling scream and ran from the room. Prince kept a straight face as I looked down to see what happened. Sitting atop the mess was a spider — not a small spider, but a hairy one about half the size of my hand with legs the size of my fingers. I was immediately repulsed. By now Prince was laughing hysterically. He reached down and grabbed the thing by one of its legs as I yelled, "Don't! There's poisonous spiders in California!" It was then that I realized it was rubber. Prince had it thrown under the vacuum while we were all talking. The vacuum sucked it up, no problem. Prince and I laughed hysterically. Britt didn't speak to us for two days.

* * * *

So how did a self-ascribed nerd like me from St. Louis Park Minnesota with no experience wind up in the middle of some of the biggest deals in Rock and Roll History? It was easy — I lied my way in. I was too poor growing up to buy concert tickets so I devised a plan to bring the shows and artists to me. And providing food services backstage and in dressing rooms when the big acts came through town was the easiest way. I simply told the major concert promoters that I had a company — and they believed me — though I had no company, and no experience. No one ever got hurt because I over-promised *and* over-delivered. The real bonus was being in dressing rooms and listening to managers and artists discussing their lives and solving problems. That proved to be my college when years later I would become an artist manager.

Before I became an artist manager I was a musician on tour with a large regional hit record, a booking agent, a concert producer and promoter, a marketing man on the road with Sonny & Cher, the Rolling Stones, Alice Cooper, and the Oscar-winning actor and singer Richard Harris (hit record, "McArthur Park"). I hung out with The Who, Janis Joplin, Sly and The Family Stone, Grand Funk Railroad, Jimi Hendrix, Chuck Berry, Johnny Winter, Elvis Presley, and Stevie Nicks to name a few. Simultaneously, I formed an entertainment Ad agency and created ads for the likes of Warner Bros Records and Doubleday's top 40 radio stations across the country.

Seneca, a first-century Roman philosopher said, "Luck is preparation meeting opportunity." All my prior experiences served as preparation for that day in in the fall of 1976 when opportunity walked through my door. My instincts knew how to get Prince from point A to point B. But my business sense came from watching some of entertainment's biggest names and wackiest characters in action. Those experiences taught me how to fight for an artist, how to promote an artist, and how to do it with class. In the early days, Prince gained incalculably from my instincts and experience. After that, his light-speed genius took over and he became a music icon. Prince taught me that my early instincts about him, when no one knew or cared, were correct.

Post Prince, I continued to manage artists, earning additional gold and platinum records. I was appointed to a board by the Governor of the State of Minnesota and charged with building a Performing Arts high school in the state. My career took a turn into the corporate world as COO/General Manager of K-tel Records, International, and Sr. VP of the mega music retail chain Musicland/Sam Goody.

Today, living in Los Angeles, I buy, sell, and broker hit artist's intellectual property — Masters and Publishing — and have brokered the sale some of the biggest hits in pop history. I also teach "The Business of Music" at UCLA Extension in Los Angeles.

I'm on the seventh reinvention of my music life. Over the span of fifty years the giant wheel of life's fortune spins, stops, and I get out on a new journey. From my earliest days, my reincarnations have put me in grand rooms and uncertain situations with the very legends that invented and shaped pop and rock music. Almost every experience I lived through has a story that needs to be told. My crazy, passion-driven up and down adventures have taken me from a 900 sq. ft. childhood home in frigid Minneapolis Minnesota, to living in homes in the Hollywood Hills. Since I was 12 years old I have always lived my passion, fought for what I wanted to be, and nothing else — for better or worse. Dark, scary, and hilarious, there is also much to be learned from my life experiences.

Bringing you into these stories from my life is my eighth reinvention.

Can't wait for the ninth. Spin the wheel.

When I began writing this book I tried to remember the very first experience that put me on track to a career in music. And I remembered it all too well. It wasn't a Roy Rogers toy guitar from my parents as a Hanukah present; it began with a tragic plane crash in the summer of 1956.

The Summer of 1956

A Restless Wind — My Gogi Grant Story

The evening wind drove the acrid smell of burning homes and jet fuel through the rolled down crack in the car window. I held my hands over my nose and mouth but there was no escaping the terrifying stench. Through the windshield I spotted an orange hue, no doubt fueled by an inferno of innocent souls. It danced skyward and fanned out through the nighttime sky. In the distance, I heard the constant din of sirens from ambulances, fire trucks, and police cars as they raced back and forth from the crash site. I prayed it just was a child's nightmare — that I would wake, and cry out for my mother who would then dash into my room and hold me — but I was wide-awake and alone — in the front seat of my father's car. This was no place for an eight-year-old kid.

The day started out like any other Minnesota August day: the sun — too bright, the temperature too hot, and the morning air already thick with moisture. By late morning, the news bulletins started coming in — A Navy Jet taking off from the old Wold-Chamberlin airfield in Minneapolis had left military formation to make an emergency landing. Instead, it hit the street in front of 5808 Forty-sixth Ave South exploding into six homes and setting an entire neighborhood ablaze. The evening paper reported that twenty or more children were at play in the neighborhood when the plane crashed. They were littered with debris and flaming fuel. A child's body was found on a couch in her home. Alongside the couch was the landing gear of the plane.

By dinnertime everyone in the Twin Cities was glued to their radios, buzzing with neighbors on phone lines, or watching it live on new-fangled TVs. For the first time, every horrific detail of carnage was now brought directly into the home — courtesy of Camel Cigarettes. "Did you hear the news?" my father said as he bounded in the door from work. "Get the TV on quick! I've been listening to it in the car. Who needs radio?"

But I had been tethered to the TV set since noon. The scorched and smoldering homes, the debris, and officials and neighbors being interviewed tugged hard on me. Looking back on it now I see that I had identified deeply with those children. It wasn't just some "adult" accident like a car crash; this could have been my buddies and me. "It's just horrible." My mother said, barely holding back tears. "I just keep thinking about those innocent children and what happened to them — they were just playing outdoors." "And just fifteen minutes away from our house!" My sister added. And then and there the family agreed; we would drive to the crash site after dinner to see for ourselves. "Who needs television?" my father bellowed as we headed for the car.

As night fell our spirits soared with the excitement of adventure as we piled into our brand new '56 turquoise and white Oldsmobile. It's a wonder we didn't break out into camp songs as we rolled along to the site.

As we approached, I could see why the children playing outdoors were so badly hurt or killed. The neighborhood was a working class community filled with post-war cracker-box houses, all squeezed together. For sure, the dense population of baby-boomer kids would all be playing outdoors that warm morning. It could have been my neighborhood. It could have been my friends. It could have been ME! In an instant my excitement and curiosity turned to fear — and I understood what Mrs. Hopkins meant.

My 3rd grade teacher, Mrs. Hopkins taught us how a bear in the wild deals with danger. When it senses a strange sound or a smell an instinctual feeling in its gut takes hold. Rising up, it surveys the landscape and sniffs the air. After fully observing its environment the bear makes a fear-based decision: fight or flight. I asked Mr. Bear what to do and he screamed, "Run away Owen!"

As we drove into the crash site there were emergency vehicles stationed on every corner — hundreds of red lights flashing and blinking in and out of sequence as far as the eye could see. A policeman directing traffic noticed me in the back seat — our eyes briefly locked. As our car drove by he stared blankly, arms waving — I could sense his grief as the red lights reflected in his face. In the distance, I could make out the smoldering tops of scorched and burned out homes — while the smell of charred remains and jet fuel drifted in through the open car windows. My hands grew clammy and the sick feeling in my stomach spread throughout my body.

By now, hundreds, if not thousands of people were scrambling to the site to view the tragedy of others. They had abandoned their cars wily-nilly and were walking to the debris area like zombies. They jammed streets, alleys and lawns.

My dad hurriedly parked our car in someone's driveway about a block from the crash site. When we got out to walk closer I refused to go. Help me Mr. Bear! Through my tears and panic I begged them not to go. What was there to be gained from staring at carnage? A short powwow of elders was held and it was decided that if I did not want to go I would have to stay in the car — windows up, locks down — it was my decision. They would be gone just a minute and quickly return. I checked in with Mr. Bear and he said, "Stay in the fucking car."

I watched as my family vanished into the burning mist. Alone in the front seat my young mind filled with irrational thoughts. What if another plane crashed into our car? What would happen to me if my parents and sister never returned? What if the ghosts of the dead children banged on the car window and begged me to come out and play? Paralyzed with fear I closed my eyes, sank down in the vinyl seat, and began to cry. What to do?

Tears streaming down my face I fiddled with the car radio. To my chagrin it came to life with even more reports of the accident. Frantically pushing the station buttons I landed on a song by Gogi Grant called, "The Wayward Wind." My virgin musical ears picked up on the song's eerie blend of vocals and strings, heightened by a haunting French Horn, and fueled by a ghostly western melody. Now, married with the burning visual, the song became the soundtrack for a visceral film that was playing outside my car window. When the song ended the melody and lyrics refused to leave me alone. They continued on in an endless loop, going 'round and 'round in my head. The lingering song spoke directly to me with its restless wind that craved to wander. It left an indelible imprint within my DNA — an imprint that remains to this day.

To be fair, my family kept their word and returned to the car in less than five minutes. The ride home was simple and silent, point B back to point A; no one said a word. And no one noticed, or cared how distraught I was, and that I had been crying. Everyone was in shock. This wasn't radio, this wasn't television, this was real fucking life — and death.

I often wondered if that was the singular moment that defined the rest of my lifetime. To be sure there were many moments but that was that the first time I had decided to really trust my instincts — just like Mr. Bear. It was the moment I had decided that no one would ever again have that kind of control over me, or force into something that didn't feel right to me. I see now I had just entered survival mode and I was beginning to take care of myself.

It would be months before I had worked out the melody, every instrument, and vocal line of that song from my brain so it would finally go away. I didn't understand it yet but that was the musician side of me kicking in. I will never forget that hot, humid evening in the summer of 1956, and how that song; uniquely matching the eeriness of the night inexplicably changed me forever.

Eventually, the evening would teach me that I had to follow my passions and wander, like the restless wind, into a fate of my choosing. However, there was a price to pay as I was soon bestowed with the moniker of "troublemaker." But I loved that in my heart I was really a rebel — defying anything norm.

And that is the absolute power of music.

POSTSCRIPT FULL CIRCLE

Forty years later I was asked to consult Ktel International, the famous Minnesota-based compilation record label. We had just purchased the Era Records master song catalog from its owner, Herb Newman. To my astonishment I learned "The Wayward Wind" was one of the songs sold to us in the transaction. As soon as the delivery truck dropped off the shipment from Los Angeles I ran down to the warehouse and rummaged through the musty tape boxes. And there it was, the tattered box containing the original Master recording of, "The Wayward Wind." Full circle.

We decided to release an Era Records retrospective: "The Wayward Wind: The Best of Gogi Grant." Of course I insisted that I to fly to Los Angeles to interview Gogi for the liner notes. On the table at lunch was the original mono tape master of that very hit record that changed my life, and across the table was a seventy something, petit and brunette Gogi Grant!

As we sipped our wine and ate our salads I passionately told Gogi my story about being alone on that tragic day. I told her about the hot and humid wind, the burning stench, and the smell of jet fuel. I told her about Mr. Bear. I told her that since that faraway evening no one would ever control me or put me in a situation that made me uncomfortable again. I told her that I eventually decided that I would always follow my passion and wander into the life that I wanted — which would be music. And I told her about the successes in my life that began with her hit record, "The Wayward Wind."

Looking away, Gogi took a long beat and returned to study me — I could tell she was struggling for a possible response to an improbable tale. I grew disheartened thinking I had just spilled the beans on a story that should have been left back in 1956. After all, this was a business lunch to honor Gogi with a prized reissued CD of her career. My intent was not to make her nauseous. I shrank back, a little white around the edges. Eyes at half-mast she said, "Owen, for sure that's the creepiest thing

I've ever heard; but because of how it impacted you as a lonely and vulnerable child it expresses the sheer power and emotion that only music can deliver. And that makes it a precious story. I will never forget this lunch." We hugged, said our goodbyes, and I watched my dark past walk out of the restaurant.

School

PART I: SCHOOL BAND

In seventh grade they made everyone play a musical instrument. I chose the clarinet. Flapping my lips into a trumpet seemed too difficult and a banging drum kit in a walk-up apartment was out of the question.

Our fearless band leader was Mr. Bunseth, a thick, dark haired, beady-eyed man of Germanic decent. He often bragged how he tried out and made the Minnesota Symphony in his youth. "I vas da best of da best!" He bellowed. But after one short season he unable to fulfill his musical dream and was dropped. Now, he was regretfully teaching incompetent knuckleheads at our school.

When band tryouts came we were allowed to play what we liked and I made "first chair" — a prestigious placement in any school band. Without reading a note I could rattle off Benny Goodman's, "Getting Sentimental Over You" with the soul of a passionate artiste. I loved improvising and the freedom it brought. But as the days wore on and we were forced to sight-read standardized marching songs I crumbled.

Mr. Bunseth met crumbling with retribution. "Vat is you doing," he would bellow. "Is this not fun for you? This is music!" Every clarinet player in Bunseth's class knew and feared his punishment. You would be *Muntched*. If you didn't practice and improve Bunseth would move you down, a chair at a time, until you slipped to the second to last position next to — Morton Muntch.

Muntch was the plague and this was band netherworld. He was six feet of nasty potato-white skin and Brillo pad hair. His body odor suggested the sour stench of old bandages boiled with rotting brussells sprouts. His passing of gas was legendary. At fourteen he already looked like the pasty uncle you would run from as a kid. His baseball-mitt fingers would slap at the clarinet with the finesse of a drunken plumber. When Muntch played his instrument, thick gobs of spit and mucous spurted everywhere from the sides of his crusty mouth. Those heading towards Muntch-land were advised to bring towels or improve quickly. After a rousing rendition of "When The Saints Go Marching In" the right side of the punished one's body would be glazed with a slimy gooeyness. I knew my breakout from this impending musical cuckoo's nest would have to be perpetual practice.

I sat for hours on a wooden chair in my tiny bedroom forcing my stiff fingers to interpret the foreign language of black-stemmed notes. My fingers refused to conform. These notes, those keys, this note wrong key, that note — loud squeak. I must have repeated "When the Saints Go Marching In" a thousand times in that room. It was to be the grand finale in the looming all-school concert just two weeks away.

After a thousand and one times I grew so frustrated that I slammed my clarinet against my bed catching it on the metal frame. The rented instrument broke exactly in half. Consumed with panic I ran from room to room, tears streaming. I was looking for bits of string, scotch tape, or anything that would put my black-stick Humpty-Dumpty together again.

I remembered my mother had just bought "Super-Glue, the new space-age bonding glue used by astronauts in space." Exactly why astronauts needed household glue in space was beyond my comprehension. But it worked. Soon my little black clarinet with its shiny silver keys was fused together, good as new. I smiled with my dark little secret and began to practice in earnest transforming myself into a disciplined musician.

And like magic, the songs kicked into my brain, note by note, as musical memory took over. And then, everything clicked. I could do this! The song came pouring out of me. Overflowing with excitement I ran around the house playing "When The Saints go Marching In" to the couch, the refrigerator, the stove — any appliance or piece of furniture that would listen. Brimming with confidence I was more than ready for the looming band show-case and my exit from Muntch-witz.

The night of the big school performance we walked on to the "Cafetorium" stage one at a time to the obligatory applause of proud parents, bored siblings, and fellow students. We took our seats. Mr. Bunseth slowly raised his baton. As Muntch spit we began to play a scarcely discernable rendition of "When the Saints Go Marching In." Three measures into the song I heard a disgusting crack. The official glue of the astronauts had given way under pressure. I was left holding two pieces of half-size clarinets in my hands as the band played on. One by one my fellow musicians began to snicker as they looked over and noticed my predicament. Within seconds the song came to a halt as the entire band and audience broke into hysterical laughter. I walked up to Mr. Bunseth, showed him the two pieces, and walked off the stage in humiliation, echoes of laughter trailing me.

School

PART II: IN A DARK PLACE

I held on tight to the little glass fishbowl so the water wouldn't spill over the sides. Inside the bowl was my only friend Sammy; a salmon colored goldfish. Sammy nervously swirled inside his watery home from the uneven motion of the car. Our family was making the trek from our upper class five-bedroom home to our new one bedroom walk-up apartment. My father had just gone broke and beside him my mother sat broken.

I lay on my bed in the bedroom that I shared with my sister now. The room was barren and minuscule with two small beds and a clock radio. From the lone window I could see the McDonald's sign across the street flash proudly; "Over 500,000 sold!" My father was quick to point out that this McDonald's was one of the first in the nation — as if the view was something special. I lay there hours on end clutching that tiny clock radio, flipping through the stations listening to songs pour forth from its AM mono speaker. The songs were a reflection of the harmonious age of pop musical innocence. Bobby Darin told me he wanted a "Dream Lover To Call His Own," Leslie Gore made it clear that it was her party and she could cry if she wanted to, and all the Everly Brothers wanted me to do was "Dream."

But Sammy the goldfish would soon die, pop innocence would mutate into songs of protest, and my childhood innocence would come crashing down.

At my new school, stray hands found their way to my chubby midsection and squeezed until I screamed. Twisting fingers found their way to my nipples. And in the shower room rolled up towels relentlessly discovered their way to my testicles with an agonizing snap.

I dreaded the school bus. For me, it was the yellow train to Auschwitz. I was trapped — there was no place to run or hide and worse yet there was no one to protect me. Clinging to my books and my little brown tweed clarinet case I would scurry up the stairs and rush to the back where I would slink down and take cover.

One morning one of the school football players boarded the bus. He sat down so close I could smell his fresh bacon and egg breath. He looked at me while announcing to the bus; "Oweee is going to play us a song on his little clarinet this morning. And he's gonna play it in TWO BROKEN parts." The bus erupted in laughter. And then he sucker punched me in the gut.

My adolescent chubbiness kicked in with a vengeance, which only added to my misery. My mother, who was never fat a day in her life, made only anemic efforts to console my extreme anxiety about attending school. "You have such beautiful blue eyes and gorgeous light-brown hair." She would say adoringly. "Don't you pay attention to them." But running to the mirror all I would see staring back was a giant scoop of vanilla ice cream with two blueberry eyes placed atop a big fat sugar cone.

My classmates noticed too. They noticed that chub never tried out for any school athletics. And they noticed that his dad was slightly dark-skinned and spoke with some crazy foreign accent the few times he showed up for Christmas plays and band performances. I didn't have the heart or the balls to tell them he was from Syria. I probably would have been set ablaze and strung up from the school flagpole.

My parents were called to the school numerous times for special conferences. It was always the same theme. "We're worried about Owen," he seems to be so capable but just doesn't apply himself and act like all the other students. He's a dreamer."

One frigid January day, while taking my parka out of my school locker a band of boys approached me. "Hey Eskimo?" They said circling me. "You won't need that where you're goin'." Before I knew it one the boys grabbed my arm and began pushing me into my own open locker. Two more joined in and pushed with all their might. On the way in I noticed that one of them really needed to start shaving. I could see his brand new stubble breaking through his pocked-marked face. I wondered what he would look like all cleaned up with a shaver and some Clearasil. And then the door closed, with a sharp metal clank.

My world went dark and silent. I was jammed, unable to move, in to a two-foot by five-foot space. The stale and musty smell of schoolbooks used year after year combined with bits of unwashed sweaty gym clothing began to permeate and build up adding to my fusty experience.

Peering out through the six metal vent slats of that dark box I could just barely make out the passing parade of students in the hallway going about their daily routine. Clicks of girls giggled as they walked by in their tight red and green sweaters, boys with brand new white slide rules compared math notes, and the occasional teacher would stroll by with a pet student, extolling the virtues of something or another, arms waving in explanation.

I wanted to cry out for help but that would only incur a lifetime of mocking once the students heard me and began to assemble in front of my locker as I was pulled out.

I was scared. I imagined that I would never be found. I imagined a returning student would open her new locker the next year and a much thinner version of me — now a skeleton — would pop out. I imagined her stark-white face running, screaming down the school halls. I imagined her, years later, on a psychiatrist's couch, scarred for life, talking away — repeating that one horrific moment over and over.

I imagined that I was sentenced by a school of my peers to solitary confinement. But what was my crime? I pictured the courtroom:

"All rise, the judge is now entering."

"Has the jury reached a decision?"

"Yes, your honor."

"Very well, pass me the verdict'"

There would be a hush in the courtroom as the verdict was read.

"On the count of chubbiness in a public school the jury finds the defendant, guilty."

A gasp, as my mother begins to weep. My father is not there. He is golfing.

"On the count of lack of interest in school sports the jury finds the defendant guilty as charged."

Another gasp.

"On the count of being interested in deranged rock music and not yet being interested in girl's breasts the jury finds the defendant guilty as charged."

My mother collapses into the arms of my lawyer wailing, "But he's such a good boy. He always makes his bed."

The judge slams his gavel. "Mr. Husney. For the crimes you have committed against the St. Louis Park School System and it's students you are hereby remanded to solitary confinement in your school locker for one hour and twenty seven minutes."

My mother cries out as I am escorted out handcuffed and chained. "Owen! My boy! I'll bring you a tooth brush!" In shocked silence she watches as I am whisked back to my school to begin my sentence in the locker.

I learned a lot in the isolated darkness of that locker. When you are confined to a small dark space you come face to face with yourself. Thrust into observing the world from afar had given me great perspective on how to individuate myself from the students on the outside. From my vented observation point they all looked like little teenage robot-conformists. The boys all had identical brown corduroy pants and popular orange and red "bleeding" madras plaid shirts; every girl had red or green drop-waist pleated skirts and those tight sweaters so important during Minnesota's subzero weather. And so important to the boys.

I vowed in that moment that I would never be a robot-conformist. I would never buy into the norm. I would forge my own way, whatever that was. Looking back now I realize it was in that in those moments that I began to further define myself. I learned that people who look alike also act alike and that wasn't for me.

"You in there?" A man's gravely voice inquired.

Looking through the slats I saw an older man in a grey uniform, multiple keys jangling from the round silver holder on his brown belt. It was a prison guard.

"A couple of students saw what happened. I'm here to get ya out."

It was the school janitor, Mr. George — beloved in our school by staff and students alike. He was a thin tall man with large mechanics hands, snow-white hair, soft brown eyes, and wrinkled grandfatherly looks. Mr. George was always there to help. He had been the janitor at the high school since 1775 and could recall almost every student's name that had passed through its doors. In his eyes every student was equal. He had seen it all.

"Those ruffians better hope I don't catch 'em. 'Cause if I do I'm gonna open up a can of whoop-ass on 'em."

"Thank you so much, Mr. George." I said, knowing enough to hold back the tears as I stumbled out of my cell. For a boy, crying in the school hallways would have been the same as running naked through the school. It just wasn't done.

The remaining four months until the school year ended I arrived just as my first class was beginning, and left immediately after the last class. During recess I stayed outdoors and froze my ass until the bell rang. In class, I tried to stay invisible by not volunteering answers or talking to other students. I left on the last day with the fear of returning for my junior year eating away at me.

What I didn't know was that Rock music was looking for me.

Metamorphosis was just around the corner.

Revenge was near.

Enlightenment Part 1 — 1963

MICHAEL ROW THE BOAT ASHORE, HALLELUJAH!

We stood in the creaky shelter and pulled back the ragged blankets of the slumping cot. On the bottom sheet were thirteen yellow concentric circles of urine — one for each day. "He's been sleeping in this mess since the first day of camp," the Director said. As we clung to our noses, he continued, "Poor kid. We see it all the time, too embarrassed and afraid to tell anyone they're a bed-wetter. They crawl back into the same bed and it happens all over again. Why parents send their kids here to be humiliated without giving us a heads up is one of the great camp mysteries."

I ran for the door, retching all the way.

"Hey Owen, before you bolt, grab that plastic bag over there and load the sheet in. It'll have to be burned."

"Huh?" I said, between gags.

"You heard me. And when you're done with the sheet take the mattress out back and hose it down. It's plastic — the urine slides right off." I needed to run but there was nowhere to go; I was trapped deep in the woods. This was not what I had signed up for.

In the spring of 1963 I was purposeless and still reeling from the humiliation of the past school year. My mother encouraged me to sign up to become a counselor-in-training at Camp Tikvah, a Jewish overnight camp in Aitken Minnesota. I saw this as the perfect escape. There would be no pay but at least I would be able to get away from the jerks at school, divert my personal pain for the summer, and perhaps make a few new friends. I signed up. But things got off to a rocky start almost immediately.

I spied several students from my school as we stood in line for the bus to take us up north to Aiken, Minnesota. Hiding behind another kid I overheard one of them whisper, "It's that goon from school. He better not be in my cabin. If he is, I'm calling my mom and telling her to come get me." I shuttered. This was familiar territory for me. Once again, I climbed up the steps and hurried to the back of yet another yellow bus where I instinctively cowered down.

The bus ride north through a loop of endless sky and flat farmland took forever. While the kids sang songs and giggled over nothing, I plotted my way back home. I would spend the night and call my parents in the morning. The little campers hadn't arrived yet, and I could get the hell out.

A few hours later the bus pulled down a single lane dirt road lined on either side with peeling white birch and towering evergreen trees. It rolled under a sign made from dried tree branches that said, "Welcome to Camp Tikvah," and jerked to a stop at the very edge of a pristine blue-green lake. Another sign read, "Camp Tikvah, a Jewish camping experience." I remember thinking how odd it looked to see "Jewish" and "Camping" in the same sentence. And I remember thinking how the dirty white cabins, circling a flaking mess hall, resembled the workers quarters on a Southern plantation. Holy shit, I was being sent away to become a slave!

When cabin assignments were made I was put in with the two guys from school that vowed to go home if I was in their cabin. That night, not a word was said. I was completely ignored as we removed the clothes our mothers had packed so neatly for us. Catching a whiff of familiar laundry detergent I all but broke into tears of homesickness. But knowing that I'd be returning home in the morning gave me some solace. So, I carried on, and spread the musty camper's sheets on my flimsy bunk bed while the floor beneath me creaked with uncertainty. I was miserable.

But then, I blurted out a joke about the cleanliness of our cabin. "Well, it looks like we've all gone broke and moved to

Mississippi!" To my astonishment the guys doubled over in laughter! It was an old trick I used from a difficult childhood. Whenever life thrust me into a dark spot I used humor to get out. It worked like a charm. From then on the one-liners flew out until they begged me to stop — lest they piss their pants. Yes, pissing is a form of male bonding. Maybe I would stay here after all.

One of the school guys in my cabin was Cliff Siegel. He was a slight, thin-framed dude with rugged good looks and a tough cockiness that I dug. Cliff talked music unlike anyone I'd ever known. He not only knew about the current acts and singers but about the old blues guys and the roots of rock n' roll. We questioned what Jimmy Gilmore and the Fireball's "Sugar Shack" really meant. People believed it to be a secret hideaway but we knew it was pussy. We agreed that "Fingertips" by this genius-kid, Little Stevie Wonder, was the coolest thing going. We talked surf music and how a few rock bands from England were starting to take hold by spitting American blues songs back at us. Suddenly, life became tolerable. Cliff confided to me that one day he'd like to be a drummer in a band. And that was one of the coolest things I'd ever heard.

Two weeks into the camp session three scruffy young men emerged from the shadows of the forest. Tattered guitar cases slung over their shoulders like returning soldiers, they marched with purpose out of nowhere. No one knew where these nomads in the middle of the night came from or how they even got there.

The Camp Director rushed to question them. "Sons, this is private property. What are you doing here? You'll have to leave immediately." He said, defending his base. The "leader" spoke up. He was a tall lean kid in his early twenties with frayed blue jeans, red flannel shirt, and three-day-old stubble. "Sorry to bother you sir, we're traveling musicians. For a night's lodging and twelve bucks we can lead the kids in singing camp songs before moving on." And so it was announced that after dinner all counselors and campers should gather around a campfire at the edge of the lake, "For a very special musical performance and camp sing-along."

The nomads took their positions "on stage" in front of a roaring bonfire and broke into something like "Michael Row The Boat Ashore." As they sang and strummed I noticed these swarthy musical dudes loved what they were doing. In that moment, nothing else mattered to them but their music. They scarcely looked at their guitars, while their faces contorted in meaningful expression as they busked.

Observing the "audience" I noticed that the girls woke up from their camper's indifference. They were spellbound, and never took their eyes off those bad boy player-singers. As the golden embers from the campfire flew into the nighttime sky, and the raging fire reflected in their faces they sensed a new sensation — a forbidden erotic burning. And even though they too were singing along, the boy campers looked annoyed and jealous at the thought of losing their girls to these nomads.

I woke up too. Passion is a funny thing. It can lie dormant, sometimes for years, and then suddenly leap into action with the fervor of a furious fire. You don't know you have it until there's a trigger. If music could fill me with passion, cause girls to desire me, and make the schoolboys jealous — then why the fuck was I working as a slave on this plantation? And god-forbid someone should pay me for that passion!

That night, as I lay my head on the musty pillow I imagined my life on stage like the groups Cliff and I had talked about. I thought of the freedom on the road, the adulation from the throngs — and the girls. The next morning I ran to the window and watched those nomads vanish back into the forest with their twelve dollars. And for the very first time my life had real purpose.

So when the director told me to wash down the urine stained mattress I quit camp on the spot. A day later I hitched a ride home with the first session campers and returned to St. Louis Park. My life was just beginning.

Enlightenment — Part II

WAKING UP

Who was this new person waking up inside of me? Was he always there, or did something grow inside of me like in the movie *Alien*? Were those vagabonds who appeared from nowhere from another planet, and I was their impregnation experiment? Either way, I felt less vulnerable. I felt stronger and more in control. My guess was that this "badass" was always inside of me. It just needed the right vehicle to emerge. Years later I would help others find that vehicle that exists in all of us.

Back home, I ran to my closet and pulled out the broken clarinet. This time I ever so carefully glued the two jagged pieces together and put black color over the cracks to conceal them. When the glue was dry I shined it up, and carefully placed the instrument back in its tweed case.

"How much do you want for it my son?" said the guy behind the counter at Bud's Used Instruments in Hopkins Minnesota. "Well, I'd really like to trade even up for that solid body red electric guitar over there on the wall." I said. "Son, I don't know if you realize it but that's a Silvertone guitar. Made exclusively for Sears and Roebuck. It's a mighty fine instrument but I don't think I can make that trade without a few extra dollars from you." I had to think fast. "Tell you what, I'll give you the case to my clarinet for free and you can forget the case for the guitar." "Alright son, but don't tell a soul!" How he bought that logic was a mystery to me but I had just made my first deal in the music business!

Floating home From Bud's with my red guitar I felt a tap on my shoulder. I turned around to see the football player who locked me in my locker. He was winding up a sucker-punch for me again. "Hey fatty, you gonna break that guitar in half or should I do it for ya?" This fucker was not going to touch my guitar. As he reached back for the punch I instinctively put my foot behind his ankle and shoved — hard. He lost his balance, reeled backwards, and hit his head on the sidewalk with a horrendous crack. I ran my ass off, and was about half a block away when I heard him cry out loud. I turned around ran back. He was lying there holding his head and wiping away his tears. Our eyes locked for an instant — just enough time for me to spit in his stupid face. Then, I walked away — slowly.

The next day, I picked up a copy of "The Mel Bay Easy Way to Guitar" book for $1.25. That night, in my bedroom, I played a D chord for the very first time. The next morning it was down to my parent's basement where an abruptly retooled Philco TV set became my new amp. Drrrrrrrrrring! I played that D chord over and over until my fingers bled. I even wrote a one-chord song and pretended that I was a one-chord man in a one-man band. And the song started out like this; Drrrrrrrrrrrring!

As sub-zero winter approached I took up permanent residence in our basement. I learned every sun-filled surf song of the day. *Surfin' Safari, Surfer Girl, Surfin' USA*, and *Surfer Joe* filled that basement with warmth and filled me with hope and determination. I eventually moved on to the blues. I started reeling off songs by Muddy Waters, Howlin' Wolf, Lightnin' Hopkins and every other Bluesman whose first name ended in an apostrophe.

I was so driven that food no longer mattered and the weight melted off. And by the fall of 1964 I emerged from the depths ready to rock. But since I couldn't drag my parent's TV set around to gigs I needed an amplifier. No money equals no amp.

I got a job delivering chicken for Chicken Delight. My work attire featured a Colonel Sanders style bowtie and a chicken-beak hat that both said, "Don't Cook Tonight! Call Chicken Delight!" And, I got to drive the Chicken Delight delivery car! It was the owner's car; complete with a bright yellow three-foot red-beaked chicken perched atop the vehicle. I raced around town like a chicken with my head cut off delivering deep-fried goodies and collecting tips. The faster I could deliver, the more tips I made. Once, in the dead of sub-zero weather I came flying down an icy hill, went into an uncontrollable skid, and smacked almost head-on into a car that was on the way up. The plastic chicken, released from its shackles, became airborne, and the beak punctured the poor guy's windshield head-on with a loud craaaack! I laughed uncontrollably to the screams of "You mother-fucker" over and over as he tried in vain to pull the chicken and its beak from the splintered window.

Within months I had my new amp. It was a small used Montgomery Wards Airline tube amplifier. I had my gear, a job, and a Chicken hat. Now all I had to do was start a band. *But how the fuck do you do that?*

Revenge Is A Dish Best Served With Music

WAS MY MOTIVATION TO BECOME A MUSICIAN NOTHING MORE THAN RETALIATION?

High school letter jackets give me the fucking creeps. The sight of one in a thrift store, or a vintage clothing store sets off a decades old form of PTSD. The source of such trauma was born in my Jr. high and early high school years. Specifically, it was a black jacket, light black sleeves, with a large orange letter P in the upper left corner. The jacket meant that an unwarranted put down, a sucker punch, or sometimes both were about to come my way. For me, the fear that was brought by the guys wearing those jackets conveyed the high school equivalence of the Hitler youth movement.

But did the jacket also represent something on a deeper level, something that was more personal to me than the guys wearing them? Back in high school, the boys who wore them seemed so confident of themselves, so proud, and so fucking manly as they stood around talking and laughing together in the school halls. They spoke of sexual conquests, winning, and the big game coming up on the weekend. They stood tall in those jackets with their crisp blue shirts underneath, neatly creased tan pants, and polished brown loafers. I can still remember the dude who "hated me the most." He'd roll in, park his new Mustang in the school lot, and stroll up the school steps with his girl on his arm. His cool act hammered home my own sense of loneliness, insecurity, and non-achievement. It meant that I was "less than." That's why I hid the brown rusted out Corvair I shared with my mother on the street, and scurried in through the lunchroom door.

So, who was I? An ex-chubby late bloomer who preferred to hang alone in his parent's basement and listen to music? What was wrong with me that I didn't want, or even know how to be like them? They were together, a team. And because I was not a member of any team I was a loner — in a dark place.

Looking back, it's easy to see why I was the perfect object for them to put down to feel better about themselves. I guess it didn't take much. And it made total sense that these guys would plot their move against me when they learned that I was in the band playing the upcoming homecoming dance. Did I want to be one of them? Hell no, they were bloody conformists. The problem was there were so many of them and only one of me.

"Did ya hear? That nerd clarinet player who spit in Bill's face is a guitar player in a band now — and he's playing the homecoming dance in two weeks! How could the principal allow it? It'll be a school embarrassment and ruin the dance! So let's give 'em our own little show that night. We'll show up, draw blood and break his little fingers. The minute he walks on stage it'll be lesson time. Spread the word!" The word spread throughout the school like wildfire. The word spread to me, and I could almost hear the devil-like chortles as they strategized their attack. So the night of the homecoming dance the entire high school showed up, not to hear my band, but to witness the "main event."

Self-defense implies that you must protect yourself. Revenge implies that someone came after you and now it's your turn to go after him — only he doesn't know it. I don't premeditate retaliation. It is innate, never immediate, nor obvious. My revenge will come at you when you least expect it. It will be in a form that is not only stealth-like but also unanswerable. In the movie *Carrie*, a bullied high school girl seeks her retribution at the school prom, destroying everyone and everything in her path. In my case, it was the St. Louis Park high school homecoming dance. Only the perpetrators never knew what hit them. I crushed them in one night without throwing a punch or firing a single shot.

NOVEMBER 1963:

I went searching for a band armed with my Sears guitar, my Montgomery Wards amplifier, and my new delivery job at Chicken Delight. At first, I thought I would be a jazz musician like my best friend Randy Resnick's older brother Art. Art was so cool. He was tall and thin, carried himself with a touch of arrogance, and was reputed to be a jazz keyboard virtuoso. He appeared so avant-garde to me in his black Italian "continental suit" with slanted flapless pockets, thin lapels, and double venting in the back. I marveled at his straight cuff-less pants and black pointed half boots. Art was so cool that I was afraid to talk to him the few times we met. The one time we went to hear him play in Minneapolis I realized that his talent for Jazz was way over my head. At the gig, the guitar player advised me: "Look, if you want to get chicks in bed it will be much easier if you learn the three basic chords of rock music. Don't fuck around trying to impress them with some jazz-bullshit-augmented 9th chord. Trust me, I know." The man shed words of wisdom that ultimately proved to be too true. Rock and Roll was going to be my life. The problem was, I had all the passion but no idea how to play a full song.

Randy was learning to play guitar at about the same time. I remember trudging the five blocks through the snow to his house with my guitar and little amp to see if we could learn a song and start a band. "Let's try and learn *Johnny B. Goode*, the Chuck Berry song," he suggested. He dropped the needle down on the 45-RPM disc as we tried in vain to find the right key for the song. "Maybe we should tune our guitars first," I said. "But how do we do that?" "I dunno." So off to the music store we went to buy a tuner that you blow into like a whistle and a book of guitar chords.

"I get it!" Randy said almost as soon as our guitars were in tune. Randy grasped almost immediately how the chords fit together. "Look, it goes from E to A, then back to E, then to B, down to A, and back to E." "Huh?" I was deflated. I just didn't get it. Randy was clearly the better musician. But I'm a competitive guy.

I returned to my basement with a resolve to kick ass. Alone, in the cold cellar, fingers bleeding, I not only learned the song, but added a few of the lead guitar parts. And within a few weeks I was back at Randy's house ready to start a band — even though Randy was a far better musician.

If you can learn three basic chords you can start a rock band; so, with two other guys from high school we formed "The Rivieras," — A Modern Musical Trio. We never played a gig and just as quickly I was thrown out of the band along with the business cards I just had printed. When your passion overrides your talent you do what I did; you retreat to the darkness of your basement with thoughts of killing yourself.

But then I remembered Cliff, the good lookin' kid at camp that liked to sing and wanted to be a drummer. We had formed a strong bond and had a similar taste in music. "Cliff, you wanna start a band?" I said, calling him out of the blue. "Ya, come on over." Following his directions I drove up to a tiny house on Louisiana Ave in St. Louis Park. As I approached the house I heard loud blues music coming from behind a screen door. He didn't hear me, so I walked in unannounced and noticed something quite odd that I loved. I could see him in his tiny bedroom pantomiming to the song; using his clotheshorse as a mike stand. He brought it close to his lips and then let it go rocking forward, then returning back to his lips as he mouthed the words to the song. Damn, this dude is the real thing I thought. Just then he noticed me and quickly stopped the music and the performance. "You caught me red handed!" He said, more than a little embarrassed. "I got a five dollar gift certificate for graduation and went to the record store to buy Jerry Lee Lewis's *Greatest Hits*. The clerk played me some songs by this new group, The Rolling Stones and they blew me away! I bought the album and just learned every song. But I'm really a drummer."

"So, lets start a band," I said; not yet understanding just how keen my musical intuition was. Cliff was the real deal.

We set up a jam session with me on lead guitar, Rick, another fellow from our high school on rhythm guitar, and Cliff pounding away on drums. It was unanimous; Cliff was terrible on drums and should never, ever touch a drum set again. "Dude, I'm so sorry that you just bought that drum kit, but damn, take it back — you suck." There simply was no time to waste if we were going to be rock stars. And then, I remembered Cliff with the clotheshorse, and how cool he looked. "Why don't you just try singing, like that guy, what's his name, Mick something?" "Yeah, I like that," he shot back with a smile. "I already know the words to "Route 66" from the album, so let's give it a try." Thanks to Randy, I already knew the simple 12 bar blues arrangement. With Cliff hollering above the guitars the three of managed to get through the song. When the song ended we froze and looked at each other in disbelief. "Did you hear that? We actually sound like something! And Cliff looks and sounds like a rock star!" Rick said, not even trying to hide his emotions.

David "Z" Rivkin, another fellow musician with a big Twin Cities band (who would go on to engineer and produce the Prince demos for me and engineer many of his future hits) recommended a drummer named Doug from Southwest, a competing high school. "I'll come by if I can bring Jay along to play keyboards." Then get the fuck over to Rick's and let's jam!"

My chicken delivery money gave me enough money to buy a real Fender guitar just like the one I dreamed of owning. Another few deliveries of golden fried goodness and I was able to purchase a Fender Tremolux amp. Although minus a bass player we set up a jam at Rick's parent's house with Cliff singing through one of the amps. "Okay, let's try Johnny B. Goode," Cliff said. "One, two, three…" We got through three quarters of the song and stopped cold. Not because the song was a chaotic mess, but because something bigger than us just happened: the fusion of two guitars in sync with the high end of piano notes — all layered with a steady beat of drums and cymbals — shot through the room like a freight train. And when Cliff came in on vocals it was like an out of body experience with all of us attending a concert — not newbies grappling with a song for the first time. We emerged from Rick's basement and sat in his living room — smiles around. "You boys look so happy!" His mom said. "Why are you all in such high spirits?" And from that moment on we were known as The High Spirits. The name would prove to be prophetic when the psychedelic age crept in a few years later.

We added another guy named Rick on bass and began to rehearse in earnest. Opting out of the cutesy harmony songs of the day, like the Beach Boys (I was a big fan though), we favored more blues oriented songs adapted from the old masters. This was mostly due to Cliff's vocal style and his amazing ability to pick songs. We were also the first band to have a stand-alone lead singer, which set us apart from the wedding and Bar Mitzvah ensembles. And rounding out our sound was a kickass piano/organ player.

The undefined magic of rock bands in those days was that you didn't have to be virtuosos to succeed. Much of your success came from the total "Wall of sound" created by band members working in sync, not individual Mozarts. I watched as many musicians, those with far greater talent than our band members, fall by the wayside due to over thinking, over practicing and trying to get it exactly right. That's selfish reasoning. We never over thought anything. But we intrinsically understood one basic secret: think only about your audience and what they want and need. Then give it to them with fucking attitude.

OCTOBER 1964:

After months of rehearsal we loaded our gear into our cars and drove the short distance over to the high school. We were confident, but no one really knew what to expect. Earlier that month we played a fraternity house on the University of

Minnesota campus. We played on the floor in the living room, it was a short gig, and the kids were so drunk that we could have played *Hava Negila* for the forty-five minutes and no one would have noticed. So the real test would be tonight at the homecoming dance. The dance was held in the school "Cafetorium," a combo lunchroom/auditorium. The lunch tables and chairs were moved to the side and neatly stacked, a stage was set, and there were even a few lights and spotlights. And the homecoming committee had strung crepe paper across the ceiling in our school colors — orange and black. I pictured the crepe paper being yanked from the ceiling while students screamed, "Make a tourniquet! He's bleeding to death!

I never shared my fear with the other band members regarding my impending demise. The jitters of performing in front of our peers was enough. Would they have backed out? Would they have been prepared to fight? Either way, the band would not have played. But I knew the school would be packed that night. Everyone would be there to witness the melee because everyone loves a good car wreck. And that meant a big audience. Then, while we were setting up word came down that the football team had lost the big game and everyone was on the way to the dance. Fuck, I thought, now they're going to get extra liquored up in the parking lot and take their super-testicle testosterone induced torment out on me. This is bad.

As the students filtered in we were back in the kitchen putting on the outfits we had chosen in unison: blue sear sucker suits, white shirts, and thin maroon ties. Cliff would dress differently since he was the front man: pants, a patterned shirt unbuttoned to his navel, black vest, and signature sunglasses. I peaked out and saw the place was packed wall to wall. The blonde homecoming queen came out, thanked the football team, and muttered something about, "Even in losing there's winning." Then she said, "It's not often we have the pleasure of having a real rock band play at our homecoming! This is a real honor. Let's put our hands together for The High Spirits!"

We climbed up on the stage and took our positions to tepid applause. After all, the band wasn't the main event, my imminent death was. Cliff wasn't on stage yet; he was to make his entrance as soon as the music started. I scanned the audience and breathed a sigh of relief. I didn't see one letter jacket in the crowd. But when bass player Rick counted down the song there was a sudden commotion in the back of the room. "Hey, get outta my way! Get out of my fuckin' way!" It was the "guy who hated me the most," and he was running ahead of a pack of Nazi letter jackets. The seas parted as he shouted, "This one's for you — you little clarinet creep." He rushed the stage and began to climb up. "I'm gonna cheach you a lesssssson." He said through an intoxicated rage.

There's an instinctual mode that takes over when someone comes between musicians and their instruments. It's the same mode that a parent uses in shielding a child from danger. He struggled through his drunkenness to crawl onto the stage. I waited until his inebriated head was at ear level with my amp. Then, I opened the volume up full and hit a piercing high D chord. Drrrrrrrrring! The sound shot deep into his skull, penetrating and splitting his ears. It was just enough of a temporary shock to send him reeling back towards the audience. At that point our keyboard player grabbed his mike stand, and without hesitation, pushed it down on jacket boy with just enough force to send him flying off stage and on to the floor.

Cliff ran out on stage and hollered, "Start the music! Start the music!" Rick counted down, "1..2..3..4," and I played the intro guitar part for Johnny B Goode. The band struck up, and Cliff came in on vocals. The other jacket boys ran to the stage but were blocked by girls making their way up to the front because something magical was happening. They wanted to see us!

Like I said, the musicianship of The High Spirits was not in our individual virtuosity. But our collective sound was raw, visceral, and pounding — the key elements in a pleasurable sexual experience. Without even understanding it we reeked of carnal nastiness.

The girls positioned themselves at the front of the stage moving in unison to the music and dancing with each other. The non-jacket boys, sensing an opportunity, made their way to the front to dance with them. The jacket-boys, humiliated in their double defeat that night, shrank to the back of the room to begin their careers selling insurance. The High Spirits were on their way.

I don't recall if this was a dream, wishful thinking, or reality but from stage I swear I saw the very janitor who freed me from being locked in my school locker. He was in the doorway at the back of the room; the same grey uniform and jangling keys affixed to his belt. Our eyes met briefly through a cloud of smoke. And just before he walked away he gave me the thumbs up.

After that evening St. Louis Park high school claimed The High Spirits, as their own. I was invited to sit at the "popular" lunch table in school. I was protected because the jacket-boys would have never dated again had they come after me. And, I parked my rusted Corvair right up front and walked gracefully up the front steps of the school.

We played almost every available dance at the school. In addition, word spread to other high schools and soon, we were playing every weekend two and three times around town.

A few months later we borrowed five hundred dollars from Cliff's uncle and went into the recording studio. We cut a white-boy garage band version of "Turn On Your Love Light," originally recorded by bluesman, Bobby "Blue" Bland. It was picked up by SOMA Records in Minneapolis and released to WDGY, the local pop station. Hoping they would give it a spin I lined up our female fans and asked them to call in and request the record should the DJ give it a play. "If you hear it, keep calling and requesting it. But remember, to change your voice every time you call back!" He tested it late one night and the phone lines "magically" lit up. "I think we have a true hit here," the DJ said incredulous. The record was then added into regular rotation and was picked up by the competing pop station across town, KDWB.

As the record spread to other markets across the Midwest and down south I still kept my job delivering chicken for Chicken Delight. After we made our first television appearance on "Date with Dino," I had to get my ass back to my job. Donning my chicken hat and Chicken Delight bow tie I made a delivery to two teenage girls. "You look so familiar," one of them said as I pulled the steaming chicken from the box. "Wait, didn't we just see you on TV today? You're famous!" "Ah, no that was someone else," I said backing away from the door in humiliation. "It happens all the time." If I was famous and on television, why would I be delivering fried chicken?" I hightailed it back to the store where my boss yelled at me for being late. "You have a responsibility to be on time. This is the chicken delivery business, when you fuck up we fail! Got it Husney! How are you going to ever amount to anything?" I looked him square in the eyes and said, "Fuck you asshole! I'm a rock star!" Whereupon I took off my chicken hat and threw it, hitting him square in the face. It slipped off his face and fell directly into a new batch of batter. We watched as the stray hairs from my head sank into the thick golden liquid with the hat. I walked out and never looked back.

1968 — My Jimi Hendrix Experience

The night Jimi Hendrix was born did the moon really turn a fire red? — I'd soon find out

"See, this is a sign we're on a fool's errand!" The lights flickered again in the old Sheraton elevator as it chunked its way skyward. The bowl we just smoked making sure every clink and bump was intensified. I stared at an empty seat and lever, once home to an elevator operator from a bygone era. I imagined him feeling so proud in his red uniform as he took travelers to their temporary homes in the sky. Kiki, willing the elevator to move faster, stared at the push buttons that had put the operator out of work. "It's one in the morning, this could be a real bummer!" I said. "I told you O, it's all groovy. It was destiny that brought us to this place, it's not up to us anymore." "Well maybe Destiny can give us a fucking ride home!" I said. "This is a bad idea." Kiki produced a bit of crumpled paper. "Look, his drummer wrote, 12th floor, Sheraton Hotel," she said in a hushed tone. I let her know that I was more than skeptical of this late night expedition. "I told you, O, I have the secret code." "Fuck the code, babe. Do you want to wind up in jail, or worse yet beat to a pulp by security?" The elevator chunked on.

It was November 1968, and we were supposedly on our way up to party on the wild side with Jimi Hendrix and his band — ground zero of psychedelic rock — and ground zero for my personal rebellion. Earlier that evening The Jimi Hendrix Experience performed in triumph to an insatiable audience of frozen hippies at the Minneapolis auditorium.

* * * *

It was a dark journey that drove me to the music of Jimi Hendrix. And the roots of that journey began in the early sixties.

The assassination of President Kennedy and the beginning of the Vietnam War left me scarred. Both events destroyed any remaining shred of my childhood innocence. I waved goodbye to Howdy Doody, Gidget, Frankie, and Annette, and woke up to little John-John, dressed in blue, tearfully saluting farewell to his slain father. Words and phrases like: Mai Lai, Vietcong, Hanoi, Civil Rights, and "Four Dead in Ohio" punctured their way into my existence.

By April of '68, Martin Luther King would be gunned down. By June, Robert F Kennedy would be shot at point blank range. I saw my childhood friends drafted, and shipped off to a distant jungle only to return zipped up in body bags, or disabled for life. In his hit record, "Vietnam Song," Country Joe McDonald asked us what were we fighting for — and then told us we're all going to die. The world turned two shades darker for me. I desired to know the "why." And I didn't trust anyone over thirty because their attitude was, "Why not?"

Our parents locked us away in split-level cul-de-sacs, and drove off to passionless jobs. Our fathers came home from work complaining about their "Nazi-bastard boss," walked past us clutching a scotch, and collapsed in front of the one-eyed antenna monster. Our mothers made sure dinner was on the table, and cleaned up after everyone. They tucked us in at night, warning about the dangers of smoking marijuana — then downed a big red Seconal, and passed out in bed reading *Valley of the Dolls*. On Saturday nights they dressed up in black suits and brown formal dresses and sucked down olive martinis at stiff cocktail parties. Any dreams of a wonderful future for them — or the world in general — had long since vanished like the last drops of their vodka.

In Minneapolis, young members of the creative counter-culture found each other like B-movie zombies gathering in a farmer's field. We sought each other out because we had bitter fights with our parents, had been beaten by the cops in the streets, or watched in horror, as our contemporaries were tear gassed — or worse yet, killed on campus. For me, being the Americanized son of a Jewish-Syrian-immigrant meant that my father and I were ships passing in the night. We had neither cohesive glue nor common history. So my glue was making music, and standing in protest for my civil rights. Banding together with like-minded brethren, our common theme was simple: those with authority had it wrong. So, we either metaphorically fired bombed them or actually fire bombed their institutions.

It seemed like the whole world, not just a hippie-musician like me was turning on, tuning in, and dropping out. Even in Minneapolis smoking dope, and dropping acid were de rigueur. The idea was not to get fucked up and party, but to expand our minds and see the world through a more prescient lens than our parental predecessors.

With the arrival of the pill, teen girls were free to explore their sexuality. They too rebelled, changing their names to "Flower" and "Moon" — and started experimenting with rebellious guys with new names like "Zoner" and "Freaky Davy".

Freed from our cages, we were rebels with a cause. Together, we progressed from making out to freaking out, and full on guilt-less fucking. Music, outdoor love-ins, and the sweet smell of incense and earthy patchouli oil were our new life — a life that was our own. Together, we expanded our minds into the next state. Music was our united flag of nonconformity and we proudly waved it loud.

In 1958, Patti Page asked me, "How Much is that Doggy in the Window?" Now, in 1968, a counter-culture freak is asking me, "Have You Ever Been Experienced?" Our parents had their Bing and their Sinatra and we had our Hendrix, our Dylan, and our "Stones." They were fucked up — and we were on a fucking journey.

The summer of 1968 was also a beautiful interval for me. For a brief moment it felt like the real "truth" of my existence had joined together in harmony with flower power and love. It wasn't the drugs fooling me — it was really happening. It was possible to protest, make music, and instigate real change.

But in the end I learned "the man" has more money and machinery than a bunch of broke hippies. Nonetheless, I was giving it my all that summer — and it was a glorious effort.

Kiki and I, friends since high school, had a chronicle of some pretty mind-blowing adventures and misadventures to our credit. Like when her father caught us naked in the men's sauna of the family apartment building on New Year's Day. When we heard his voice, Kiki ran out and pretended to be a man at the urinal and was immediately caught. I sat in that sauna for hours, dehydrated and shriveled beyond prune, afraid to come out.

Our adventures were more like a dying person's bucket list. And, though very much alive, we managed to check off a lot on that list by our 22nd birthday. Kiki referred to it as, "Creating your personal understanding of the human experience — on your terms." Kindred spirits, we felt that we were part of the breakaway generation. A new generation that would resist inheriting our parent's pathetic ideology at all costs. Crew cuts, nine to five jobs, and war were not going to be the motivations for our existence.

Kiki was a free spirited soul who floated into every new experience on the wings of butterflies. Brought up in a comfortable Jewish household outside of Minneapolis, it would have been easy for her to slip into the traditional route of marriage and babies in the 'burbs. But when the Age of Aquarius took over Kiki seized it and left for Los Angeles. It was there that she blossomed into a blue-eyed hippy-princess. Her shoulder length hair was English rock star: blonde, feathered, and untamed. Delicate in body, tantalizing blue eyes, and just enough precarious cleavage gave Kiki an all-access pass to most male-dominated situations — especially famous musicians in a sixties rock and roll world. Once in, she used her earth-mother instincts to nurture even the most hardened man-child musician. Neither a groupie nor a saint Kiki was a selfless, gifted muse who was smart enough to walk into a room and light it up — with your light.

Once a neatly trimmed and chubby Bar Mitzvah boy I let my hair grow to my shoulders and sprouted a raggedy beard. As a rebellious hippy musician, I relished showing up at family functions wearing frayed pink bellbottoms, a stained, tie-dyed t-shirt and a scruffy fringe vest. I loved it as my parents and relatives gagged on their brisket, repulsed at the bloodshot monster seated next to them on Jewish holidays.

When Jimi's first album, "Are You Experienced," came out I was certain he had created that album just for me. From the first distorted lick of *Purple Haze* to the intro of Hendrix's distant echo-vocals I was beyond spellbound. Every euphonious lick from his guitar was utterly groundbreaking. This man was not just playing typical staccato notes; his guitar was alive and singing to me. It felt like each note entering my ears was like a drug hitting all the right pleasure spots. I felt the music. I breathed the music. Here was a blues-based African American singer/songwriter/guitar player singlehandedly changing the face and sound of rock music forever. I got high daily and played my guitar until I learned every lick and note on that album. At the same time in Los Angeles Kiki became friends with Jimi Hendrix's band and briefly met Jimi.

So, in November of 1968, when Kiki came back to Minneapolis for the holidays, we were again thick as thieves. And when it was announced that Jimi Hendrix was playing the Minneapolis Auditorium she made a call to his drummer, Mitch Mitchell, and we were in the front row, feeling both the exhilaration of the audience and the raw energy of the artist at close range. Just before he played "Foxy Lady" Jimi gave a shout out to "Some lucky lady," and dedicated the song to her. Kiki touched my arm and whispered; "I think he said that to me."

The elevator screeched and clanked to the 12th floor. As the door slowly limped open we saw throngs of stoners standing and milling about in in the hallway. Kiki and I were unexpectedly adrift in a sea of multi-colored scarfs, bright psychedelic shirts, and bellbottoms. Everyone looked like Jimi Hendrix! A dude with jet-black hair to his waist lit up a loosely rolled joint. He giggled endlessly as he passed it along to a too-white girl with dark circles under her eyes. In another dark corner of the hallway a guy and his girl were peeling little purple dots off of a piece of paper swallowing them whole as they gazed into each other's eyes. Before us on the floor was a filthy, shirtless guy with stringy dishwater hair. He was rocking back and forth in a fetal position muttering something about a magical experience. The people who could still walk were all waiting to get into the party room that looked like it could handle maybe twenty people. I pulled Kiki back in as the elevator door was about to close.

"This ain't my bag babe." I said. "I'm more about tripping one on one. This scene has a bad vibe." "I know," she murmured. "Is there a room number on the piece of paper?" Kiki unfolded the scrap of paper — her eyes opened wide — and she broke into a smile. "Yes!" She belted. "And it's on the 14th floor — not the 12th!" The elevator door closed on the Fellini scene and all was quiet as the elevator chugged on.

Maybe it was fear of the unknown, maybe it was the bowl we smoked, but as we ascended a dark wave came over me. I suddenly felt like the victim in a horror movie. You know, the one where we all know the monster is in the attic but the poor dupe naively climbs the ladder armed with only a flashlight. The audience screams, "Don't go!" Filled with panic, I reached over to push the button for a return to the lobby. But it was too late and the elevator door opened. We peeked out, and there was no one; no druggie hangers on, no bicep bursting security, no groupies waiting for a carnal taste of stardom — just a musty faux French hallway before us.

The directions brought us to the end of the hallway where we found a small grouping of tired suites. Each had its own name, one for each of the Great Lakes. On the piece of paper was scrawled, "14th floor, Lake Superior Suite." I told you he gave me the right room, didn't I?" Kiki said. "But I don't hear a party in there!" I said, as I started to bolt. Grabbing my arm she put her other hand to the door and made a sequential tapping sound with her long fingernails, Di di di dah, di di di dah. Kiki gave me a self-assured smile and whispered, "That's the secret code!" "What good is the secret code if we're dead? We're not supposed to be here!" I shrieked back in a whisper.

From the inside the room came the lone clink of a drink landing on a glass table, something being zipped up, and the sound of footsteps nearing the door. "That's it, Kiki. I'm out of here!" "Who is it?" a male voice said, as a chain and multiple locks were unlocked. "Fingernails." Kiki said. The door opened wide.

Jimi fuckin' Hendrix stood in the doorway — a freshly lit cigarette in the corner of his mouth — a trail of smoke spiraling upward. He wore a pink and red paisley shirt open to his navel that presented us with a preview of the countless strands of red, turquoise, and black beads that encircled beneath. His wrists and fingers were adorned with silver bracelets and turquoise rings. I recognized the dark blue bell-bottoms, the purple scarf across his forehead, and the trademark brown fringe jacket from his performance earlier that night. His neatly trimmed "fro" was back lit, illuminated by a lamp in the suite. I gave out a gasp at the sight of this album cover come to life and hoped he didn't notice.

"It's cold", Jimi muttered in a hip-cool voice, "C'mon in." "Welcome to November in Minneapolis" Kiki countered as we entered Jimi's suite and found ourselves in a dream. The normally sterile hotel room was alive with a surrealistic radiance. Yellow, blue, and magenta scarfs had been swathed over each and every lamp and chandelier. Kiki gave Jimi a lingering hug and I sank into the hotel room sofa in utter disbelief.

"What's your name, man?" "I, uh, I'm…ah…Owen…" I said, breathless from intimidation "My pleasure, Owen. Cool pants, man." Jimi fuckin' Hendrix noticed my pants! I picked out my favorite body-hugging pink bellbottoms especially for the potential of this occasion. Kiki floated in and took over. "It's so groovy in here. I absolutely DIG your home away from home Jimi!" "Yeah, I wish Mitch and Noel dug it but they won't even stay on the same floor with me." Guess they're mad 'cause I won't party with 'em."

Kiki and I were expecting a rock and roll party, but here we were, alone with Jimi in his suite. I thought to myself, the man who asked me on his album if I'd ever been "Experienced" was handing me the fucking experience of my life.

"Hey, you guys wanna do some purple Owsley from San Francisco? One hundred percent pure." Jimi offered. "I'm already trippin'." Kiki and I huddled. We decided that if we did acid, especially Owsley from Jimi Hendrix, we might not be able to function let alone trip. The whole thing could turn into a bummer and we'd have blown our once in a lifetime opportunity. "No thanks." Kiki replied. "We've smoked a big bowl on the way over and we're doin' alright here with you. Mind if we smoke some more?"

Jimi flipped through the three available channels on the television set in the suite and landed on an old Laurel and Hardy movie. He took off his famous fringe jacket and plopped down on the couch next to us. We all giggled as the duo performed their famous "tit for tat" antics on the small screen.

I couldn't help but think that perhaps Kiki and I were the Laurel and Hardy of visitors that night. Our comedic antics had placed us in a position that most people would die for. And what were we doing with our opportunity? We were sitting on a couch like chuckleheads with one of the most celebrated icons in all of rock stardom. I needed to say something.

"So, as a musician do you like to…." "Yes," Jimi said, looking directly at me. "I love jamming with other musicians. I really don't like the confines of my band and having to churn out three-minute songs for radio." "So you feel that…" "Yeah, Jamming with other musicians is the most freeing thing I can do." I was in shock. Jimi was completing my sentences. "Are you considering….?" "Yeah, I'm seriously thinking about it. I'll probably do just one or two more tours with Mitch and Noel and then take a new direction."

Jimi wasn't being rude. In fact, he was a great guy. What struck me most was how easily I accepted and understood was happening in the moment. What separated Jimi from the rest is a rare gift. Call it mystical; call it unspoken-word shit, it didn't matter. I knew I had that same ability but I was afraid to disclose it to anyone for fear of being labeled a nut case — so I buried it deep — until this moment. I would have otherwise never experienced this phenomenon as a young musician living and working out of Minneapolis. This was my Confirmation, college, and graduate school all rolled into one singular evening.

Jimi and I bonded that night because he knew that I knew. Jimi, cracking a Cheshire cat grin, said, "Hey man, you're one of us." "Holy shit! Jimi and I were "One of us!"

Opening up and delving deeper Jimi told us that he had experimented with mescaline when he was in Los Angeles. "I felt alone in the midst of all the hangers-on man, so I dropped mescaline and went up to the roof of the hotel. As the sun set, the moon came up and turned a fire red and I felt reborn."

I knew his words to us that night came from the lyrics for "Voodoo Chile" on the "Electric Ladyland" album. I speculated that the "hell red moon" might have been just another Los Angeles sunset filtered through smog. Smog creates spectacular, deep red sunsets. A simultaneous rising full moon would most assuredly benefit from the same occurrence. I often wondered if Jimi ever figured out that his "rebirth" was born from the particulates of LA smog.

Kiki got up and walked into another room. A few minutes later Jimi followed and I could hear them talking and laughing in the back of the suite. I didn't want to follow them. I wanted a souvenir. I had taken chances and fought hard to be in this room tonight so there should be a reward. I noticed that Jimi had been playing with a guitar pick earlier and put it back in the pocket of his jacket. And the jacket was right next to me. What's the harm I figured? Surely he would give it to me, but asking for a souvenir guitar pick from Jimi Hendrix would be like a fan asking for an autograph, and we were way beyond that stage tonight.

I slowly reached over and put my hand in the jacket pocket and soon had the souvenir pick in my grasp. Just then a door opened in the back of the suite. Holy shit, Jimi and Kiki were coming back into the room! I quickly pulled my hand from the jacket pocket but it caught inside. The famous Jimi Hendrix jacket went flying halfway across the room and guitar picks splayed everywhere. I flew to the floor on all fours scrambling to fix my idiot situation. What could I possibly tell them; that in their absence I had decided to roll around on the floor on Jimi's jacket and guitar picks as some sort of religious experience? Their voices grew louder. In one motion I swept my arm across the floor sweeping the picks into my hand. In another simultaneous motion I grabbed the jacket and flew back to the couch stuffing the picks back into the pocket. Breathless, I sat on the couch as if nothing had happened. Not bad for a guy who had just smoked a big bowl.

Jimi came right up to me. Had he caught me red-handed? "Hey man, I'd like to ask your permission." "For what?" I said. Was he going to kick me out? "I'd like to hang with your lady tonight, if, ah, you know what I mean." "I'm cool with it. What'd Kiki say?" "She's cool with it." "Hey man, you're Jimi Hendrix. As long as Kiki's cool, I'm cool." "Cool. Thanks for being cool man." The "cools" won out and at 5 AM I descended to the lobby in the old elevator — thrilled with the anticipation of speaking with Kiki as soon as she got home.

The elevator stopped on the 12th floor and a bleary-eyed hippie dragged himself through the door. "A real bummer man." He muttered. "Hendrix never even showed. Someone said he flew off to Chicago after the show." "That is a bummer," I said. "Maybe next time."

On the drive home I reflected on the craziness of the night and what brought me to this point. It felt as though I was in just right place during truly a magical time in history; a time that was born from a demand for change in our societal beliefs. Everything in our system was being questioned and challenged: how we looked, the jobs we had, how women and minorities were being treated, the environment, what we ate — would it all come crashing down some day? Today, Kiki and I were free, floating without a care on the wings of butterflies, but in the future would we find ourselves wandering without a cause? Would we all be locked away in a cul de sac with short hair, 2.3 children, and a boss we hated? Or would we carry some of this newfound freedom forward.

I awoke at noon and called Kiki. "You're not going to believe this," she said, breathless. "While we were fucking "Foxy Lady" came on the radio!" It was a magical moment that I'll never forget — ever. Remember when Jimi dedicated "Foxy Lady" to a special woman in the audience? I knew it was my destiny and I'm still shaking in disbelief." Afterwards, Jimi had to leave for the airport, but he said I could stay in the suite as long as I wanted to. Then he kissed me softly and told me that everything was going to be alright." "That is so cool." "We've done some pretty crazy things in our lifetime, eh?" I said. "There's gonna be more, O. This is just the beginning."

As usual, Kiki was right. That night, I learned from Jimi that I was, "one of us." Jimi was one more mentor for me on my path searching for light at the end of the music tunnel. What he gave me was confidence in my instincts, and the will to keep going in an impossible business. And Kiki was right; Destiny brought us there that night — and refused to drive us home.

Maybe there was hope for the future after all. Woodstock proved to the world that our generation was on the right track — a half million people gathering in peace, sharing love, and listening to music. The 70's were just around the corner. And the Stones were planning a similar peaceful festival at a place called the Altamont Speedway in Northern California.

The following is a review of Jimi's show that appeared the next day in *The Minneapolis Star and Tribune*:

"THE MUSIC by Hendrix and his two white sidemen was loud but not too clear. Among his songs were "Foxy Lady," which he dedicated to some lucky lady, and "Are You Experienced," which he dedicated to "all the narcotics agents and detectives and a few other bastards." People sitting in the balcony probably had no trouble seeing Hendrix. For those sitting up front it was quite difficult because of those rude, smelly long-haired kids who pushed their way up to the stage, completely intimidating law officers and Andy Frain ushers. It was possible to see if you stood up, but Jimi Hendrix isn't worth standing up for."
— Allan Holbert, November 3, 1968, Minneapolis Star and Tribune

Suddenly It Was Over

WE HAD A GREAT RUN BUT IT WAS TIME TO MOVE ON:

In almost five years The High Spirits played every school and teen dance, small hall, and concert venue in the states surrounding Minnesota and well beyond. In markets like Kansas City, where our hit, "Turn on Your Love Light," achieved top ten on the charts we were true rock stars. Then, one day in 1969 I phoned our booking agent, Dick Shapiro. "There's nothing on the books! Where are the gigs? You guys are lame!" "Well, there is something," Dick said, trying to sound enthusiastic." "Great, it's about time, where do we go next?" "To the Holiday Inn in Duluth." "Is there a big event there?" "No, it's in the lounge. And you're there for a week." So this is where bands go to die I thought. My ego would not accept the reality so I told Dick, "Thanks but no thanks, you suck," and I hung up.

The band was over and I had no place to go. All my money had been spent on sports cars, women, and drugs — and I was stone-broke. I moved into an apartment with friends who had no furniture and slept on their one smelly makeshift couch. I desperately needed a job but working at the local McDonald's was out of the question because I still was a rock star in my mind. I simply could not be seen asking, "Would you like fries with that." In desperation I called Cliff, our lead singer and explained my woes. "Dude, I got this great job working in a basement phone room on Excelsior Blvd selling aluminum siding. No one sees you, and no one knows who you are!" "Dude, that's perfect — a dream come true!"

I applied for the job and was hired on the spot by a man named Neil Rowe, a chain smoking, anorexic wisp of a man with black greasy slicked-back hair and pencil-thin mustache. "All you guys have to do is call people and lie," Neil said, in a nasally high-pitched voice. He then took a long pull from his filter-less cigarette and exhaled the smoke, with a hint of alcohol, in our faces. "We make calls in the afternoon using this reverse telephone book so you know their names. That's when the housewives are home. You tell 'em were putting siding on a home in their neighborhood. That gets 'em reeled in. Then you tell 'em that rather than haul all the equipment back to the main office you'll give 'em a big discount to keep the gear and workers in their neighborhood. Your job is to make appointments for the salesmen to come out to their house. If they make the sale, I put an X next to your name on that blackboard behind me. The more X's the bigger bonus you'll get in addition to your $2.50 per hour salary. Now here's your script, memorize it, and get to work.

I made at least fifty calls and couldn't get a nibble. Most of the women hung up on me mid-sentence. I returned to my couch despondent that night. Laying there in the dark it hit me. This is Minnesota, so why not use a Minnesotan accent when you call the women! I called Cliff and told him of my plan. "Great idea, Hus. Let's start tomorrow."

"Ya, is this missus Christianson? How are ya dere dis mornin? She's a nice day, huh? Oh, and how are da kids doin? Oh, you have grandkids? Geez, that's wonderful ya know." I continued my spiel in Minnesotan and not only did I keep them on the phone but made appointment after appointment. Cliff came up to me during the break and said he was wildly successful too. Both of us left work excited in anticipation of the next day. The next morning our chain-smoking phone room boss met us at the door. He was all smiles. "You guys did a great job yesterday, just look at all the X's on the board by your names. We looked up and our smiles turned to astonishment. There were lots of X's all right, but he had changed our names at the top of the board from Cliff and Owen to Jew boy #1 and Jew boy #2. It was time to move on.

I called the booking agent I'd hung up on and asked for a job. "What makes you think an out of work hippie musician like you deserves to work for me?" "Because I studied every way that you screwed my band for over five years — and I know all your tricks." He hired me on the spot and within two years we'd become partners.

Richard Harris

LATE SUMMER, 2016:
THE EDGE OF DOWNTOWN LOS ANGELES

As a sinking sun mirrored in distant skyscrapers, Lauren and I, balancing lawn chairs and a picnic basket, jumbled our way down the rocky incline into MacArthur Park. Dodging a dead rat here, a glob of litter there we trudged our way to a bandshell that was fronted by an expanse of patchy lawn. As we approached, folks were setting up camp in front of the bandshell; some sat on blankets, others had elaborate tables with fancy wine coolers atop.

Bob Merlis, music P.R. maven, invited us to the outdoor event via Facebook. We were there to hear songwriter Jimmy Webb perform at the very park where he had penned the hit song of the same moniker back in 1967. It was a free concert, and Bob was assembling a group of comrades in music to join in. "Just bring chairs and food, and we'll picnic," he advised. The song, "MacArthur Park," was of remarkable significance to me. It represented a time in 1970 — almost forty-six years to the day — when I first learned that I could fib my way into a major showbiz deal.

* * * *

By 1968, Richard Harris was already recognized as a truly gifted actor and singer. He was best known for his roles in *Camelot, A Man Called Horse,* and *This Sporting Life* — which earned him an Oscar Nomination. But he achieved ultimate fame at the time with *McArthur Park*, an unheard of seven-minute song written by Jimmy Webb about the breakup of his love relationship. When *McArthur Park*, from the album, "A Tramp Shining," skyrocketed to #2 on the Billboard Hot 100, Richard left out on a national tour with a full orchestra in tow.

I was twenty-three at the time, and intrigued by a curious seven-minute hit recording by an Academy Award nominated Irish-born actor. When the show hit Minneapolis I hustled a couple of free tickets from the promoter and left to the Hennepin Theatre downtown. But halfway through the performance I noticed something odd; my date and I almost doubled the crowd! How could this be? His performance — a combination of great songs, spoken word, and stellar orchestrations — was over the top good. Richard was tall and lean with piercing eyes, cheekbones to die for, long, light brown hair, and trimmed beard. And he looked as if he could be equally as comfortable fronting a rock band, or as a knight in King Arthur's Court. How could a handsome actor with a hit film and a hit record have only a one-quarter audience?

After the show I discussed the empty audience situation with my partner, Dick Shapiro. We decided to write a letter to Richard Harris and drop it off at his hotel before he left town. In the letter we told him that I was a marketing person with a stellar background in promoting touring acts. It went on to say how pitiful it was that his audiences should be so sparse. "Shame on your marketing staff!" I said, like I was the foremost marketing guru in the nation. The next afternoon I received a call from Richard's manager in Los Angeles. "Richard read me your letter. You're damn right. Can you do everything you stated in the letter?" "And more" I said boldly. "Alright then, Richard and I need to meet with you in his suite at the Fontainebleau Hotel in Miami." "No problem. When?" "The day after tomorrow and bring your plan. I'll arrange a plane ticket." "Don't you worry; I'll be there!" I hung up the phone and ran into Dick's office. "What's up? You look like you've just seen a ghost! Did you ever hear back from Richard Harris?" "Yes, but..." "But what?" "Holy shit" I shouted, "I just lied my ass off and they hired me! Now what do we do? We've never done this before!" "You got us in to this, so you just do it," Dick said with a grin.

As the plane sailed towards Miami Beach, a feeling of panic came over me. I don't really have a plan, I thought. Take out some print ads? Buy radio spots? Those aren't fucking plans. They're just ways of spending money — and besides they're already doing that. Maybe I should just volunteer to walk outside of each venue with a sandwich board that says "See Richard Harris — Tonight Only!" Think Husney, or they're gonna beat you to a pulp for conning them! Think! Of the two hundred people who were at the show, who were they? What did they look like? Picture the fucking audience!

In my mind's eye I saw an audience of upscale thirtyish women and men who, I speculated, were married or close to being married. Many people, myself included, assumed the disjointed lyrics of "MacArthur Park" were hippie driven, but this was definitely not a "Hendrix" crowd. And, it felt to me like the men were attending the show at the behest of their significant others. The women in the audience also seemed to be clapping louder and longer than the men — and they were swooning over the handsome actor turned pop star.

I got to work and scribbled out a promotional plan on the back of a piece of paper. Basically, I determined that Richard's target audience was a thirty-five year old female — possibly a stay at home mom with young kids. I decided I would go into each market a week before Richard's gig and line up all the midday women's TV and radio shows for in-studio appearances by Richard. In addition, he would do "phoners" from the road to local press. Either the day before the show, or day of, he'd knock down everything I set up. The best part of the plan was that not one dime would be spent on buying TV, radio, or print advertising!

I presented the plan to Richard and his manager as the Atlantic Ocean glistened before us from the top floor suite of Miami's Fountain Bleu. "So, you're sure you can do this?"

Richard's manager offered. "Absolutely, I said, crossing my fingers behind my back." "Great, here's Richard's tour schedule, all you have to do is go into each market one week ahead of each date and line up the interviews. Just call in at the end of your day and let Richard's tour manager know where Richard has to be. Then, you'll come back into the city and get him to the interviews." "Huh? That means I'll be crisscrossing the US several times a week!" "Hey bud, it's your plan not mine. You're the one with experience. Just make it work. Here's the itinerary." I stared at the remaining dates: Cincinnati, New York (Johnny Carson show), Atlanta, Miami Beach, Buffalo, Columbus, Gaithersburg, Cleveland, Detroit, New York, Hartford, Philadelphia, and back to Los Angeles. Not a bad ride for a kid who just fibbed his way on to a major tour — with no experience.

Truthfully, it was easier than I thought to line up interviews for Richard. The midday radio and TV shows were hungry for the star of Broadway, the silver screen, and now a man with a hit song. Additionally, they all wanted to speak to Richard about his Irish roots, and his connection, if any, to the IRA — the Irish Republican Army. Simply put: The IRA was a movement that believed the whole of Ireland should be independent from the UK — and would use any violent means necessary to accomplish its goals. I was to advise interviewers and hosts in advance that the subject was taboo and that Richard would not discuss it — period. But Richard could take care of himself. At one radio interview in Cincinnati the male announcer thought he could buck the edict and asked Richard directly if he was involved with the IRA. "You were told in advance that I would not speak on this subject weren't you!" Richard fired back, Irish temperature rising. "Yes, but don't you think the radio audience has a right to know where you stand on the issue?" "No, I don't!" Richard responded, turning beat red. "Any more than your listeners should know that your hand has been trying to creep up my inner thigh for the past five minutes — and it's disgusting!" There was no seven-second delay in those days. And just like that the interview was over.

Suddenly, theaters were filling up and I was looking like the maharishi of marketing. My efforts were easy to confirm; advance ticket sales were sluggish. But because we were doing interviews on the day of the show the walk up sales at the door were huge. It was all great stuff, but there was a lesson to be learned about the rigors of the road and human behavior.

Because I had identified Richard's target audience as a woman in her mid-thirties, and directed all marketing and promotion in that direction, guess who showed up outside the station after a midday television or radio interview, or at the stage door for autographs? What I didn't know was that my efforts to attract these women to Richard's interviews and shows also meant that I had unwittingly become a pimp for this hard drinking, rabble-rousing, and womanizing star. If Richard spied a beauty in the crowd he'd call me over and have me, "Fetch her" for him. And it didn't seem to matter; if you're a 35-year-old housewife, happily married, with three children living in Omaha, and Richard Harris tells his "pimp" to tap you on the shoulder — you join Richard in his limo. I can't tell you the number of times I'd watch as woman after woman slipped her wedding ring into her purse as she followed me to Richard's car. I'd bet this parade of women would never, ever think of cheating on their husbands — but fuck it, it was Richard Harris, and so they followed me. It was a once in a lifetime opportunity — perhaps a break from the mundane — and besides, no one would ever believe it if they told them anyway. I often wonder how many 80-year-old women around the US today are still keeping that Richard Harris carnal secret.

Richard also had a special talent for consuming mind-boggling amounts of alcohol. Guinness and whiskey, or Guinness and champagne were his liquids of choice. There were many times after a show where I would watch him hit a local bar and down at least fifteen drinks. His drunken bleariness was something I had never seen or experienced even at the height of my druggie band days. Richard's relationship with Ann Turkel, a Jewish beauty, sixteen years his junior, was tumultuous to say the least. And, depending upon his most recent conversation with Ann, Richard's demeanor was either extremely cooperative, maniacal to the point of explosion, or where I thought he'd just plain drop dead from alcohol poisoning. People have reported that the two didn't start dating until later, but I remember Ann's name being mentioned frequently. Richard seemed quite jealous and stated many times, through a cloud of alcohol, that possibly his "girl" had met, and was dating one of the Beatles. The whole thing finally came to a head after a *Tonight Show* appearance with Johnny Carson.

After the *Tonight Show* (then taped in New York) we went to Richard's favorite bar where Vinnie the bartender poured glass after glass of Guinness and lined up shots of whiskey — six at a time. Some fifteen shots in Richard started jumping on tables, screaming lines from Shakespeare, and punching customers in the face until the police were called. He then ran from the bar and disappeared into the New York night. I was worried that the press would get a hold of this story. But comforted because Richard always asked for my room key before we went out. After he'd disappear from a bar I'd find him passed out in my hotel room, splayed naked across my bed — sometimes with a pool of vomit on the floor below. I'd check his breathing, remove the key from his floor-bound pants pocket, and retire to his suite. It was a great plan to avoid the press, and I got to sleep in some amazing hotel suites.

In late March the tour arrived early in the day in Buffalo New York. Richard was to be honored before his gig by the Roman Catholic archdiocese. Two hundred Priests and Nuns had gathered in a rustic lodge that looked more like the dinning hall in a Boy Scout camp. There was to be a dinner and subsequent speech by Richard. I felt honored when Richard asked me to sit on the dais with him. We were there about ten minutes when Richard excused himself to "take a leak." Twenty minutes later, still no Richard. I grew nervous. The bathroom was not connected to the lodge, and the outside temperature was twenty degrees. *Did Richard slip and fall on a patch of ice? Was he mugged on his way back?* I knew he hadn't been drinking because the event was very important to him. But Richard was my responsibility now. As the head Priest was delivering the last speech, Richard suddenly appeared back on the dais. "Whew! That was a close one," I said, "For a minute there I thought I was going to have to deliver the speech myself! And this doesn't quite look like a crowd that wants to hear what a twenty-three year old Jewish kid from Minneapolis has to say!" "Not to worry, Owen. Just watch the front door." Huh? Within a minute the door opened and in walked a Nun straightening her habit. "Are you fucking kidding me?" I whispered. "Got her from behind right up against the outside wall." Richard whispered back. He then got up and delivered his speech on the wonders of growing up Irish-Catholic as I sat speechless. I never knew if Richard was telling the truth or not, but I had personally seen him in action before — and he had no reason to lie.

The tour ended and I returned back to Minneapolis a star of sorts. When I was in New York I purchased a fedora and people thought the whole show biz thing had gone to my head. And they were right, I had moved up a notch in my career. But then, show biz reality set in.

My American Express bill came in the mail about a month later and the amount due was just over five thousand dollars! I called Amex only to find out that the bill was for a full week at the City Squire hotel in Manhattan. "Yes, Mr. Husney it says here that we have your signature on file. It's for ten rooms, a suite for a Mr. Harris, plus food and taxes. And you know, Mr. Husney, the amount is due immediately. Thank you very much, Goodbye." The bill might as well have been for a million dollars; I was just twenty-three in 1970, living on a shoestring, and could scarcely pay for gas, which was all of thirty cents, a gallon. I was immersed in anxiety and tried to think of how that could have happened. Was I a sleepwalker who loved to pay hotel bills for wealthy people? And then it hit me; the person responsible for paying for the hotel had maxed out his card and I was fresh young bait. I knew who he was — it was the fucking road manager. He always had a key to everyone's room for emergencies and I remember him coming into my room in the middle of the night. I awoke, and asked him what the problem was. "Oh, nothing Owen, I just entered the wrong room, so sorry." But the jerk came in, took my card, and charged the entire week's bill to me. Okay, perhaps the asshole forgot to pay me back. It didn't matter; in my mind I was facing the destruction of my career, debtor's prison, or both. But soon, my young boy's angst turned into an "eat, or be eaten" show business rage. I fired off an incendiary, "look what I've done for you and this is how you treat me?" letter, with the American Express bill attached, to the tour manager's company, Richard Harris, and Richard's manager. And all three paid me the five thousand dollars. I used the "profit" to start my own business, and almost immediately performed the same marketing function for Alice Cooper and Sonny & Cher from my new office. Touché.

* * * *

Jimmy Webb poured out his soul that night in MacArthur Park. He was infinitely more gifted than I had imagined — playing a Steinway grand piano with a pop fervor, yet a classical master's sense. He churned out hit after hit he had written for others: "Wichita Lineman," "Galveston," and "By The Time I Get To Phoenix." He then called up two members of the Fifth Dimension to sing one of his biggest hits, "Up, Up And Away." And then, he launched into a minute and a half piano intro to "MacArthur Park." The intro not only mesmerized the crowd on the lawn, but I'm sure would also have brought an audience to their feet at the posh Dorothy Chandler Pavilion less than a mile away.

After the outdoor performance I tried to get backstage to say hi to Jimmy and tell him how the genius of his song "MacArthur Park" gave a twenty-three year old kid from Minnesota the credibility to start a business. I wanted to tell him that that early experience on the road with Richard Harris had lead to my eventual discovery and management of the artist Prince. But the young security guy at the door only saw an old man with a lawn chair and told me to go away.

Elvis, a Bed, and Me

1971 was a tough year for American rock n' roll icons from the 50's. They were the true talents who fashioned, founded, and forged the template for all of pop music. By then the Katrina of musical storms known as The Beatles and the subsequent British invasion had swallowed them up and cast them upon the shores of yesterday. And as if that wasn't enough they were further engulfed by the quake of the Psychedelic firestorm. Music from The Doors and Jimi Hendrix was definitely not your parent's Bill Hayley and the Comets. Few artists of that era endured — most were consigned to the graveyard grind of oldies shows. There was one artist however who had clung to the lifeboat of popular musical culture and reigned supreme. He was the undisputed King and I was about to learn how to do the impossible for rock n' roll — and win.

"I'm bringing Elvis Presley to Minneapolis for two nights to the Metropolitan Sports Center. Are you the guy to handle the local preparations? If not, lets make this a very short call." The voice on the other end of the line had a thorn of a New York accent and a brash assertiveness that intimidated me from almost two thousand miles away. I knew who it was. He was Jerry Weintraub, the showbiz impresario who at the time either managed or promoted the likes of Frank Sinatra, Neil Diamond, Led Zeppelin, John Denver, and countless other major acts. The son of a gem dealer, Weintraub was born in Brooklyn in 1937 and was raised in the Bronx. He was so big in the biz that a little piker like me would never even think of calling him by his first name.

"Of course Mr. Weintraub, I'll line up the usual; limo, security, food prep, anything else?" I said. "Anything else? Are you fucking kidding me?" Mr. Weintraub belted one back at me. He was a legendary pro and I was scarcely learning to crawl. "This is the King schmuck. I can tell you're not the guy." Seeing this opportunity abruptly slip away my voice broke and squeaked out, "But I am the guy!" I needed this one for my résumé. Mr. Weintraub was right, this was ground zero, the King of rock n roll, and being able to tell other promoters that I had just worked with Elvis Presley would go a long way for my career. "Look, you were recommended to me so then be the guy, prove it, and listen to me." He said. "Yes, Mr. Weintraub."

"We take the whole wing of the hotel and it must be sealed off for security. Elvis, the Colonel, and I get in a day early and Elvis will need a separate place to rehearse so line that up and make sure its secure. Got it?" "Yes Mr. Weintraub." "There will be strict food requirements sent to you in advance and I want to know who the chef is so send me résumés, referrals, and any additional culinary suggestions." "Yes Mr. Weintraub." "I will come in to Minneapolis a week in advance of the show to check hotel security, limo service, food, and the rehearsal space." "Yes, Mr. Weintraub." "Mr. Weintraub?" "Yeah." "Can I watch Elvis rehearse?" "NO ONE is EVER allowed into Elvis's private rehearsal! Can you just be the guy and do your job?"

I really wanted to attend the rehearsal and meet "Colonel" Tom Parker. The Colonel was Elvis's infamous ex-carnival barker manager who outsmarted everyone in his path and manipulated Elvis Presley to the top. I knew from studying him that we both loved P.T. Barnum, the circus owner and master of controversy. It was rumored that P.T. would send shills out on to the circus grounds to tell people that the bearded lady in the tent was a fake. Curious throngs would then flock to the "bearded lady tent" to pay good money to see for themselves. I thought of Elvis gyrating his hips on the Ed Sullivan show forcing CBS execs to ordain that he only be allowed to seen from the waist up on future appearances. And I remember millions tuning in to see for themselves. In show business controversy – money. "Yes Mr. Weintraub, whatever it takes." I said.

With the precision of a Swiss watchmaker I lined up every minute detail for Elvis's arrival and counted the hours until Mr. Weintraub's inspection date. He met me at the Marriot hotel across from the venue. I had booked and arranged for security at the hotel and fought with management to seal off an entire wing.

"Now, lets see Elvis's suite," Mr. Weintraub barked. I took him to the top floor. Beaming, I opened the door of the suite. "Perfect, huh?" I said. "Are you fucking kidding me?" He shrieked. "What is it Mr. Weintraub?" "Do you think the King is going to sleep on that bed?" "Well, ah, it is a king bed" I pointed out. "When I come back next week I want to see a bed fit for the King, or you are out. The last thing I need is amateur hour in Minneapolis to destroy this tour for me!" "Yes, Mr. Weintraub, I already have a great idea." I said. "Good, then get it done."

But I had no idea. How could Mr. Weintraub be so disappointed? Why would he push the envelope so far over a freaking hotel bed that Elvis would only sleep on for two nights? I immediately called the hotel manager but he had no ideas. I called bedding store after bedding store and they had no ideas. In desperation I called my father and explained the situation to him. "Oh, you should call Moishe in St. Paul, he's had that furniture store since the 30's. He'll know what to do." Desperation will force you to call Moishe in St. Paul. "Come on over and see what I have." Moishe said with a thick Jewish accent.

The spider-webbed 1880's basement of Moishe's Bedding and More in downtown St. Paul yielded a jumble of unsold crappy furniture, pieces of scratched and dented wood scattered along the floor, and dust-laden broken lamps. As I listened to the creaky melody created by the footsteps of the customers walking along the wooden slat ceiling above I wondered if I should instead ask old Moishe for a job. This adventure was going nowhere. Was this really rock and roll?

"I'm in trouble Moishe." I said. "I need a bed fit for a king." Gesturing towards a murky corner of the basement he said, "Don't you worry, I have just what you need my boy." Let me get this light on it." Moishe grabbed the dingy shade of a light hanging from the ceiling by a threadbare cord and pushed the shadows out of the way. And suddenly there it was, the holy fucking grail of beds! Standing up against a wall, covered tightly in vinyl was a massive round bed that was 10 feet by 10 feet in all directions. I was beyond euphoric, and doubly thrilled to be back in show business. "Look, no one wants this bed, no one ever wanted this bed so you gonna give me twenty-five bucks, pay for the delivery, and its yours my son. I'll even throw in the custom-fitted round sheets and blankets. And for you I'll throw in the pedestal for the bed — no extra charge. Just get this thing outta here." I remember thinking how apropos the pedestal was for my King as I hugged old Moishe.

Mr. Weintraub showed up a day before Elvis's gig and asked to see the King's suite again. Throwing the door open his eyes gazed in elation at the spectacular colossus of a round bed that lay before him. "You get it, don't you? You did the impossible to make it happen!" "Yes Mr. Weintraub." "You have a natural feel for the business!" he said, putting an arm on my shoulder like the grand master so proud of his student. "Yes Mr. Weintraub. Thank you Mr. Weintraub." "So, I guess we'll be seeing you at the private rehearsal?" He said. "It will just be you, the Colonel, and me watching Elvis and the band." "Yes, Mr. Weintraub. Thank you so much Mr. Weintraub."

What Mr. Weintraub didn't know, or anyone else for that matter was that I paid the twenty-five bucks for the bed; therefore I owned the fucking bed. Two days before Mr. Weintraub showed up in Minneapolis I had struck a deal with the local rock radio station. After Elvis Presley left town they would giveaway the King's bed in an on-air contest during ratings sweeps. I would receive ten thousand dollars, five thousand dollars up front and five thousand dollars upon delivery of the bed to the station. I was just 23 years old and had just made ten thousand dollars for two hours work, which was exactly ten times my fee from Mr. Weintraub. If I would have thought about it I would have cut up the sheets into one inch squares and sold them for ten bucks apiece. Yes, I loved show business! Thank you Mr. Weintraub. Now I was the king.

I Killed My Childhood Friend

I killed my dear childhood friend in the winter of 1971. He was the only daily comfort I knew growing up in a tumultuous household. I lost my temper in the heat of the moment and he was gone. I can still see his face in death like it was yesterday. I swear I didn't do it on purpose.

This is my confession:

By 1971 my partner, Dick Shapiro, and I had built a nice business catering food backstage for major rock acts when they came through Minneapolis. Bands like Three Dog Night, Cat Stevens, and Steppenwolf dined in their dressing rooms on our spread of neatly folded bologna, white bread, chicken wings, various Wisconsin cheeses, and tiny meatballs.

The big money however was not in folding bologna but in actually being the promoter of the shows. We saw the promoters come into Minneapolis with their fancy suits and walk out with ten of thousands of dollars a night and we wanted in on that action.

I called Barbara Skydel, the legendary booking agent at Premiere Talent in New York. Our plan was to bring The Who to the Minneapolis Auditorium sometime after the first of the year. "And what promotion experience do you have?" Barbara said. "We do food backstage for all the major acts when they come to Minneapolis." I said. Hardly containing her laughter she said, "Chicken wings, tuna, and slaw hardly qualify as promoter experience. We do have a process though if you have money or investors." "I'm all ears," I said. "I'll let you start with one of our lesser acts, see how you do, and if successful we'll move you up the ladder to the major acts." "OK, where do we start?"

"Howdy Doody and Buffalo Bob Smith." You remember the kids TV show from the 50's?" "Of course, it was the biggest children's TV show ever." I said. "I grew up with Howdy Doody, but is he in a band these days?" "No, it's a baby-boomer nostalgia thing. 'The Howdy Doody Revival' staring Buffalo Bob Smith. It's gaining popularity with college students and doing big business in small auditoriums and college campuses. Buffalo Bob talks about the TV show, plays outtakes and clips, and answers questions from the audience. The kids love it!" "Well, OK, if that's what we have to do. But it's not exactly The Who."

Dick borrowed the money for half of the fifty percent show deposit and advertising budget from his father. The second half would be paid directly to Buffalo Bob from ticket sales before he went on stage. Dick and I were on the hook personally and we could now call ourselves promoters.

We booked the old twenty-six hundred-seat Orpheum Theater in downtown Minneapolis and set about buying advertising in all the local college campus newspapers and on local radio. We organized on-air radio interviews with Buffalo Bob, and arranged for clips of the old Howdy Doody show to be aired on local TV. It seemed as though everyone wanted to talk to Buffalo Bob and share their childhood memory of watching The Howdy Doody Show. Reporters and radio interviewers who previously never had the time of day for me were calling to talk to Bob. They fell over themselves reminiscing about Howdy, Clarabell the clown, Princess Summer-Fall-Winter-Spring, Phineas T. Bluster, and Pepe Mint. It was truly exhilarating and we were truly on our way in show biz.

One week before the show we realized we were in deep shit. Dick asked me what the pre-sales were and I answered, "Seven." "Seven hundred!" Dick said. "No, seven."

The evening of the show was no better. It was snowing heavily and we knew we were on the frozen titanic. "There's got to be a line outside the box office," Dick said. We hurried to the front door of the old Orpheum but outside there were only another seven people buried in snow.

Buffalo Bob showed up in his famous fringe jacket and quickly disappeared into his dressing room. I followed him and asked if maybe he could start a little later to allow all the ticket holders to get to the theatre since it was snowing. "I called Barb Skydel," he said. "She wants the other half of my deposit before I go on or there will be no Howdy Doody Revival. There's no one here!" I tried to reason with Buffalo Bob but he wouldn't hear any of it. Beneath the veneer of that famous leather fringe was a businessman who didn't want to get screwed. And we stood to lose $15,000 that we didn't have.

Dick made a hysterical phone call to his father from backstage and begged and hustled the other half of the deposit from him. He explained that the show must go on at all costs since anyone who showed up and bought a ticket would help cut our losses. Dick then drove full speed through blinding snow to pick up a check which he personally delivered backstage to good 'ol Buffalo Bob. All Bob said was, "Great." Dick left post-haste to check the ticket count in box office.

Meanwhile, backstage with Buffalo Bob I noticed an American treasure sitting on his dressing room table. There he was, Howdy Doody, my childhood idol, my daily dose of comfort growing up. I strained to count the 48 freckles on his face — one for each state. How remarkable I thought, that comforting puppet from my childhood is giving me diarrhea causing me to lose my ass.

"One minute to show time!" the stage manager bellowed. As Buffalo Bob got up and headed to the door I noticed that he wasn't taking Howdy Doody with him. "Bob, don't you think you're forgetting something?" I asked. "Oh, Owen, I'm sorry. Didn't Barb tell you? I don't have the rights to use Howdy. The rights are owned by NBC and they won't let me use Howdy in the show. It's just a Q&A with the audience." Turning beat red, I screamed, "But if you don't bring the fucking puppet out on stage the audience will want their fucking money back!" "I can't do that." Bob shouted. As the shouting progressed outside of the dressing room Dick and the stagehands came running. I lunged for Bob and he instinctively picked up Howdy Doody to protect him like he was an actual child. "You're taking the fucking puppet out on stage." I said, as Bob held on tight. "No! I can't take him out there, I told you!" By now, I was insane and pulling on Howdy. Buffalo Bob was pulling back. I grabbed Howdy's head and pulled hard. All of a sudden I pulled Howdy's head right off of his body. It was just a head with a wooden post in my hands. Howdy's eyes were wide open as he stared up at me in death. Everyone froze in disbelief. One of stagehands screamed, "My God! He killed Howdy Doody!" There was a collective gasp from the stagehands and crew. I thought there would be a riot. Bob, ashen-faced, ran back to his dressing room with the body parts and slammed the door behind him. Dick went out on stage and told the now seventy-five people in the audience that there would be a slight delay due to a minor "technical difficulty."

Buffalo Bob eventually emerged, went on stage for about twenty minutes, and just as quickly left for his hotel. We refunded the money to our patrons.

That night I learned my first lesson about show business. When you put your money and your head on the line in the entertainment business there is an excellent chance it's going to get chopped off. Just ask Howdy Doody and me.

Al Jarreau and the Impossible Concert

SEPTEMBER 2010:

Marilyn, my wife, and I were herded like cattle through the bowels of the Walt Disney concert hall — the acoustic masterpiece in Los Angeles designed by Frank Gehry. "This way to the green room," said a guy with a uniform and an all-access pass. "Mr. Jarreau will be right out to say hello. He's just taking a few minutes rest after the show." After some twenty minutes the doors in the back of the green room opened and in walked Al Jarreau — multiple Grammy award winner, and the most innovative jazz vocalist of our time. He entered with poise, wearing his signature black beret, a black vest, white shirt with sleeves rolled up, and a thin black tie — loose and open. But close up I could see that years of touring had taken its toll. He looked so exhausted and road weary that I was taken aback. Al said a few obligatory hellos to his fans and signed a few autographs. But as soon as he saw Marilyn and me he lit up, cracked an ear-to-ear smile, and spread his arms wide. He hugged us in a big group hug and said out loud, "Oh ya dere Mr. Husney den. I can come fix your roof on Toosdee den — geezus she looks like a big job ya know!" We all broke into laughter while his fans and my wife looked on in bewilderment.

Al was remembering a time in Minneapolis, back in the early seventies, when he was dating Marilyn and the three of us were thick as thieves. I taught him how to speak "Minnesotan," a Midwestern accent the Coen Brothers would eventually make infamous in the movie Fargo. Al was from Milwaukee, so no stranger to Germanic accents. But he adored Emo, my character that would come to your house and fix anything. That is — as long as it was on a, "Toosdee, Wensdee, or Fridee." Marilyn said something through our laughter. Al leaned forward and said, "I'm sorry, I didn't get that." "You too?" Marilyn said. Marilyn then reached to her ear and produced a hearing aid. Al then reached up and produced one from each of his ears. I watched in astonishment as they compared hearing aids. Then, we all laughed again. It suddenly hit us how far we had come from a time, almost forty years prior, when the three of us were the hippest of the coolest of the hip — living and working in Minneapolis, a town on the cusp of becoming one of the leading pop music capitols in the world.

MARCH 1973:

I sat alone in my office behind a locked door. Tears, like rain, fell from my eyes — splashing on my desk. It was just so sad. She didn't deserve to die. She was so young and vibrant, and they were so in love. And then, her life was snatched from her. When his estranged father came to help it was too late. The father started to apologize to his son, but the son stopped him and uttered the very words his wife said before her death, "Love means never having to say you're sorry." I closed the last tear-stained page of the book and put my head down on my desk.

My girlfriend suggested I read Love Story. We first met when she was a rock singer in a local band and I was her booking agent. One afternoon, she came to my office with her boyfriend but stayed, and left with me by nightfall. From that moment on we experienced a kind of romance that in my youth I would have thought corny, but in my early twenties never thought possible: staring into each other's eyes, making snow angels, and giggling under the warmth of a blanket as a fire roared in the fireplace. We were as happy as could be, and I was experiencing a love I had never known before — not at home, not anywhere. Could my true love be snatched away from me in death? My eyes welled up again. Just then, there was a knock on my door. "Who is it?

Go away!" "Owen, there's someone on the phone named Shelly. He manages a jazz artist and he really wants to speak with you." "Get his number and I'll call him back!" I barked. Whoever he was there was no way I could speak with him in my frail condition.

Dick Shapiro's office was in the Towers apartments, a new high rise in downtown Minneapolis. From my office I could see the expanse of our small downtown and the only two skyscrapers in the city; the Foshay Tower, a 1928 replica of the Washington Monument, and the sleek new towering IDS building just completed. It had been just a few years since I'd lied my way into the production services business. I answered the phone one day. It was from Golden Star Productions in San Francisco. "We're bringing Three Dog Night to the Minneapolis Auditorium. Someone gave us your number and said you could supply us with a local band as the opening act." "Absolutely," I said. "And, of course, you know about our producer services?" I said. "Not really, please explain." "We handle all logistics for you locally. That includes hotels, limousine service, security, and even food backstage in the artist's dressing rooms." "What a great service! Of course we'll use you. What do you charge?" Since I had never done anything like this before I said, "It's on a case by case basis according to the artist and the venue. Can I get back to you tomorrow?" "Of course," came the reply from the excited promoter. I hung up the phone and ran into Dick's office. "We just started a new business and I don't know what the fuck to do or how charge the guy!" I said, both motivated and scared shitless. "Tell him six hundred bucks and go figure out what to do."

I remembered the doorman to our office telling me he bought a used limousine and would do airport runs for the folks in the building — so I called and hired him. I phoned a local company that provided security for sporting events and hired them. And of course they would all pay me a "small reimbursement" for using their services. As for backstage food, I would do that myself. Deli trays and a grocery store run would suffice. I wanted to be alone in the dressing room with the acts. It would be an education listening to the banter of the acts, their roadies, and managers as I sliced cheese and folded meats into crust-less sandwiches. Eventually, Golden Star hired us on a permanent basis. And I wound up backstage with the likes of: Three Dog Night, Janis Joplin, and Steppenwolf as they toured the Midwest. Eventually, I wrote ads, bought media time on local radio stations, and designed print ads for the promoters. And, of course, put local acts on the bill whenever I could.

"Shelly? This is Owen Husney, Central Booking Agency, calling you back. Sorry I couldn't talk earlier but we were in a routing meeting." I said, drying the tears from my eyes. "Thanks Owen, I'd like to come by your office with Al Jarreau. Al's a jazz singer who's had some success recently and we'd like to take it to the next step." "You're welcome to come by Shelly, but we book local rock bands and provide producer services for national concert promoters. Jazz is not what we really do." That's okay. Do you mind if we come by at two tomorrow." I liked that Shelly wasn't giving up, so I agreed.

Although I'd never heard of Al Jarreau, I felt I was in the presence of greatness when I met him. He was physically beautiful: a tall and sleek light-skinned black man with a warmhearted smile that you couldn't help but answer with your own smile. To me, he looked like a movie star. Shelly explained that Al had a Bachelor of Science degree in Psychology and a master's degree in vocal rehabilitation but his passion was singing. He said that Al had appeared on Johnny Carson but he was having trouble converting that exposure into a solid career. "To experience Al is to see him live," Shelly continued. While Al thumbed through my water logged copy of Love Story Shelly played some live recordings from Al's club dates. I knew in an instant that he was the shit. He wasn't just singing jazz classics and a few original songs; Al was mimicking various instruments. "That sounds like someone putting an elbow on a conga drum." "Well, it's Al doing that vocally." "And who's playing bass?" Again, that's Al." It didn't take long to realize that an angel of vocal supremacy had just floated into my office. Al was a brilliant one-man vocal orchestra, and I wanted in.

"So, what can I do for you?" I said, wishing there was something I could do but not knowing what that would be. "I want Al to open for a national act with a large audience so he can gain exposure and hopefully get noticed by industry execs. "So why come to me?" "We came to you because you provide major promoters with opening acts," Shelly said, doing his manager thing. "We do, but the promoters we work for have acts like Steppenwolf — hardly your audience." "It doesn't matter, Al will hold his own." I thought Shelly was nuts so testing him I said, "Well, all I have at this time is an opening slot with Canned Heat in Winnipeg Canada. And that's in two weeks." I fully expected them to turn down the offer cold when Al, still holding the book, jumped in; "That's great, we'll take it!"

"Listen, Canned Heat is like a hippie-blues-biker band. I think their name implies drinking Sterno to get drunk or high or something — I've seen their audience, they'll beat you to death or eat you alive — take your choice. Have you ever seen the lead singer Bob Hite? He's a giant grizzly of a man. I can't let you do it. You're a classic jazz performer in every sense. It would be a suicide mission." "Great we'll take it," Al repeated with a smile that again demanded a return smile. Al put down my Love Story and they left. I called the promoter, Golden Star Productions, and talked them into letting Al open. Shortly thereafter Al rehearsed with a couple of Minneapolis's finest musicians and headed for Canned Heat in Canada.

I paced back and forth backstage that night in the Winnipeg concert hall. Soon, the Canned Heat audience piled in to the theater. Scared for my life I peered out from a small break in the curtain. It was an out-and-out array of motorcycle jackets, lumberjack shirts, and boots with thick buckles on the side. The pristine concert hall stank with the smell of cigarettes, pot, and belched up beer. What the hell did I do? I thought. I'm not only putting Al's career on the line but his very life will be at stake once these folks get an eyeful of him. I cringed as the house lights went down and the curtain came up. Al walked out confidently, introduced himself, and launched into an original song replicating a bass guitar with his voice. After a few little heckles and laughs I couldn't bear to watch and retreated to the safety of an unused backstage dressing room. Alone in the dark with my mistake I could hear muffled screams traveling through the heating grate from the stage. The screams grew louder. I imagined poor Al being torn to shreds by ravenous wolves on a bone while he continued to sing with his last breath. And then, I remembered that fateful night when the letter jacket boys showed up to beat the shit out me when we performed at my school homecoming dance. I burst from the dressing room like Superman ready to save poor Al's life.

The screams grew louder as I approached the backstage area and I thought I heard a gunshot. I imagined the crowd running from their seats, stepping on each other in the crush. A stagehand ran past me and said, "Did you see that?" Fear bordering on panic came over me.

But there was no gunshot. As I approached the stage all I could hear was applause — wild applause. I didn't know it but Al was on his third ovation and encore performance. The audience was on their feet! A roadie for Canned Heat tapped me on the shoulder and told me to get Al off the stage. "He's just the fucking opening act," he screamed above the applause. "No one is gonna want to see Canned Heat! Get him off now or I'll do it!"

Al, Marilyn, and I hung out that following summer. He was dating Marilyn and the three of us were inseparable. I dubbed us the "Minnesota Mod Squad." We engaged in all manner of the 70's Minneapolis hipster experience: endless music and limitless pot. We loved antiquing at house sales in Kenwood, the old 1800's neighborhood of mansions where Marilyn and I were neighbors. We'd sit around and critique Marilyn's taped radio show. It was called "Marilyn's Scene." I figured that she should come backstage with me and try to get taped interviews from the acts while I made veggie trays for them — perfect access. I sold the star-studded interview show to KQRS FM, the emerging powerhouse of album oriented rock radio. And Al continued to rehearse and play gigs around town with his all-star band of Minneapolis musicians. It was all capped off when Al performed on a live radio broadcast from a local recording studio. Thousands of people heard the broadcast and fell in love. It turned out that Al's style and talent crossed every border and appealed to all audiences. Greatness is greatness.

By the end of the summer it was evident that Al needed to move on in order to foster his career. You could effectively formulate your career in Minneapolis, but sooner or later you have to move on to achieve true national or international prominence. My client, Golden Star Productions, who at great risk agreed to put Al on the Canned Heat show, loved Al as much as I did. Together, we put him on as an opening act for as many shows as possible and the results were always the same — standing ovations. We decided to fund a trip to Los Angeles for Al to find management while continuing to have him open for national acts.

It never occurred to me to manage Al. I knew his manager Shelly had taken him as far as he could go because Al discussed it with me in private. It was apparent that a change was in order. And from my backstage experience — listening to acts and their managers — the last thing I wanted to do was feed the unending narcissistic needs of an act that could fire me at will. Backstage food can't fire you. And though Al was a great guy, somehow managing acts was low on my list of future career activities. Around that same time Patrick Rains, also a local Minneapolis promoter, headed to Los Angeles to manage a local hard rock band. Pat was competent, disciplined, and efficient. So with initial funding from Golden Star Al was on a plane to LA where introductions were made.

"Owen, Pat Rains is on the phone from Los Angeles!" my secretary squawked from the intercom. "What's up Pat? I said, grabbing the phone from her hands. "Last night Al played the

Troubadour," he exclaimed. "Yeah I know, a friend called me from LA and said you got Al a gig there. What happened? A standing ovation?" "Better," he said. "Mo Ostin, the chairman of Warner Bros records was there and offered us a recording deal on the spot!" "That's great Pat!" I mumbled. "Please tell Al I knew it all along!"

I hung up the phone and slumped down in the chair; my face in my hands. I was unable to hold back my sadness. This time there would be no Love Story to blame for my tears. I was jealous as hell and felt like a damn fool. I knew Al was the shit, so why wasn't it me who got him the deal? Yeah, I didn't want to be a manager but the reality of what just happened hit me like a freight train. Why wasn't I there instead of Pat? I can spot talent, promote that talent, and make it happen for them. What the fuck was I thinking?

I vowed to myself that if another artist of ultra-talent ever walked through my doors again that I would manage that artist. I'd be the one to bring them to Mo Ostin, the Chairman of Warner Bros. But seriously, how many ultra-talented people the likes of Al Jarreau would ever cross my path again in Minneapolis? Surely it would be a one in a million shot — which meant never. My eyes welled up at the thought.

A Little History:
Twin Cities Music

"Y ou don't get to choose where you'll be born, or if you even want to be here at all.

Your parents get it on and from there it's all the luck of the draw."

The random quirk that planted so many talented people in Minneapolis, Minnesota defies the odds of population percentages. And, in an added gift of irony, the relentless Minnesota winter presents that talent with a colossal boost to their creativity.

The prolonged cold creeps in by the end of September and struggles to let go on the heels of May. The first snowfall is beautiful — picture any Christmas card. Come midwinter, the once pristine snow turns brown with the soot of belching chimneys. Roadways turn black from exhaust and the filth of unwashed, salted cars. The temperature can dip to twenty below zero and beyond. The sun barely makes an appearance.

Outdoors, everyone is bizarrely equal. Trying to look hip is for idiots. Only fur lined and hooded military survival wear keeps you alive. If you have means you get the hell out for a month and flee to warmer climes. But if you're young, gifted, and poor there is no escape. It's a microphone, your instrument, and a heater in your bedroom or basement that offers you the only way out. Like an unrelenting taskmaster the interminable Minnesota winter keeps you focused, and empowers you to become a better artist.

You know Bob Dylan, Prince, The Time, Vanity Six, Jimmy Jam and Terry Lewis, Jesse Johnson, Andre Cymone, Jayhawks, Mint Condition, The Sounds of Blackness, Apolonia, Lipps, Inc., The Replacements, Alexander O'Neal, Semisonic, Marcy Playground, Hüsker Dü, Soul Asylum, Paul Westerberg, Peter Himmelman, Chameleon featuring Yanni, Bob Mould, and The

Jets. But did you know, beginning in the late 50's, the Twin Cities was already becoming a vibrant music scene spawning charted hits? The Fendermen, Korner, Ray, and Glover, Dave Dudley, The Trashmen, Bobby Vee, The Castaways, The Underbeats, Gypsy, Crow, The Accents, The Chancellors, The High Spirits, and The Gestures, all hailed from the frozen tundra with local, US, and worldwide hits.

The Twin Cities was also home to 3M, Pillsbury, USBancorp, General Mills, IDS, Target Corporation and Best Buy. These Fortune 500 corporations did their best to support the arts and donated generously. If you lived in the area you didn't realize it but you may have been the recipient of their grants to local community centers where bands could play live.

There was also a community of booking agents, clubs, and a wealth of recording studios to lay down your tracks. There were radio stations that would play your record, and a record label with powerhouse distribution to get your music into the hands of the public. Ground zero was SOMA Records, owned by the Heilicher Brothers.

The sons of an immigrant Hebrew teacher, Amos and Danny Heilicher, hailed from the North side, a predominately Jewish area of Minneapolis. The area was acknowledged for being "lenient" in renting to minorities, aka Jews. In the 1930's, while still in high school, they saved enough money from odd jobs to buy a small printing press. At first they printed calling cards, an early form of business cards. Then, they began printing scorecards with game dates for sale at University of Minnesota Gopher football games. They pressed them up in their basement, worked every street corner near the stadium, and made $150.00 per game — a tidy sum to help support their post-depression family. Then, one-day things changed. As Amos put it, "There was a house of ill repute across the street on the North side's Plymouth Avenue that needed music for the jukebox. The customers kept complaining about hearing the same songs over and over. Danny and I offered to change-out the music every so often for a fee and they agreed". Soon after, the Heilicher Brothers were changing out music for every jukebox in the Midwest and making a small fortune. "We had this little truck and Danny would drive around throughout the five-state area delivering music and changing out machines, the cash was rolling in! And it was a cash business! Soon after, with a loan from our uncle, we bought our first five jukeboxes. Eventually, we owned a jukebox in every soda shop in the Midwest. One day, we were sitting in our office and Mercury records called. They asked if we would like to distribute their product to retail stores and jukeboxes and we agreed. Soon after, RCA and Columbia Records called and we added them to our route. We didn't know it but at the time but we were among a handful of people who invented rack jobbing and record distribution."

One day, while reading a local newspaper, Amos came across an article about a small record store in Duluth Minnesota that had gone bankrupt. "Danny, what if we bought this store named Musicland, and combined it with our record store?" By the late 60's, Musicland record stores were stuffed into every new mall in America. Musicland would evolve to become the largest record store chain in the world. Within a few short years the Sam Goody chain was bought out and the operation renamed Musicland/Sam Goody.

By 1970, Amos Heilicher was considered one of the most powerful people in the music industry, landing that year on an Esquire magazine list with Mick Jagger, Paul Simon and Motown founder Berry Gordy. At one time the Heilichers moved 20% of the records sold in America. Amos, Danny, and Amos's son Ira could also take a local record such as the Fendermen's "Mule Skinner Blues", The Trashmen's "Surfin' Bird," the Castaways' "Liar, Liar" or Dave Dudley's "Six Days on the Road" and make it a national hit on their SOMA record label (Amos spelled backwards). "We could get the airplay, prominently feature the record in our stores, and distribute it nationally to other retail stores. Then, we'd sit back and watch it climb the charts." In 1958/59 their first hit, "Mule Skinner Blues," reached the top 10 on the Billboard charts. "To facilitate the hits we bought Kay Bank, a recording studio on the southeast side of town." By 1963, hits by pop and rock bands were rolling out of their offices on Glenwood Ave at the edge of downtown Minneapolis. My group, The High Spirits, grew to large regional fame thanks to Kay Bank studios and SOMA Records. The Heilichers opened the door for the next generation of artists, record labels, and studios. Within a decade, other strategic labels like Twin/Tone Records would come to life and spawn major indie acts like, The Replacements, Soul Asylum, The Suburbs, and The Jayhawks.

The Jewish population on the city's North side left to the suburbs in the late 60's early 70's. And, with the still "lenient" rental and sales practices, other minorities were able to rent and own in the area. The same was happening on the city's south side. Within those areas another genre of music was taking hold. Soul artists and bands like The Valdons, Haze, Cohesion, The Lewis Connection, Prophets of Peace, Willie Walker, Jerry Hubbard, Morris Wilson, Bobby Lyle, The Stylle Band, The Amazers, Walter Lewis and the Blue Stars, Ronnie Robbins, Herman Jones, Mind and Matter were writing, recording, and releasing records. They paved the way for the next generation of Funk artists. Soon, bands and artists like Flyte Tyme featuring Terry Lewis and Jimmy Jam, Grand Central featuring Prince, Andre Cymone, and Morris Day, Alexander O'Neal, Sue Ann Carwell and Cynthia Johnson would be breaking onto the scene. Most of these bands and artists were well known in their communities but off the radar for larger club owners, managers, and booking agents. By the mid 70's things would change as the two worlds of music collided. The stage was set for the musical big bang.

The big bang was not the result of a battle of the races, or a battle of genres — not even a battle of the bands. It was the cohesive bonding of forces — the force of super talented artists and business people with a passion for music. Though they may not have known it at the time they were all contributing to the creation of a new sound that would soon explode upon the world.

Prior to Prince, engineer and producer, David "Z" Rivkin was recording many of the soul and R&B bands in town, bringing their hit talent to light. I credit David as one of the true founding fathers of the emerging music scene. Soon after, I became aware of the real music wunderkinds who were emerging from the North and South side of the town. I started hanging in clubs like the Elks lodge and the Nacirema (American spelled backwards) and was blown away by the sheer amount of talent.

Across town, small studio owner Chris Moon would soon give of his studio and his time to young artists by negating many of the studio costs. Like Berry Gordy in Detroit, Sam Phillips in Memphis, Gamble and huff in Philadelphia, and Chess Records in Chicago there must be a business infrastructure to support the creative talent. If not, the talent leaves for places like Los Angeles, New York, or Nashville. I like to think that working together we all found our small place in history by keeping the music in the Twin Cities. Together, we lived our passion, worked hard, and helped create what would become known to the world as the "Minneapolis Sound."

This Chapter Is Not About Prince — It's About Me

PART ONE: DECEMBER 1975:

There was a blizzard howling outside that night when Cliff Siegel brought Russ Thyret — his boss, and VP of Warner Brothers Records in Los Angeles, around to my house in Minneapolis. Cliff, the lead singer of our 60's band had landed a most coveted job as regional promotion man for Warner Bros Records. His job was to get records played on radio stations no matter what it took. Brilliance, supreme knowledge of pop music, and a super personality were necessary attributes of the gig — but sex, cocaine, and money usually did the trick.

Russ was a big deal in the biz and directly responsible for the success of many acts of the time including the enormous success of Fleetwood Mac.

My wife, Britt, and I had a beautiful cabin-like home across from Cedar Lake on the cusp of downtown Minneapolis. Its large bubble stone fireplace threw off enough heat and glow to give the cabin a super cozy feel. It was just enough comfort to give an LA dude respite from his stark hotel room in the frozen tundra.

Russ was portly, with freckles on a roundish face, and red hair. When he spoke, he looked me directly in the eyes, and the words flew out at a hundred miles an hour. I had the feeling that if I didn't listen closely I'd miss something of great importance. This was a man of overriding passion, intellect, and heart — all coupled with the drive of a speeding locomotive.

That evening, over beer, drugs, and rock and roll the four of us bonded in the way survivors of natural disasters do. Russ was most appreciative as we said our goodbyes in the wee hours, and we promised to keep in touch.

Less than a year later I wrote Russ a letter and told him of my desire to relocate to Los Angeles and work for WB in their marketing department. With the help of Cliff he gave me a test. WB needed an ad campaign for Randy Newman's album "Good Old Boys" and Little Feat's new album, "Feats Don't Fail Me Now." My ad agency, The Ad Company, had just enlisted an 86-year-old woman, Ruth Sherman, to do a series of radio ads for a local record store and head shop, The Electric Fetus. We made her, "The Mother of Them All" for the Electric Fetus. The campaign took off in a big way. The ads were so successful that she became the toast of the town — throwing rolling papers off the stage at an REO Speedwagon concert in St. Paul, and riding in the Gay rights parade in Minneapolis. Why not use her for Randy Newman's, "Good Old Boys" album I thought? I demoed the spot and Cliff shipped it off to Russ. The answer came back, "Fantastic, we'll use it nationally!" Within a month, I was on a plane to Los Angeles to see about working at Warner Brother's Records.

A DREAM COMES TRUE:

I spent a week inside of Warner Bros Records in Burbank. At night we visited with artists and managers. An afternoon with Stevie Nicks at her house in Hollywood proved to be my new appearance as a comedian; "My doctor warned me against the evils of snorting cocaine," She offered out of the blue. "He said I could develop a deviated septum that would destroy my voice." "Sounds like good advice," someone in the room injected. "The doc said, if I had to do it I should take it in suppository form." Not missing a beat I responded with, "But then you'll get a deviated rectum." The room broke out in laughter and Stevie, laughing out loud, suggested that Russ send me back to the "Corny" Midwest on the next plane. We dined with legendary manager Alfred Grossman (Peter, Paul and Mary, Bob Dylan, Todd Rundgren, The Band, and Janis Joplin) at Roy's on the Sunset

Strip, and hung out with writer/producer Norman Whitfield ("Ain't Too Proud to Beg", "I Heard it Through the Grapevine," "War," "Car Wash").

Being on the inside of WB was everything I had hoped for with one exception; I never slept. In the 70's, cocaine ruled the record biz. It seemed nothing got done without the magical white powder. Almost every artist, manager, record company employee, and radio station program director survived on the stuff. It was the powdery grease that made the giant gears of the music biz turn. I had been a musician-hippie in the 60's and no stranger to drugs, but I was naturally super-charged and had no need for the stuff. And after a week of snorting my way through Los Angeles I'd had it. My teeth hurt from grinding, I was a nervous wreck, and the lack of sleep made me feel like donning a camouflage outfit and killing someone. If I didn't get back to Minneapolis quick I was sure I would die, or worse, wipe out a whole neighborhood. Russ could tell that I wasn't cut out for the gig too. I don't know, maybe it was my red eyes and gray complexion. I told Russ, thanks but no thanks, and he didn't disagree. But he still believed in me and I told him that because of his generosity, belief, and warmth that I would make it up to him. But I had no idea how — until…

Six months after returning to Minneapolis Chris Moon, a young, small-studio owner brought me a rough demo tape of a young kid named Prince Rogers Nelson. I was knocked out. It was then that I hatched the plan to make him part of the WB family. Yes, it's quite possible that Prince was signed to WB because I didn't want to die from cocaine and wanted to make it up to Russ, the man I knew who could take him to the top. It's just a possibility.

SEPTEMBER 1976:

Chris Moon was humble and almost apologetic as he walked in to my office. He was in his early twenties, of fair complexion — tall and thin but not lanky. His light brown hair was cut almost in a Beatle mop top but more hip-exec. It worked well with his blue eyes and a moustache that stretched straight across his upper lip almost to his cheeks. A sweater swung over his shoulders lent him an almost preppy look. "I'm so sorry to bother you Mr. Husney but I thought you'd be interested in this project that I recorded in my 8-track studio" he said, in an accent that defied origin. I couldn't tell if he was English, Australian, or perhaps South African. Whatever it was he used it for full effect. Chris reached into his briefcase, produced a single cassette and popped it into my player. From that moment on my life, the lives of everyone around me, and the course of music history would change forever.

I spotted Chris just two days before. He was sitting on the couch in the reception area of my office reading a magazine. I noticed him when I came back in a huff from a client meeting for the ad agency I co-owned with DJ Rosenberg. The client just told me that people like to buy Chevrolets because they are, "Chevys and nothing else." I just told him that was bullshit. "People who want a car in that utilitarian price range want a low payment in a color they like, period. And that's your campaign, take it or leave it," I bellowed. The client said the meeting was over and I agreed. When I returned to my office I walked right past Chris, into my office, and shut the door.

The intercom fired off a loud beep and my receptionist barked in that a gentleman by the name of Chris Moon was waiting to see me. "He said he has something really big for you. Something about Stevie Wonder." She lowered her voice, "And he's been waiting a very long time for you to return." "Tell him he can come back tomorrow with his big thing; maybe it will be smaller by then. Get the creative team in here! We're sticking to our guns with this asshole car dealership."

The next morning Chris was back on my couch when I came in to work. The minute I got into my office the receptionist beeped in, "Chris Moon is here and he's been waiting…." "I know, I have eyes," I said, firm in my self-importance. "Tell him this afternoon sometime." When I left for lunch Chris was on the couch, and when I returned he was still there. I buzzed into the receptionist, "Does this guy ever eat or sleep? After I tell the client what's good for him I'll see this guy Chris."

I stayed resolute with the client, and even enhanced my point of view. "Can't you see it? I can. We're gonna circle the city with billboards." The client mumbled something inaudible but I continued. "Why billboards? Because this is 1976, everyone drives now; and drivers are captive audiences. The streets are like one big giant outdoor theater that everyone has to go to every day." "What're they gonna say?" The client questioned. Knowing that I was reeling him in I slowed down the patter. "I see simple white block lettering on a black background, ten words, that's it. Drivers have about a three second window. Forget the balloons and the hotdogs. We'll have billboards ringing the city that say: — BUY A LOW PAYMENT IN A COLOR YOU LIKE SUBURBAN CHEVROLET." The pause on the other end of the phone let me know that he liked it. If he didn't, he would have shot back a negative immediately. To play power games at this point and make me sweat would just be a waste of time. He just needed to save face in the moment. "Can your art director mock it up so we can see what it looks like?" "Done, we'll have it for you in two days." I hung up and told my receptionist to, "Send in that Chris Moon guy with his big thing."

I started The Ad Company in 1972. It grew out of my buying media time for major concert promoters when they brought the big acts in to town. By 1976, I was just twenty-eight years old, we were billing in the millions, and had fifteen employees. DJ and I had just taken over the first floor of the old Northwestern Life Insurance building, a gorgeous Beaux-Arts building built in 1924 on the edge of downtown Minneapolis. The offices overlooked the two small lakes of Loring Park. Our client list included Warner Bros Records, Doubleday rock radio stations across the country, high-end fashion stores, and of course car dealerships. In addition, I owned a music management company and was promoting concerts at The Marigold Ballroom, an art deco nightclub downtown.

Chris pressed play and messed with the volume while I shuffled through the papers on my desk. I had been to this party before. Usually it was the artist themselves, a band, or the parents of some young kid. They were all hoping for the big time so they came to see me, the music guy. Stopping the player mid-song my answer was always the same, "That shows real promise but it's not quite ready yet. Come back in maybe three to four years." But as Chris's cassette rolled on I was compelled to hear more. It was that feeling when you bite into something so great you immediately take two more bites before swallowing the first one. Or, the first time you try cocaine and it works.

As a former musician I listened with a different set of ears than most. I was able to pick apart subtle nuances that separated greatness from fiction. It was hard to fool me. What struck me about the song was that the intro was not only memorable but also methodically original. For sure, the demo was not record ready, and possibly too long, but someone had endeavored to create a new instrumental sound and tonal quality. Whomever it was they were obviously borrowing from sonic elements of the day; Sly and the Family Stone, Santana, perhaps a bit of Hendrix — but the end result was they had created something entirely new. With a mix of guitar and keyboards — working together harmoniously — the music defied comparison to other acts of the day. The vocalist came in singing something about angora fur, the Aegean sea, and a soft wet love with such an endearing and vulnerable male falsetto that I wanted to simultaneously hug him, protect him, and sign him — even though I had no idea who he was. I could tell the singer was black but the song itself crossed many barriers where most artists of the day either refused to go, or just plain lacked the ability to get there. It was definitely a fusion of R&B, Pop, rock, and Soul. I was in shock and remember thinking; damn I hope he's not nasty looking!

"What's the title?" I asked, as the song drifted into the chorus. "Soft and Wet," Chris replied, like someone who had lived with it for so long it had finally become an appendage. Perfect, I thought. Whoever crafted this track knew exactly what they were doing with the title. Yeah, it could mean that, or it could just be your dirty little mind going there. Plausible deniability — pop music genius!

"So, who's the band?" "It's not exactly a band," Chris shot back. "Shit, you mean it's a bunch of studio musicians?" "No, not exactly." "Then what is it?" Chris cocked a sly smile and looked directly in my eyes. "It's one kid. He's just turned eighteen, and he's playing all the instruments and singing all the vocal parts. We co-wrote the lyrics and recorded it at Moonsound, my 8-track studio just down the road. Still in shock the only question I could muster was, "Does he have a name?" "Yeah, Prince Nelson." "Really!!" I said, almost losing my big man cool. "You come in here telling me you've got a Stevie Wonder one man band, who writes the music, sings everything, and he's the Prince of some country? How does the fairy tale end?" "No, he's from North Minneapolis. He and his friend Andre both live in Andre's mother's basement — Prince is his real name."

I hunkered down in my couch while Chris carried on; "He came to my studio last year with a band called Champagne. We struck up a relationship during the process. After a week or so he absorbed all the information he needed to record by himself."

I desperately wanted to believe this fairy tale. "So, what did you do?" "I gave him the keys to my studio. I told him he could let himself in after school and do whatever he wanted. Our deal was that in return we'd work on songs together, make a demo tape, and get him recording deal." "And what's in it for you?" I said, the wheels turning. "All I want is co-writing credit." "And what can I do for you?" Just then my receptionist came through the intercom. "It's the Chevrolet client and he needs to speak with you ASAP." "Tell him I'm out of the office and take a message," I said, muting the speaker. "Chris, what else is on that cassette? Let's hear everything." We both sat silent as, "My Love Is Forever" and "Aces," filled the room with undeniable talent. "How old did you say he was?"

I already knew what I could do for Chris and the vulnerable artist on that tape. But first I had to meet this Prince Nelson. "Where is he now can we call him?" The one thing I learned in this business is that if you're in to a project you move fast — no, you move at lightning speed. If you don't, you lose. "Right now he's at his sister Sharon's place in New York." Chris said. "We've been trying to get a record deal with the demo but we're not having any luck." Chris continued. We just can't believe that no one gets it. That's why I'm here to see you." Chris continued, looking a bit dumbfounded. "We need a music business and marketing guy. We need you." Once his spiel was over Chris too sank into the couch. "Then we need to call him right away. Here, use my phone. Just dial 9, and call straight out. Don't worry about the expense."

"Prince, it's Chris, I'm here with Owen Husney at his office." I overheard a deep voice on the other end mumble something. Was this the same voice I just heard singing in that vulnerable falsetto? Wow! "You know, the music guy I told you about. He likes the tracks we cut and would like to say hello." The deep voice mumbled something and Chris handed me the phone.

"Hey Prince." There was a long pause and the deep voice spoke. "Yes." That was it? Just yes? "I really like what I heard," I said. "Thank you." That's it? Thank you? There was nothing mean in his response. In fact, he was quite polite, if not a bit calculated. "Well, I'd love to get together with you when you're back in Minneapolis and hear some more music. What I just heard was great." There was another long pause for me to wade through. "Okay." "Okay then, and Prince?" "Yes." You're young and this is a funky business. I will protect you." I don't know why I said that; it just came to me from deep inside. Chris got back on the phone, "Uh, huh, yes I will Prince. Okay bye."

Chris put down the phone, turned to me and said, "He'll be back next week and he said to tell you he'd rather come to your home than meet in your office." After Chris left I sat back down on my couch and listened to the demo at least another twenty times. It was then that I decided if Prince Nelson signed a management contract with me it would take every waking hour of my time to get him signed. And then the thought hit me again, gosh, I hope he's not nasty looking.

In my car and at home, I must have listened to the demo tape two hundred times waiting for Prince to return from New York. I put on headphones and gave it the supreme test — I rolled up a big fatty, smoked it, and listened. I listened to it straight. I got high and listened to it again. The music never grew old. In fact, the more I listened the more nuances of greatness were revealed. On "Soft and Wet" I thought I heard him say that someone came too quick and they left too soon. Holy shit! Was that the lyrics of a slightly older Chris Moon influencing the young impressionable Prince — or was it the other way around? I had to know. In the chorus there was that low voice I heard on the phone call balanced underneath that vulnerable falsetto, "You are soft and wet — Love is soft and wet." And who the fuck is bold enough to say these things? I'd never heard so much care put into the construction of a demo song — period. Chills ensued.

I waited at home that weekend for the call from Chris Moon like he was someone setting me up on a date with his beautiful cousin. Every time the phone rang I jumped up and answered it only to be disappointed by my mother calling to ask how I was, or someone selling aluminum siding.

Monday morning at work I was the same nervous wreck. I was buoyed only by my complete confidence that I could protect, and get this vulnerable kid a record deal   providing he wasn't nasty looking. On Tuesday Chris called and we agreed that the three of us would meet at my house the next day at 2 PM.

I stayed home that day and made sure the house was ready to receive the Prince. Newly married, my wife Britt and I had just rented the bottom half of a gorgeous early 1900's duplex just up the hill from the Lake Harriet bandstand. It was located on a quaint tree-lined, "slice of Americana" street at 4248 Linden Hills Blvd. in the heart of old South Minneapolis. The house had hardwood floors, high ceilings, and leaded glass built-ins indicative of the era. From our front window, and beyond the screened porch, one could almost visualize horses and carriages carrying families to and fro back in the day. The house was already a "musicians home" with acoustic and electric guitars and amps scattered about, my huge record collection and sound system, and an upright piano in the dining room. At precisely 2 PM the old doorbell rang with a sharp ding-dong.

I could see Chris's neatly arranged Beatle-cut hair through the upper door window but where was the Prince. What the fuck, my heart sank. Was Chris here in person to tell me that the Prince had backed out? Why didn't he just fucking call; I needed to be at my office with my staff! As I reached for the handle I peered through the window of the door. Just below the window I noticed the top of a huge fro. The Prince was hiding and playing a joke on me.

I opened the door and offered a hearty, C'mon in guys!" thrilled that this kid of few words was a practical joker. But as the old door creaked open I noticed that this was no practical joke. The Prince couldn't have been more than five foot two. He was wearing nothing special — a jean jacket, brown t-shirt underneath with some sort of medallion necklace, and blue jeans with unremarkable brown boots poking out. These were not the clothes of a wealthy man but it was obvious that he had spent time in preparation; everything was clean, coordinated, and neatly pressed. The Prince obviously knew his way around an ironing board.

As Chris made the introductions I couldn't help but notice the Prince's deep brown eyes. Even though their shape seemed to be a little larger than his face could handle they only served to enhance his gorgeous appearance. Set beneath very thick eyebrows, their almond shape immediately gave off a sense of intelligence and understanding — but there was an underlying intensity, directness, and a sense of fire. I was reminded of the early publicity shots of Little Richard. There he was posing in a group with his fellow band mates. They were all smiling and looking off in different directions — and then there was Little Richard. He was staring directly into the camera with a force that said, "Oh yeah, I'm here motherfucker".

At first, I thought that the Prince could be of Egyptian roots. His eyes, light skin, and high cheekbones, reminded me of drawings I had seen in books depicting the early pyramids and the Pharaohs who built them. Was Chris Moon really a mad scientist who had cooked up this musical phenom in his laboratory? If I went to Chris's studio would I see Chris in a lab coat surrounded by electronic medical devices instead of recording gear? Prince and Chris were such an odd couple that that could be the only possible explanation. What was I getting into?

More often than not I use a device to break the ice in new situations; it's called humor. Never premeditated and always spontaneous, the humor-device saved me many times as a child growing up in a tense household. My brand of humor can often be sophisticated, sarcastic and riddled with double meanings — some people get it, others don't. The Prince got it. My unfiltered comments slipped out and the Prince of few words laughed — out loud; I looked at this youthful, beautiful, talented creature with a smile on his face and thought, oh my God, I'm in love.

The Prince played a few songs on my guitar, tinkered at the piano and then asked if I wanted to hear another "rough" song. This was no amateur musician playing his heart out — this was an early genius letting us in on his gift. I guess it didn't matter to me who was actually writing the lyrics. Chris told me it was a joint effort and I believed him. What was important was the songs were great, and these two, working in Chris Moon's laboratory, were creating one hell of a monster.

Our meeting concluded with the three of discussing a little biz. I closed the loop again by telling them that I was here initially as more of a protector than manager. "You're very young and there are too many wolves in waiting as you meander through the musical forest," I explained in passing. "The two of you need to be one hundred fifty percent creative right now. I'd like to walk ahead of you and carry the rifle."

I also brought up that just the name "Prince" alone worked perfectly. There was no need to use "the" Prince, Prince Rogers Nelson, or even Prince Nelson. They told me they had discussed that same concept earlier so we agreed that all future references would be just Prince. "Great, because when I make the record deal it amplifies the mystery and that means more money." Prince nodded in complete agreement. Damn, he was into commerce too!

I stood on my front porch and watched as Prince and Chris headed to Chris's car. Was I on the cusp of something historic, or was my desire to score a major record deal pushing me into a fantasy of biblical proportions? What was it about this kid that made me suddenly want to put my life into him and trust him? I remember Chris telling me that after a few initial recording sessions he had handed the keys to his studio over to the young Prince and told him to come in day or night. When he first told me that at my office I thought that Chris had taken an unusual risk with a complete stranger. But soon after our initial meeting I too would be handing over the keys to my home to the young Prince.

As they drove away I remember thinking that I could not do this alone. This effort would take a team. But who would believe me and be there to help?

Bar Mitzvah 1960 *The Syrian Husney lineage: (L to R) Ed Husney, Rabbi Eli Husney, chubby Owen, and my father, Irving Husney*

High Spirits 1965 *The summer our record hit the charts. A town somewhere - yours truly on the far left.*

On the Road 1965 *"Turn on Your Love Light" started running up the charts in many cities and we were Jr. rock stars.*

On Tour 1966 *Kansas City: Last publicity shot before we became wild musician hippies.*

Minneapolis Tribune

Rock facing trial at 'Stones' concert

By Brian Anderson
Staff Writer

Owen Husney's phone has been ringing more than a senior citizen's ears at a rock concert.

"I've never in my life got so many calls," said the 25-year-old rock-concert promoter. "People who used to beat me up in high school even are calling for tickets."

The tickets the callers are seeking are for the June 18 Rolling Stones concert at the Metropolitan Sports Center.

Although most callers realize that the 17,100 seats for the concert were sold in less than four hours after they went on sale May 24, they hope that their high school buddy, good old Owen Husney, can dig up a couple of tickets for a few friends out of the past.

Owen Husney

But no such luck.

"I've had people offer $35 and $50 for a ticket," said Husney, who as head of Owen Productions is the local producer for the concert. "But there aren't any tickets left." (Tickets were priced at $6.50 each.)

The concert promises to be not only a big day for rock enthusiasts, a field day for ticket scalpers and a long day for security officials, but possibly also the "last chance" for hard-rock concerts in the Twin Cities area.

The Rolling Stones, an English rock group second only to the now-disbanded Beatles in popularity, is making a 30-city tour of North America this summer.

The group opened its tour Saturday night in Vancouver.

Concert continued on page 11A.

Rolling Stone 1972 Made the front page of my hometown Newspaper - my father wanted to know why I was arrested. School bullies who beat me up now wanted free tickets.

Concert Promoter 1973 Don't do drugs.

IF YOU THINK IT WAS A GREAT SUMMER . . . WAIT 'TILL YOU SEE WHAT'S COMING UP . . .

You've Already Seen Jethro Tull The Rolling Stones Alice Cooper Emerson, Lake & Palmer

Howard Stein Presents at the Minneapolis Armory August 28: Black Sabbath September 12: Allman Brothers Band September 23: Yes & Eagles

Owen Productions

1409 Mount Curve, Minneapolis. 377-0574 • 374-2638

Promoter and Producer Services 1974 *Self promotion is always good.*

Al Jarreau 1975 *The greatest jazz singer, the greatest guy. Got him gigs, should have managed him, cried when Patrick Rains signed him to WB.*

Bobby Z 1976 *On my sailboat, Lake Minnetonka, just before all hell broke loose.*

Chris Moon *The man with the machine that started it all.*

Prince Sound 80 Studios 1976 *First pic just before the first demo session*

Santa Monica 1977 First trip to Los Angeles.

Prince 1977 Second trip to Los Angeles. My friends Mimi and Ron's
House with daughter Kate - Brentwood

Moped Man *Third trip to Los Angeles. Santa Monica.*
The labels want us! Forerunner to a future film?

The Ad Company 1977 *My staff who did all the coordination, artwork,*
and graphics for the launch of Prince.

Lee Philips 1977 *The best attorney in the biz!*

Prince 1978 *CBS Records didn't believe Prince could play all the instruments so they put him in Village Recorders to find out.*

Al Coury
President
Chief Operating Officer

May 19, 1977

Owen R. Husney
American Artists, Inc.
430 Oak Grove, Suite 110
Minneapolis, Minn. 55403

Dear Owen

The enclosed material on PRINCE has been reviewed by
our A&R Department and although we feel there is
great potential, it is not the type of act we are
looking for at this point in time.

Thanks for your consideration.

Sincerely,

Al Coury

Al Coury

AC/lw

Enclosures

RSO RECORDS, INC.
A Member of the Stigwood Group of Companies
9200 Sunset Blvd., Suite 505, Los Angeles, Calif. 90069
Telephone: (213) 278-1680

Too bad for you RSO.

Prince Travel-Mate *Fourth trip to Los Angeles and Prince needed a companion so my wife made one*

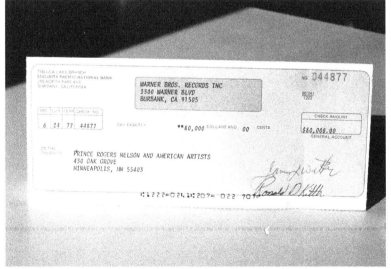

Warner Bros Check *Prince is signed to the biggest record deal in history for a new artist.*

Signing Party *Celebrating the deal in Minneapolis: (L to R) Cliff Siegel, me, my wife Britt, Prince, his date, Susan and Gary Levinson.*

Prince Takes a Moment *Reflecting on what he just accomplished.*

Signing Luncheon *Warner Bros celebrates the arrival of Prince: (L to R) WB Chairman Mo Ostin, Sr VP Russ Thyret, Prince.*

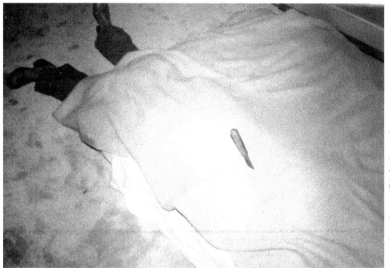

Stabbed In The Back *An evil prank gone wrong: Prince, David Z, and I play a nasty prank on our executive producer Tommy Vicari in San Francisco*

Inner Sleeve *Prince planned the inner sleeve to the album by stripping down at my house and superimposing three of him.*

The Grammys 1978 *With the first album almost complete we head off to the Grammys. Shown: Prince and Britt.*

NEWSPAPER

Billboard 87th YEAR®

A Billboard Publication   The International Newsweekly Of Music & Home Entertainment   Oct. 30, 1982 • $3 (U.S.)

Manager Owen Husney: Minneapolis Has A Sound

By NELSON GEORGE

MANAGER OWEN HUSNEY SAYS
The Minneapolis Sound Is Here

• *Continued from page 51*

Minneapolis Sound 1982 *Like Detroit, Nashville, and San Francisco Minneapolis is now on the musical map.*

The Time *The Minneapolis Black Music Awards: (L to R) Jellybean, Terry Lewis, Me, Morris Day, Jimmy Jam, Monte*

Jesse Johnson 1986 *Backstage with Jesse and the band somewhere in America. His record had just hit #1 Urban in Billboard.*

But Wait, There's More! *Is it a golfball finder, a marijuana finder, or an explosives finder? It doesn't matter — it's a scam!*

High Spirits 2015 *Lauren Siegel rocks out at the 50th reunion of*
The High Spirits, St. Louis Park, Minnesota   Full Circle

Lifetime Achievement Award *Presented by*
The Rock-Country Hall of Fame Minnesota

The Team

PART TWO: "WE WERE JUST DOING WHAT WE LOVED. WE HAD NO IDEA WE WERE CREATING HISTORY." — DAVID "Z" RIVKIN

G ray November skies vanished beneath early nightfall as I drove south along Lyndale Ave. to Chris Moon's studio. Earlier in the day Prince called and asked me over to hear a new song — so at 5 p.m. I bolted out of The Ad Company. This would be our second meeting, and I was more than curious to see where two guys had labored deep into the night unearthing a mysterious new sound. I was also happy that Prince felt comfortable enough to invite me into the inner sanctum.

As I drove along I kept the radio silent so as not to taint my ears for the virgin song I was about to hear. Before me, mostly bare trees relinquished their last leaves of red and gold as the fall winds picked up. They danced across my windshield in a sweeping gesture — gliding to the ground in their final act. And, in my forced silence, I sensed the earth turning on its axis, foretelling a change of seasons; and I knew the axis of my being was also beginning to turn — a new season for me, shifting the course of my life forever.

Following Chris's directions, I turned right, across Hennepin Ave, and then left, on to Dupont Ave South looking for 2828. Pulling up the short driveway through a crunch of leaves, I noticed the studio was in one of those late forties industrial buildings next to an auto impound lot. It was the kind of plain red brick building and car lot you'd expect to find alongside tracks on the outskirts of town — not in the midst of a tree-lined street of early 1900's homes.

The small studio was dim and unremarkable, unlike the larger and shinier 24-track studios across town. But there was this dark-cool and creative vibe to the place — you'd almost expect candles to be lit in every corner. The cramped studio was meant for hard work — by musicians who probably couldn't afford it's meager rates. But I had heard that Chris looked the other way when it came time for payment. What the little studio lacked in shininess and big league quality it more than made up for in heart and soul.

I stepped into the control room. Prince and Chris were seated at the soundboard while a song was playing back. They were twisting knobs in helter-skelter fashion — arms flailing — as if an octopus had been hired to mix the song. The minute they saw me they stopped the playback. It was like I had accidently walked in on someone entering the nuclear codes. This very new song was top secret and not yet ready for curious ears.

I couldn't help but notice that Prince's 'fro had grown even larger since our first meeting! He was wearing the same blue jeans — crisp crease down the middle — and the same brown boots. But this time he wore a black t-shirt with a Superman logo over a black, long sleeved shirt. This t-shirt—on-shirt look was not unusual for Minnesotans. The frigid northern air was beginning to make its appearance and we were all adding layers.

Chris spoke first, in a full on British accent. "We finished another track last night mate. Would you like to hear it?" "Fuck man, I thought we were here to record my group, Big O and the Gypsy Cowboys," came my sarcasm. Prince laughed out loud. "It's called, "Make it Through The Storm," Chris said, slightly annoyed by my humor. He pressed play on the big tape machine.

The cascading intro of keyboard and guitars was nuanced and layered; and fed immaculately into Prince's delicate falsetto. The overall result was neither pop nor soul; "The world's a cold and empty place without a love to keep you warm. Hold me in your arms tonight, don't cha know we'll make it through the storm." I hung on every note and vocal line until the end; and asked Chris to play it again. Prince had no use to hear the song again. He'd delivered this baby and was already on to the next.

Without a word he exited the control room and headed back into the studio with a meticulous gait. This is a guy who would rather walk through fire than break his cool I thought. Does he plan every move? I watched through the glass as he headed over to the piano and tinkered a bit. He then went over to the guitar, ran a few licks, and then kicked it with the drums for a minute. Had he contrived this little display of cool for me?

Chris leaned in close, and said in a hushed tone, "Prince has no confidence in his voice." "Bullshit." I said, waiting for the punch line. "Really Owen, when we were recording the vocals I thought there was something wrong with the microphone; I could hardly hear his voice. We did another vocal take and the same thing. I checked the mike again, and it worked just fine. I asked him what was wrong and he said he wasn't sure he should be singing lead." "Look," I said, incredulous. "I don't think I should be singing lead either, but I don't fucking' sound like that. How'd you get that performance out of him?" "I went to the room in the building where I sleep and grabbed some bedding and a pillow. I put it on the floor of the studio, made him lay on it, and turned off all the lights — it was pitch black. While he was lying there I pushed the mike right down to into his face. I ran back to the control room, pressed record, and told him to have a go at it. You just listened to the end result, mate." "Well, if that's the case lets buy him a fucking bed for the studio. I haven't heard a distinctive vocal like that since Curtis Mayfield."

"Getting Prince signed has to be first class all the way." I told Chris. Do you have any idea what this is going to take?" Without hesitation Chris replied, "That's why we came to you Owen. We tried and failed. You have music business experience and con-tacts, a marketing company, and most importantly, a suit."

Chris nervously thanked me for backing him up on using Prince Nelson as his stage name. "Well, that's his name isn't it? And I'd prefer he didn't even use his last name." Chris took a moment to regain and said, "It was the biggest argument we ever had. One day I told him that he had the greatest stage name ever in Prince Nelson." "Did he agree?" "He said there was already a 'King' of rock and roll, and a Prince was less than a king." "And what name did he want?" I said. "Mr. Nelson," Chris mumbled. "Mr. Nelson?" "Yeah, the only thing I could think of at the time was to tell him that there was already a Mr. Nelson — Willie Nelson." "And did he agree?" "No, he walked out and didn't speak to me for weeks." "Boy, I can't wait for his response when I tell him I'm pushing his age back a year," I blurted. "Why would you do that?" "The labels will cough up even more dough when they realize all this is coming from a mysterious seventeen year old named Prince — from fucking Minnesota — with no last name."

Prince returned to the control room and I explained that we needed to get a management contract together. "Owen, you gonna make a slave?" He responded, with an intentional smirk that belied a too serious undertone. How could an unknown guy, sitting in a tiny studio in Minneapolis — on the property of an auto impound lot — display the courage of a lion? "No, I'm gonna protect your creativity, fight for you, and make you one of the wealthiest young men in America."

I drove off reflecting on the meeting. Here was Prince, a lone eighteen-year-old kid living in Bernadette Anderson's basement on the North-side of Minneapolis. And I had just made a promise to him; a promise to help him rise from the basement, garner the attention of the biggest record labels in the world, and shine as a new musical giant. In my heart, I believed he could pull off his side of the bargain. But the weight of my new promise fell solely on me. I should have been scared, but I wasn't; I was stupid — I never thought about not being able to do this for him.

While at the studio I was sure that Prince picked up on my hunger to score a big deal in the biz; he understood it on a very primal level — it was the same obsessive desire that burned within him to create music. And he knew that I was prepared to get him the deal his creativity deserved.

There's a quote somewhere from Hugh Hefner. He said that if someone had told him how fucking challenging it would be to build the Playboy empire he would have turned around gone back to bed. But passion, drive, and stupidity make you oblivious to the hazards that lurk ahead. You blindly run into the burning building of risk, never knowing if you'll come out a hero, or a zero. But you do it anyway, because at the time you could care less about the cost or the consequences.

I even had a litmus test upon meeting new artists that went like this: Would you bag groceries at the local store if your career failed? If they said yes, I wouldn't work with them. But I knew Prince was my man, without even asking; there was no way I could envision him bagging groceries if all failed — or myself for that matter — we'd rather die first.

But Prince was an anomaly. He wasn't part of a road-dog band that had played hundreds of gigs on the "I'm Cold & Starving Tour." Nor was he part of a band of finely polished studio musicians and writers who decided to cut a record. There were many Soul and rock bands in Minneapolis — each with their standout "stars,"— but Prince was off the radar and a complete unknown. If there were a buzz I would have found him. Besides a few proms, party gigs, and the few dates Bernadette had arranged at the local YWCA and elsewhere, he had never been on the road, never cut a full album, and from what I understood — had never put his own true band together. He was raw, uncharted talent — an uncut diamond, freshly plucked from the musical mines of Minnesota. And because of that, I knew I couldn't go it alone; this was going to take soldiers and money. I needed to enlist dedicated people who would also give of their time, their lives, and their pocketbooks to get Prince signed. And they had to work on nothing but fumes of belief in his talent. They needed to fully comprehend how I felt — that we were all living one split-second before the big musical bang.

The next day, demo in hand, I went on a moral support tour. There was one Minnesota fellow, Don Powell, whom I had known for years. Don moved to Detroit in the 60's training to become an airline employee. While attending a party he had a chance conversation with Motown head Berry Gordy. Berry saw something in Don, believed in him, and eventually handed Don an impossible job; managing a thirteen-year-old blind musical genius who was throwing tantrums in the studio. Don wound up managing Stevie Wonder almost from the start; co-writing hit songs with him along the way. He had even co-managed David Bowie and Iggy Pop. Don was now living back in the Twin Cities running his family's car dealership business. There was only one other successful person in Minneapolis who had done what I wanted to do. And it would wonderful to get Don's blessing as I ran into the burning building.

"I really think you got something there bud," Don said, as we looked out at the shimmering new '77 Ford models. "I've never heard anything like this; sort of rock-R&B, a voice higher than Curtis Mayfield, and it's funky as hell!" He said, somewhat stunned. "What does he look like?" When I played Prince's demo to people I never showed pictures of him. The music had to do the talking. If people asked what he looked like I knew I had them. "Would you like to meet him and see for yourself? He's obviously a big fan of Stevie." "Sure thing bud." Don said, as I stuffed the demo back in my briefcase. "First, I need to get him signed to a management contract then I'll bring him by," I said, protecting my territory. "What's your plan?" "I'm gonna raise money for him and do this first class. First, he needs to get out of the basement. Then, I'll redo the demos you just heard in a 24-track studio with an experienced engineer. I'll buy him the instruments he needs, create a knockout press kit, and then lie my way into the major record labels." "Sounds like you got a big road ahead." "I know. But somehow I've been chosen." "Hey Bud." "Yup?" "I have a funny feeling Stevie is going to know who this Prince kid is one day."

Fortified with Don's blessing I left the dealership with an even more passionate resolve to get Prince a deal. I knew I could coordinate the management, recording, creative direction, and marketing side; it was in my blood. But to live up to my promise to protect Prince would require that the legal and business side also come together — fast.

PART III:
WHO WANTS TO BE A SOLDIER
IN THE ARMY OF PRINCE?

My wife and I had become social friends with Gary Levinson and his wife Susan. Gary was a few years older than me, and the brother of the rhythm guitar player in my band in the 60's. The four of us hung out, had dinners together, and traveled together. Gary was bright, and an up and coming business attorney at a prestigious law firm in downtown Minneapolis. His slight cherubic face, close-cropped beard, and statuesque stance were the perfect Zen balance to my longhaired business-hippy look. I could be wildly entrepreneurial and histrionic; but it was hard for Gary to act in anything but a stiff, professional manner. I'm sure that beneath it all he was as batty as the rest of us, but his tailored three-piece suits made for exquisite camouflage. If I could get Gary to come aboard and handle the legal and related biz we'd be whole, with legal, management, design, and marketing. I knew Gary loved music. But would he get this? I asked him to come over to my house one evening. Twisting up a big fat joint I said, "Take a couple of hits of this shit and then I want to play you something."

"What does he look like?" Gary said after listening to the demos for the third time. "Would you like to meet him?" I said. "Absolutely." "Gary, this is going to take a ton of work. Prince is young and gifted but not seasoned. We have to support him from the ground up." Without missing a beat Gary shot back, "Owen, promise me that we'll go for a homerun without stopping and I'll handle the business side — just take care of him." It was an easy promise for me to make.

Prince, Gary, and I met at Bridgeman's Ice Cream restaurant on Hennepin Ave. Outside, random snowflakes scurried to replace the falling leaves. Yes, Minnesota folks eat ice cream in the cold. Prince arrived alone. He was neatly dressed in a jean jacket, turtleneck underneath, and a thin silver necklace dangling to mid-chest. As usual, his limited wardrobe was crisp neatly pressed, and well thought out. I could tell Prince had prepared for this meeting and wanted to handle it alone.

Prince said nothing as we all slurped down chocolate malts and talked of what it would take to get him signed. Though he scarcely looked at us, his focus on every word, and composed intensity, meant he was grasping everything that was being discussed. He was there to check us out and had no intention of hearing how much we loved the *Moonsound* demos. When we were finished, someone picked him up and he was gone. We watched as Prince strode out of the restaurant like he was walking off-stage after a killer performance. "He doesn't say much does he?" Gary said. "No, but you need to understand, he just absorbed everything you said," I shot back. "I'll get a management contract written for you to review."

While Gary was getting the contract together I decided to pay Prince a visit at Andre's house. I learned from Chris that Prince had run away after many conflicts with his stepfather. There was a stop at his aunt's house, and by his mid-teens he wound up living at Andre's mother's house after the two met in school. Chris told me that Andre (Anderson) Cymone was Prince's music mate, band mate, and soul mate. Together, they jammed incessantly in Andre's mother's basement. They had formed the band Grand Central that included Andre's sister and Prince's cousin Chazz — who was eventually replaced by drummer Morris Day.

I was concerned about the environment they were living in. If this was going to be a risky situation I wanted to know about it before making any kind of investment. I drove "over North" to Russell Ave. Like many areas, North Minneapolis had once been a post-war neighborhood of Jewish immigrants before they fled in one last pilgrimage to the suburbs. The houses looked like any middle class neighborhood in America.

Standing outside Andre's the door I could hear raised voices and my antennae went up. I knocked, and the door opened a crack as if someone was expecting an intruder, or maybe the police? A handsome teenager introduced himself as Andre, and I remember thinking, damn, he's good looking too. Who's cookin' these kids up!

Once inside, Andre introduced me to his mother, a hefty, serious woman who studied me like I was a con artist ready to pounce. North Minneapolis is predominately black, and the sight of a white, long-haired, sort of nerdy Jewish guy could only be suspicious at best. "This is Owen Husney," he said. "He wants to manage Prince and sign him to a record label." "Nice to meet you Owen. I'm Bernadette Anderson. Sorry, I was just yelling at these kids. Homework has to be done and this place needs to be cleaned up!" I could tell that Bernadette was special. This was a woman of strength and dignity — and probably a woman you didn't want to mess with.

Prince appeared and showed me around the house, including the famous basement. It was neat and clean, and the beds were made per Bernadette's orders. I thought about how the house was so much bigger than the house I grew up in as a teen. Prince was a lucky guy. He found a caring family, a strong parental figure, and a roof over his head. Additionally, he had Andre. It was obvious that Andre was far more than a trusted friend; he was a musical co-creator, and an unfailing companion. Andre and Bernadette were the co-founders of Team Prince.

As I was leaving I asked Prince to come out to my car. "You're going to need some money for expenses, so here's a hundred dollars," I said, producing a check from my shirt pocket. Prince looked up at me, eyes open, with a sort of a half-cocked smile and said, "Thank you Owen, but first I'll need to open a bank account." "No, problem Prince, we'll do that tomorrow.

Driving away I couldn't help but think how naive I was for not reading the situation. But something else came over me that actually frightened me; I would probably have to walk out of the business I had built tirelessly for the last six years to make this all happen.

I named the new management company American Artists, Inc. Gary drew up the management contract and I dropped all my other management clients so that my sole purpose would be the management of Prince.

It's always a tense moment when you have to present a contract to an artist. Truth be told, you are marrying each other after a very short dating process. There are many, "I love you's," but the consequences of a wrong decision are worse than an actual divorce. If you're the artist you could wind up paying your ex for a very long time. And even risk putting your career on hold. If you're a manager you could be putting all of your time, energy, and money into something that has more promise of going bust than making it. And that's reality, but you both choose to take the gamble. And then there's always that one moment.

"Hey Prince, it's Owen." "Owen." Came the one word response on the other end. "Gary's writing up a contract and we'd like to meet with you and go over it. "This ain't no slave deal, is it? "No, but you'll need someone who isn't a slave to review it before you sign." Prince laughed out loud. "When?" He said. "Today is Wednesday, could you meet us at Gary's house, say next Monday?" "Okay, someone will bring me over." "Sure thing." After we hung up I felt a rush of exhilaration. Prince and I weren't married yet — but we were well on the way to being engaged. The following Saturday my phone rang at two AM.

"Owen." "Yes?" "It's Prince." "You sound far away, and what's that noise?" "Some people flew me out to Los Angeles. They want to manage me. Right now I'm at a club in Century City and I just saw Lainie Kazan perform — and I met her. They gave me a gold guitar, just wanted you to know. "I'll be back on Sunday." I lay there in bed starring up at the ceiling in disbelief.

"Well, okay, then we'll see you on Monday?" I said, burning with angst. "I think so." Prince said, and hung up.

I think so? As I lay there unable to sleep I wondered; did I just get played? Did a manager I know just rip me off? Was this a contrived ploy by Prince to get me and me to sweeten the deal? And besides, Prince didn't actually say he was going with the golden guitar people. It didn't matter, I was fuming; and when I fume it's not fucking good.

On Monday evening Gary and I stood in the living room of his beautiful Tudor home just off lake Calhoun in south Minneapolis. We waited and waited for Prince and his "friend" to show. Outside, fresh winter snow was pummeling down and the temperature was rapidly dropping below freezing. Inside, Gary had the contract in hand and was ready to explain every paragraph and clause to Prince — if he showed.

I was staring out the front window when a car pulled up leaving a trail of tire tracks in the freshly fallen snow. A very skinny dude, someone I'd never seen before, turned off the headlights and almost slipped on his ass as he got out of the car. Prince departed the passenger's side and pulled a guitar case from the back seat. "Is it them?" Gary said from the living room. I turned and yelled, "Yup — and here comes the fucking golden guitar."

Stomping the snow off his boots Prince looked almost pained as he made brief introductions. "Owen and Gary, this is Eddie Anderson, Andre's brother." "Nice to meet you Eddie." We stood awkwardly in the living room for a minute then made our way to the living room. Prince asked if I wanted to see the guitar. He handed it to me and I played a few blues licks. "So this the famous, golden guitar?" There it was, a fancy white electric with gold plating on the trim and tuning pegs.

I handed the guitar back to Prince. "Here ya go, it's a beautiful guitar." "Thanks," Prince said, as he carefully placed the instrument back in its red velvet-lined case. I didn't know if this was a setup, pure bullshit, or there was really another manager come to steal our artist. It didn't matter because I was fuming. "But one thing, Prince," I said, looking him directly in those beautiful eyes. "You need to know that I'm not here about a fucking golden guitar or to have you meet yesterday's Lainie Kazan. If you can be bought, and that's what you want, then go sign with them. I'm here to protect you and to get you the deal your talent deserves. So I think the both of you better get out right now."

I watched as Prince and Eddie trudged through the snow and drove off into the blustery night. I felt that I'd just kicked the love of my life out the door. Gary turned to me with a — what the fuck did you just do look on his face. "Just sit tight Gary. Just be cool and sit tight, I'm not worried in the least."

Four days passed with no sign of Prince. I couldn't eat or sleep. I was like the guy who had dumped his true love and suddenly regretted it, *Where is she? Why doesn't she call?* I was sick to my stomach, yet I knew I couldn't blink. Saturday morning, I get a call, and Prince says, "Owen, alright, let's go. Let's go do this." And just like that we were married. We joined forces and never mentioned the incident, or the fucking golden guitar again. Prince learned that I had a bottom line.

After that, I wrote Prince a check for living expenses every week and he spent almost every day at my house while I was at work. I had a state of the art tape machine so he would record works in progress and leave them for me to listen to. He'd always hide the tapes for me to find. It wasn't a game. He just didn't want to be around for my commentary.

One day I had "the talk" with him. His recordings often went on for five minutes or more — typical for most talented artists. But to get a record deal, the songs needed to be three-minute nursery rhymes at most. "Think of the Beatles 'I Want to Hold Your Hand,' that's the simplicity that's needed to get over." I argued. Prince called for someone to pick him up and stomped off into the night. The next morning there was a cassette on my doorstep with a note that read, "Here you go asshole." The song was a two and a half minute ditty titled, "I Like What You're Doing." It was perfect — my suggestion, his genius.

I immediately set about laying the groundwork to get Prince a record deal. There was one problem however, money. Sure, I had been on the music scene over ten years and enough of a street-hustler that I could pull in favors, but this was going to require a real investment. Prince needed to get into his own place. There would be recording expenses; and he needed clothing, instruments and gear, not to mention travel expenses. I brought a financial forecast to Gary that totaled over $20,000, and together we made a list of perspective investors. Armed with a few clumsy pictures, and Chris and Prince's demos we dialed for dollars, scared up a few meetings, and hit the happy money trail.

To our shock, our sure-fire music-star dream was falling flat. After every "young genius/next Stevie wonder" dog and pony show we'd hear the same answer: "Excuse me, but you want me to put my money in an unemployed, eighteen-year-old kid living in a basement over North? Thank you, but I think I'll keep my money in the bank." It was the same defeating answer day after day. Desperate, I knew if I didn't raise the money fast I'd probably lose Prince to some shark manager — even with a contract. Money talks, bullshit walks.

After three weeks of rejection I had exhausted all my contacts. In near despair I pleaded with Gary to think of anyone who would help us finance what I thought was an obvious slam-dunk. "I'm about to call the bullies who beat me to a pulp in high school. "And you should be calling your grandmother." The next day Gary offered up a last resort plan. "I've got a couple of childhood friends, a doctor and a lawyer, they both love music and maybe they'll get what we're trying to do.

I had my art director whip up a quick but impressive foldout presentation piece with some pictures taken at Moon's studio. In one black and white photo Prince was seated at an electronic keyboard, head tilted to the side — Stevie Wonder style. In another Black and white he was at the guitar with his Superman t-shirt. I put the *Moonsound* three-song demo cassette in a matching black and white package. Yep, we were getting our presentation shit together and prepping for the big time.

Gary and I met with the doctor and lawyer. We had our talking points together; I was the successful entertainment dude who painted a picture of a future music business utopia — one that included Prince at the top. And Gary was the serious business lawyer dude who would make sure his friends investment was protected. We gave our spiel and let it all roll.

This time, our natural roles, and our prepped presentation worked. Within a week the money was wired to the account of American Artists, Inc. The doctor and lawyer became the newest members of the army of Prince.

We learned a valuable show business lesson, don't talk about basements; talk about a positive future, real numbers, throw in show-biz sizzle for the close, and let the music do the talking. I now had the very plan I'd use for the presentations to the major labels. But this time around with funding, I'd kick ass. It was now time to get the rest of the kick-ass team together.

I'd known Robert Whitman since grade school. We attended Fern Hill Elementary in St. Louis Park, and both went on to graduate from St. Louis Park Senior High School in 1965. Photography was an early passion for Robert and he was a rising fashion photographer in the Twin Cities.

Robert had a keen eye for shooting pictures of women. Our clients loved him. He just didn't "take pictures" but had an uncanny way of capturing the raw emotion of the moment. I used Robert for all my management clients too. In 1974 he took shots for me of a singer songwriter duo named Muske and Raths, an exceptionally talented singer/songwriter duo from the Twin Cities. We had an expensive near miss getting them signed to CBS (Columbia) Records in Los Angeles. The painful experience did much to teach me the ropes of the major label dance.

On a snowy day in December 1976 I sat in Robert's car and played him a cassette demo of young Prince. "Is he good looking?" Robert asked, more than amazed after "Soft and Wet" concluded. "Good looking? I'd marry him if I could," I said. "But being good looking is one thing and being able to have that transfer to the public on film is another. "Yeah, you're right." "That's why I need you." "Take him around town, c'mon over to my house, do whatever he wants, and let's see what this kid looks like in the eyes of the camera. We're gonna need to make a press kit that's as much of a knockout as the new 24-track studio demo we're gonna make." "How much you gonna pay me for this?" Bob needed to know. I shot back, "How about I give you more fashion shoots for my ad agency and you do this for free?"

Robert ended up doing three different shoots over the period of a few days. He had a very small studio in an old ice cream building. He did the first controlled shoot in the studio; Prince with hands on his waist — his fro backlit wearing a sequence shirt, naked from the waist up, a smiling Prince, Prince with visible acne blowing soap bubbles, and Prince posing with his acoustic guitar against a white seamless. But it was the non-planned session they did downtown Minneapolis, out of which came one of the most iconic and historic images ever published. He was standing in front of a five-story wall that was painted white with music notes from top to bottom. The old brick building belonged to the Schmitt Music Company. And then they did another shoot at my house. They shot him with my dog, sitting at our dining room table, and playing the piano. There was a picture of my mother on the piano while Prince played away. I asked Robert if he would enlarge it for me to frame. I wanted my mother to be memorialized with Prince at the piano — just in case he made it big.

* * * *

It would be many years before Robert Rivkin would evolve into Bobby Z, drummer for the Revolution. By 1965, his older brother, David Rivkin — aka David Z — and I were already friends. We were also musicians in competing bands on the Twin Cities band circuit. When things weren't so great at my house I'd go over and hang out at the Rivkin's — who also lived in St. Louis Park. It was just a short drive from my parent's house — located on the poor side of the same suburb. Their mother Shirley was my second mother. Petit and thin with short dark hair and a warm smile she would always greet me with, "Oweeeee, I'm so glad to see you!" She was always there to encourage creativity, and as far as I know never really saw the downside of anything. It was a most refreshing change from the darkness that shaded my house. Shirley became my role model, or should I say, my role mother.

The Rivkin's Cape Cod two-story house was filled to the brim with creativity. There were drums in the basement, guitars and amps in David's room. And in middle brother Steve's room there were movie cameras and projectors, editing devices, and strips of film hanging from impromptu clotheslines waiting to be spliced into meaningful tales.

David and I were the older music guys who did a lot of naughty experimenting and mind expanding but always managed to keep it together for the music. When David and I smoked a joint and jammed in his basement little eight-year-old Bobby would beg to play the drums. We'd laugh as he tried to get his feet to touch the bass and hi-hat pedals. Every once in a while Bobby would manage to find a little groove and we'd join in.

A few years later when I became a concert promoter and local set-up guy for major touring acts Bobby came to work for me. He helped with backstage food and one time was even ordered to go below and hold up a sagging stage for Roberta Flack while she played away above him on a grand piano singing, "Killing Me Softly."

I soon "promoted" young Bobby to my security team at the Marigold, a 1930's art deco ballroom in downtown Minneapolis. It was there that I introduced the world to the likes of Billy Joel, Bonnie Raitt, and Foghat. Bobby once put his life on the line for me when the road crew for Foghat wanted to "Beat my ass to a pulp." Things hadn't gone well that night. Foghat was insulted that I had booked them into a 600 capacity ballroom with a small stage instead of an arena on their first American tour. Furious, band members and the road crew plotted to teach the young American asshole-promoter a lesson. After the show they jumped off the stage, circled me, and began swinging mike stands in my direction. Stepping in front of the band's road manager Bobby, with his own mike stand, yelled out for the rest of our security to get their ass over to the unfolding situation. Within seconds the rest of my team had poor Foghat and their limey-ass crew surrounded. My security team was not neatly groomed, same shirt wearing professionals but a rag-tag bunch of unkempt rough-ass stoners who would relish the opportunity for a good brawl. Sensing they could easily lose their life in a foreign land Foghat turned tail and ran — almost forgetting to collect their money on the way out.

I rewarded Bobby by making him my personal gopher at The Ad Company. He was becoming a serious drummer on the local scene with Pepe Willie's 94 East, and a band I managed, Kevin Odegard's, KO band (Kevin went on to record the guitar parts for Bob Dylan's, "Tangled up in Blue" which was recorded at Sound 80 Studios in Minneapolis). But to earn extra cash Bobby worked for me running ads over to my clients for approval, picking up my dry cleaning, and bringing my staff sandwiches for lunch.

Prince didn't have a driver's license, let alone a car, so once he was on the scene I assigned Bobby the task of driving him around town. Young Prince would now have to deal with photo sessions, purchase of new instruments, and meetings at my office to plan his future. Bobby and Prince were close in age so driving around in Bobby's green, rusted out Pinto "woody" station wagon turned out to be a real bonding time for the two would-be rock stars — especially when Prince threw up in the car and Bobby had to clean it up.

Bobby was not considered to be a candidate for the drumming gig — it was to be Prince's cousin Chazz, or possibly leftie drummer Morris Day. But while bonding in the Pinto, Prince confessed to Bobby his vision of having a "rainbow" band. This was a bold concept for the time in the Twin Cities — most bands were a binary choice: either all Black or all White. Bobby told me of the discussion, and a jam session was organized a few nights later at my office on Loring Park. After the last Ad Company employee left we pushed the office desks out of the way and made way for drums and amps. That night, I watched as Prince, guitar slung to his side, moved effortlessly from keyboards, and back to guitar without pause, or missing a note: Bobby Z was on drums, Robbie Paster (Bobby's cousin) on bass, and Andre Cymone on guitar and bass. That night, holding his own with a solid, steady beat, Bobby Z was born.

I first met Bobby's brother, David Rivkin, aka David Z, in the fall of 1963. A classmate, fittingly nicknamed named Mouse invited a bunch of guys over to his parent's house for a "study session." A friend of a friend invited me. Being the school nerd I was thrilled at the invitation to finally be one of the guys. Filing down to the basement we were each asked to contribute fifty cents for Coke and potato chips. Once paid up we were sworn to secrecy under the penalty of getting the shit beat out of us for squealing; then, we were instructed to tell his parents, if asked, that we were studying for school finals. What I didn't know was that it was Party time! It was all a ruse so we could play poker and craps, sip from the liquor cabinet, and look through well-worn *Playboy* magazines. The more daring could climb out the basement window and sneak a few puffs off a shared cigarette. It was naughty time for high school boys coming of age.

At the "study" session, David and I — mutually bored with the "boys will be boys" shit — struck up a conversation and discovered a shared love of music. As a young man David was slight, cute, preppy/"surfy," and already locally famous as a member of a popular rock band called The Chancellors. Their rendition of "Little Latin Lupe Lu," written by Bill Medley of the Righteous Brothers, was climbing the charts on Twin Cities radio. We left Mouse's house and walked the two short blocks back to David's family home. David invited me back to his house and showed me his beautiful "Lake Placid Blue" Fender Jaguar guitar and Fender Showman amp. Grabbing the guitar from its stand, he cranked up the amp, and popped off a perfect rendition of "Surfin' USA" by the Beach Boys — complete with their exact surfin'-reverby sound. David wasn't showing off — he was naturally that good. I would later learn that he was equally as soulful.

After a brief stint with my band in the late sixties David left for Hollywood. He became a songwriter signed to A&M records publishing department. He learned his craft hanging with the likes of Joe Cocker, co-writing with legendary Gram Parsons, and cut his R&B chops playing on Billy Preston's demos. By the early seventies, David was back in Minneapolis working as a promotion man for Warner-Elektra-Atlantic. On the side, he earned a commission working with local-band booking agent Dick Shapiro. David's job was to entice Twin Cities bands to make low-cost demo recordings at ASI studios — a much larger studio than Moonsound. The idea was that new bands could get hired for local club gigs if the owners could actually listen to them first via tape. It was less risky than relying upon word of mouth, or taking a blind chance.

When the recording engineer at ASI quit, David took over. With no real previous engineering experience, David stepped in and found his passion. He soon became the go-to recording engineer in town. But it was in recording young black artists where David showed serious insight and depth. David knew of Prince, and had even recorded him earlier when one of his bands recorded a little demo backed by local businessman Archie Givens. So, it was no coincidence that I chose David to record Prince's new demos for presentation to the major labels in Los Angeles.

I arranged a meeting with David and Prince at Sound 80 studios. Sound 80 was a state of the art recording facility located on the south side of Minneapolis. It rivaled many of the great studios that were found in Los Angeles and New York. Sound 80 had some history of its own; KISS recorded there, Bob Dylan recorded tracks for his, "Blood on the Tracks" album in studio B, and Cat Stevens had just recorded tracks for his "Izitso" album there.

I could tell Prince was visibly awed by the facility when we pulled up. The facility was a gleaming, modern, stand-alone building with a massive parking lot. Inside, was a lobby with a real receptionist, and fine art adorning the walls. The staff was so professional that you could almost imagine them wearing lab coats as they walked the halls.

But the only available room for our meeting that day was the tiny "dub room" where copies of tapes and cassettes were made. We stood in the cramped quarters with the heat and whir of cassette decks piled high on racks and watched as David fed Prince and Chris's demo into one of the machines. As we were listening, David started humming a possible horn line to one of the songs. Prince turned to me and whispered, "Let's go." I was deflated. What did David do to set Prince off — hum a fucking horn line? Was Prince really that sensitive? I glanced at David and we hurried out. As we got back in my car Prince turned to me and said, "David is the only person I want working with me on my songs — period."

PART IV: PUTTING IT ALL TOGETHER

The pieces were beginning to fall into place like a well-crafted song. We had our artist; our legal side, our financing, and most importantly we had the recording engineer to bring Prince's genius home. But for this "song" to truly be a hit it also needed to be accompanied by a kick-ass visual presentation piece — something that would faithfully complement Prince's new demo. And that's where the art team at my ad agency came in. I took them off task from fashion stores and car dealerships and put them on task with photographer Robert Whitman to bring out Prince's visual magic. All I needed to do was manage and guide this thing — while simultaneously taking the blame when things went wrong.

We rented Prince an apartment at 2012 Aldridge Ave. South on the edge of downtown. It was across the street from his favorite hang, Rudolph's BBQ. We filled the meager one-bedroom place with guitars, keyboards, and a new-fangled thing called an Oberheim Synthesizer. Prince viewed the synthesizer, with its ability to replicate horns and strings, as an instrument of the future. And possibly something "out of the norm" that could shape his sound going forward. I learned early on that Prince detested anything "norm," as he put it. And that was evident when I tried to pull information out of him for the presentation piece to go along with the demos we were recording.

Prince squirmed in his chair as I asked him questions in a mock interview. The idea was to catch his personal thoughts for a presentation piece — and I wanted the whole story: What was your childhood like? Who are your siblings? Were you ever bullied? What were the cloudy times? What artists do admire the most? Do you have any mentors? Any love interests? Visibly uneasy, Prince's lips began to move from side to side while his eyes darted back and forth. Then, he calmed down and elicited a single answer; "I love Grand Funk Railroad." The simplicity of that answer spoke volumes. Grand Funk Railroad was a tight, white, three-piece rock outfit. I had provided backstage food for them in the early seventies, so I was familiar with their music. I would have been hard pressed to believe that any Black artist or group would ever have that band on their radar. To me, that demonstrated Prince's willingness to embrace, and self-educate on the full spectrum of popular music. It was also indicative of the airplay in Minneapolis at the time. Rock and pop music ruled the airwaves, while traditional R&B radio was relegated to KUXL, a single, low wattage, AM station that was on air from sun up to sundown. The ironic result was a well-rounded musical schooling for young Black artists at the time. And that single answer allowed me to peer into Prince's musical future —where there would be no Black and no White — just groundbreaking music for everyone.

While Prince was comfortable making music, he was terrified of revealing anything personal, or anything relative to his past. As he fidgeted, it hit me. If he doesn't want to reveal anything, then that's the marketing plan. Simply put — that's who the guy is — so keep him a mystery and let his music do the talking.

But there needed to be something representative of Prince for his presentation package — so I nonchalantly asked him how he came to play the piano — and the floodgates opened; "When I was seven or so I would go down and pound on my dad's piano. I think the first song I ever learned was the theme from The Man From U.N.C.L.E. By the time I was eight I had a pretty good idea of what the piano was all about." "And the guitar?" I probed. "At thirteen I went to live with my aunt. There wasn't enough room for a piano, so I learned guitar. It came in handy when I started playing on stage a year later." "And drums?" "My first drum set was a box full of newspapers." He continued with a grin. "The snare was the flap of the box. It sounded good when my phonograph was up loud!" "And what about your parents, were they musical?" I said, keeping the subject on music. "My father was a swing and jazz band leader during the early fifties. His stage name was Prince Rogers. "And your mother?" My mother was the lead singer." And just like that we were done.

The best managers are those who exploit their artist for who they are, and don't attempt to change them. Prince was darling, super young, thoroughly original, and a man of few words. There was no need to make him look, act, or sound like someone he wasn't — or a clone of the artists of the day. Say very little, and keep him a mystery. This was the tactic I would employ going forward. If little was said about him in our presentation piece to the labels — yet the music slayed them — the label A&R folks would start asking questions. And once they started asking questions I would own their fucking ass.

I exploded from my office and hollered for my art director, Jeff Framakes, to get down to my office. Jeff was a large, thick man with baseball mitt hands — more football player than art director. But he was super-creative, and the fashion clients loved him. "I need a presentation piece on Prince to hand to the record labels with his new demo tape!" I ordered. "No problem, what do you want it to say?" "Nothing," I shot back. "Just a few sentences." "And what do you want it to look like?" "Almost nothing. A cover photo; one picture of him at the piano, one playing drums, one with a guitar, and a tight shot of him doing vocals — that's it, got it? And it has to be first class."

Bobby Z came by to drive Prince to Sound 80 for the sessions that had begun with his brother David. Prince left happy, and I was one step closer to not only understanding him, but also getting him signed.

The next day Jeff came into my office with a mockup of the presentation piece and my jaw dropped. It was an 8x10 all black folder, like a school folder. When opened there was a pocket on the right side that held four separate 8x10 all black sheets. Each sheet had a black and white photo of Prince with a different instrument at the top — strikingly framed with a red border. From our mock interview there would be just one sentence below each picture — a single quote in white type from Prince. Jeff explained that each folder would be hand made with special black gloss ink. "Great work Jeff, what's the cost?" I asked, ever the businessman. "My guess is a hundred dollars apiece." "I'm sorry, I thought you said a hundred dollars apiece." I said, wondering in the moment if I was going to have to sell my dog to make it happen. "I did, you said you wanted first class." I surmised that we'd need only fifteen presentation kits for a total of fifteen hundred dollars. "Okay, you got it, but if it costs any more than that its coming out of your paycheck!" I said, only half joking. I then added a forward sentence on the inside cover: "Composition, voice, instrumentation… rarely in a single musician. American Artists presents Prince." Jeff headed back to his office and I left to see how the first recording session was going at Sound 80.

When I arrived at the studio the air in the control room was so thick with disappointment you'd be hard pressed to cut it with a chainsaw. Prince was recording "Baby," a down tempo song about an unexpected teenage pregnancy. The original Moonsound demo, though limited sonically, was soft and caring: revealing a sensitive, vulnerable-male side to Prince. But for the Sound 80 demos, he wanted an actual 15-piece orchestra to complete his vision. As Mr. resourceful manager, I called WAYL, a classical music station, and cut a great deal to use their traveling orchestra.

But the WAYL Traveling Orchestra wasn't cutting it in the studio. The average age of the players was around 76, and the string parts they were playing, even though previously charted, sounded like roller rink music. Take after take ensued to no avail. Finally, the repeated sound of the recorder being rewound — with the screech of music in reverse — got to everyone. Prince sank into a corner, and David made the decision to shut down the whole session.

Prince was not about to give up. Though disheartened, he relished the challenge (possibly because he understood more about pop music than they did?). "Owen, who is the leader? I want to speak with him," Prince coolly demanded. "We're wasting precious time." I ran out to studio and found the near octogenarian huddled with the string players. "What does that kid want now?" He barked. "He'd like to speak with you in the control room." We all took a break as the two went at it in the control room. When we returned Prince was sitting with the string players and rewriting each of their parts to reflect quarter notes instead of sixteenth notes. The whole process took about a half hour, and once completed they finished "Baby" in two takes. On the way out the leader cornered me as he was putting on his overcoat. "That little kid has an uncanny sense of music. You might have something there when he grows up."

After the exhausting session we decided to celebrate the breakthrough by going out to Perkins Pancake House just down the road. Prince ordered his usual chocolate malt. When the malt came he proceeded to put one of everything at the table into it. Ketchup, mustard, steak sauce, syrup, Tabasco, salt, pepper, and my Coke all went in. He stirred the concoction and signaled for the waiter to come over. "Could you please taste this?" Prince said, fake clutching his stomach. "Is there something wrong?" "Yes, its supposed to be chocolate but I think it's the wrong flavor, please taste it." Prince sat smug, relishing in his mendacity, while we grew nauseous as the waiter brought the "sip of death" to his lips. Skeptical, the waiter took a big gulp and immediately spit the brew out on the floor hitting his own pants on the way down. "I'm so sorry, this has never happened before!" The he said, turning grey-green. He removed the malt from our bill and produced a free one for all. Prince had pulled off this layer of deception without so much as a hint of it being a joke. While everyone laughed hysterically I kept thinking — fasten your seatbelt Owen.

PART V: TAKING OUR SHOW ON THE ROAD

Working in the studio with David proved to be better that I'd ever imagined. Under David's guidance Prince had grown exponentially — both musically and at the recording board. I was learning that this wasn't a one-time event. Prince was someone who could absorb difficult and critical information at lightning speed; he was downright scary. The finished demo wasn't just an improvement from the Moon demos but an uncanny leap of musical brilliance — all within a few months! A guy who delivered a synthesizer to the studio confided in me that he thought Prince was a prima donna. When I pressed him for an answer he said, "Because Prince told me to go home after I showed him how to program the thing." But I knew that Prince couldn't help it; this was the brain he was born with. And once he had absorbed everything in your brain, and all your talent, it was time for you to go home. Nothing personal.

Within days the presentation kits arrived from the printer, and the new demo would soon be fully recorded and mixed. It was time to set up appointments with the labels in Los Angeles. Gary, handling the legal side, set up a meeting with famed LA music biz lawyer, Lee Philips. Lee, a doppelganger for Gabe Kotter from the hit TV show "Welcome Back, Kotter," was known in the biz as super bright and tough-knuckled. He was Barbara Streisand's attorney. But it was up to me to get the major labels on board. My strategy was simple: Lie my way into the labels.

I'd always held the belief that it's very important to fib in this business. No, not a destructive lie like, "Hey man, I saw your girl at the club with another dude," but a "business lie" that generates what I call "gentle-jealously." I ask you: How else would you break down doors and get your artist ahead of the pack of thousands of artists looking for recording contracts?

I phoned Warner Bros, "Hey Russ, it's Owen. I want to make sure you are a part of our presentation in Los Angeles." "What presentation?" Columbia Records is flying us out to meet a seventeen-year-old musical prodigy from Minneapolis that I discovered. While we're out there on their dime would you like to hear his demo?" "Of course, Cliff Siegel mentioned an act you were managing but I didn't know Columbia was already in," was his immediate reply. "Great, I'll get back to you with an exact date."

Once Russ agreed I phoned Columbia Records. "This is Owen Husney, we have a seventeen year-old musical prodigy and have a meeting set up with WB. Would you like to take a meeting and hear the demo?" "You have a meeting with Warner Bros? Of course," came the reply. I did the same with A&M Records, and ABC Dunhill. Within two days I had almost every major record label on board and every meeting was set.

I never mentioned to Prince or Gary that my intention was to make the deal Warner Bros Records. I had witnessed WB at work from the inside and knew first hand that it was a truly artist-friendly record label. I observed Russ Thyret in action get record after record added to radio stations across the country. And Mo Ostin, WB Chairman, and Lenny Waronker, WB President, were legendary in the business for understanding artists and creativity. Additionally, my best friend and former band mate, Cliff

Siegel was now Regional Marketing Manager for WB, covering the entire mid-section of the U.S. But first, I needed to get a bidding war started so we could drive home the best deal at Warner's for Prince.

Jeff brought the printed presentation kits down to my office and suggested that we cut out the picture of Prince from a few of the front covers and attach them to the reel to reel demo tape boxes. "This way everything will match," he said with an art director's eye. "But we're putting his demos on cassettes, aren't we?" I said, knowing that cassettes were all the rage in the late 70's. And then it hit me — if we're going first-class let's not use plastic reels, let's go all the way then and put the demos on silver tape reels. If everyone is expecting cassettes — we'll go the opposite way. We found the silver tape reels and Jeff affixed the pics of Prince to the tape boxes. It was a spectacular presentation.

Gary and I huddled together for a strategy meeting. One of the ideas was that it would be great if we wore three-piece suits to the label presentations. If everyone in sunny LA were wearing casual Hawaiian shirts and sneakers we'd cause attention by going the opposite way with three-piece suits. If we were going to make presentations in New York — where everyone was wearing suits and ties — we'd have worn Hawaiian shirts and sneakers.

Prince and I decided that "Soft and Wet," "Baby," and "My Love is Forever" would be the songs on the demo. But we agreed to have the Moonsound demo of "We'll Make it Through the Storm" in my back pocket — just in case they wanted to hear one more song. If they wanted more songs, they'd have to pay for it — period.

In March, on the edge of winter's thaw Prince, Gary, and I — our wives in tow for support — flew out to make the presentations to Warner Bros, A&M, and Columbia — the very labels I had fibbed to in order to get meetings. Gary and I went into the meetings while Prince waited in the reception area. During the presentations I said very little. The first class presentation kit with five pics and a few one-liners said even less. Prince's first-class music did the talking. The reel-to-reel demos forced the label folks to get off their ass and use a better playback machine than a cassette deck — giving the demo superior quality sound.

I loved watching the faces of the super-cool label dudes half-way through the demo; at first listen their expression became intense, then came a slight smile upon hearing greatness — which quickly retreated — lest they give away their bargaining position. And because I gave up very little info, the label execs immediately started asking questions; "Is he really from Minnesota? Is he really seventeen? Are there really black people in Minnesota? Does he really play all the instruments? Isn't Minneapolis home to the Pillsbury doughboy? Isn't it freezing back there?" My answer was always the same, "Yeah, and he sang all the vocals too." It worked like a charm. When they asked, "Where is he now?" I answered, "Right here in your reception area, would you like to meet him?" Prince would then walk into the room — a star's entrance for an unsigned kid.

I returned home from Los Angeles visibly giddy from the meetings. "It couldn't have gone much better if you had scripted it," I bellowed to my staff who were all ears, "They couldn't contain themselves when they heard the demos. And they fawned over the black lacquer presentation kits that said nothing." Everyone laughed. "They kept asking us questions, and when they asked Prince questions he just smiled that super-cute half smile — and gave them one-word answers. I retreated to my office and couldn't wait for the phone to ring with a call from Lee Phillips or one of the labels."

But as the days wore on there were no calls. Returning from client meetings I'd rush to my in-box and look for the pink "while you were out" note that guaranteed our future — but there was nothing. Despairing, I could barley look at another client's fashion ad; I missed Hollywood, I missed the action, and I wanted to get Prince a record deal and be his manager. I wouldn't dare call the labels — lest I give away our bargaining position; and I wouldn't dare call Prince and tell him nothing was happening.

How embarrassing this would be for all of us who had worked so hard.

In my passion I didn't even consider the possibility that he wouldn't get signed. Even worse, I had sent a demo tape to RSO Records, home of the Bee Gee's, and in the afternoon mail was a rejection letter. "It's not the kind of act we are looking for at this time…" It was signed, Al Coury, President. Dejected, I left the office early and went for a walk in Theodore Wirth Park; I circled the park until nightfall.

The weekend came and went. On Monday morning I returned to my mundane duties at the Ad Company and reviewed the car-dealership copy with my staff; "Yes, a black background with white lettering will pop on the billboards," I said, staring out my office window and imagining palm trees on the edge of Loring Park. But the only Billboard I wanted to be reading had chart listings of hit records, not, 'Buy a Low Payment in a Color you like.'

Cliff Siegel stopped by to say hi and inquire how it went in LA. I told him I wanted to get the fuck out of the office — so we smoked a joint, went to lunch, commiserated, and I returned to the office.

I knew that neither Prince, nor I, nor anyone on the team had done anything wrong. But I understood that this whole music biz thing was, at the very least, a giant crap shoot. To save my soul my mind turned back to advertising; maybe it should be black lettering on white background. Then, fuck it; it'll be red lettering on black background for the copy, yellow for the client's name, and white for the fucking location!

Around two o'clock my secretary buzzed in and said someone from Los Angeles was on the line. I picked up the phone with a sinking feeling. "Hey Owen," an excited voice responded. It's Kip Cohen, A&M records. Sorry for the delay, but we got feedback from our staff on the demo and we absolutely LOVE your artist Prince. We're super excited to make you an offer so please don't sign with another label until you get our offer." I had rehearsed my response in case this should happen. "That's awe-some. Please have your business affairs department call Prince's attorney, Lee Phillips." I hung up the phone and the words, "We absolutely LOVE your artist Prince…so please don't sign with another label until you get our offer," sent a rush of endorphins through my soul like a mainline of heroin.

The next day CBS Records President Don Ellis called, "We'd like to fly you and Prince out here. We've set aside time at Village Recorders so Prince can record a track — and we have a special luncheon set up." "Great, I'll let Prince know. But why the studio time?" "A few of our A&R (Artists & Repertoire) guys want to stop by and see if he can really play all the in-struments." "Interesting, I'll run that by Prince. Do you intend to make an offer?" I said, with confidence. "If he's really who you say he is — then the answer is yes." "Great, when the time comes please have your business affairs department call Prince's attorney, Lee Phillips."

With two labels under our belt I felt safe in bringing the good news to Prince, but inserted the caveat that we had to hold out for Warner Bros. "Oh okay, that's good," Prince, said. "When do we leave for LA?" "As soon as we hear from Warner Bros." Yep, the kid of a few words was also cool as a cucumber too.

It took a full week for Warner's to respond. "Hey Owen, it's Russ," came my blessing from Burbank. "I was prepared to walk into the A&R meeting and quit if they didn't want to sign Prince, but they were already there. Mo (Mo Ostin — WB Chairman), Lenny (Lenny Waronker — WB President), and I are totally in and we're gonna make an offer." But WB was going to have to step up to the plate so I could steer them in Prince's direction — it was in his best interest creatively. So now was my time to strike. "We have two other offers on the table Russ. The advance mon-ey is important but the guaranteed number of albums is strategic to his development and success." "I understand Owen, and I'm going to do everything in my power to bring him on the label." Russ said. It was obvious he had the same passion for Prince as the Minneapolis team. "So, have your business affairs people contact Prince's attorney Lee Phillips." I said.

The next week I was on the phone with either the Chairman, President, or Sr. VP of the leading record labels in the world. Not bad for a guy who just a few years before had been pinched, punched, and locked in his locker in school I thought. And it was especially gratifying to know that a young wunderkind named Prince Rogers Nelson was rising from the basement "over North".

Lee Phillips called and said that A&M offered a solid deal; two albums firm and a six-figure advance, CBS Records offered a very similar deal, as did Warner Bros. CBS offered up Verdeen White from Earth, Wind & Fire to produce the "the kid," and interestingly, WB offered the producer services of Maurice White from E,W,&F. But as far as I was concerned WB needed to get to three albums firm before I'd accept the deal.

We decided to go on radio silence for a couple of weeks and analyze the pros and cons of the offers. It would be especially important for Prince to have a say; first, his intuition was perfect and I trusted it, second, this was his life. For him, it would also be important to know his other label mates, and their success, or lack thereof. For us it was to drive home the best deal for his creativity to grow and flourish. For me, it was to steer us in the direction of WB without being obvious with my intention.

Warner Bros. was not exactly known as a Black record label. They did have Curtis Mayfield through Curtom Records, Quincy Jones's QWEST Records, famed producer, Norman Whitfield, with great tracks like "Car Wash" by Rose Royce. But they were known more for their successes with acts like Fleetwood Mac, Elvin Bishop, Rickie Lee Jones, Van Morrison, The Doobie Brothers, and Paul Simon. That was okay with Prince. He expressed many times that he did not want to be pigeonholed as a "black artist." "No color barriers, Owen. I want to make music for everyone, so please don't make me nobody's black act." He knew that Columbia/CBS Records was responsible for breaking Sly and the Family Stone — an act that had ripped down color barriers and delivered massive crossover hits. But he also knew that Reprise Records, founded ironically by Frank Sinatra and WB Chairman Mo Ostin — under the WB umbrella — had given us Jimi Hendrix. And that's how Prince saw himself. Besides, as highly competitive as Prince is he didn't want to compete with Sly on the same label — much better to break down barriers in fresh, fertile, territory.

A&M sent me a Western Union telegram; "Owen, please understand that we consider your artist, Prince a true talent and someone who we are very excited about signing. Not hearing from you is making us quite nervous. Please respond at your earliest convenience. We are attempting to make you an offer that is in the confines of our deal making ability." It was signed, Herb Alpert, Jerry Moss, and Kip Cohen. Still we waited.

To further induce us A&M flew Prince, Gary, his wife Susan, my wife Britt, and me to Los Angeles. They put us up at the swanky Beverly Wilshire Hotel in Beverly Hills. We had fabulous meals, gorgeous rooms, and limousines at our disposal. And Prince got his first taste of luxury. During the trip Prince and I disappeared and met with Russ at his house. Instead of limos, and fancy meals Russ picked us up at the hotel in his two-seater Mercedes 450SL. Prince fit perfectly in the rear seat, which wasn't really a seat at all. Russ drove us directly to his house in the Valley and offered us soft drinks. We sat on his floor and discussed the music business.

As soon as we got back to Minneapolis CBS Records flew us back out to Los Angeles and made good on their offer to give Prince studio time. "We just want to make sure Prince can play all the instruments and sing like on your demo tapes." Said Peter Philben, A&R. So on April 18th, 1977 Prince marched into historic Village Recorders and blew the minds of everyone in the room. When Prince announced that he needed handclaps on the recording everyone ran into the studio ready to clap. And that included the President of the label, Don Ellis, and A&R head, Peter Philben. I guess success has many fathers.

CBS held a luncheon for us the next day and invited Verdeen White from the mega group Earth, Wind, & Fire to attend. He made an appearance halfway through the luncheon and sat down right next to Prince. Prince turned to me and whispered, "Is that supposed to impress me? Let's get the fuck out of here." Prince had the utmost respect for E,W,&F but he knew CBS was hinting at Verdeen possibly producing him and he didn't want any part of that.

After the luncheon Russ Thyret picked Prince and me up in the two-seater and off we went back to his house. Once again, we sat on the floor and sipped Cokes. "It's important to understand that if you write a song and get it placed on the "B-side" of someone's hit single it earns as much as the "A-side." Russ advised. This was a man understood the value of a personal relationship over luncheons.

THE MAGIC OF LEE PHILIPS:

I wanted three albums firm in order to develop Prince's career. First albums traditionally don't sell well but serve to introduce artists to the world. If an artist is truly talented they will learn and grow and get the chance to record a second album — and simultaneously build their base audience. And should an artist be fortunate to get to a third album it means they have started to build a serious audience base and position themselves for a real career. My fear was that if Prince was given only two albums, and the first one didn't do well, he might be dropped from the label. But with three albums firmly guaranteed from a label Prince would be assured the best possible formula for his career. But there was one problem; record labels did not give out three album deals — ever. It was simply too risky financially. But would WB step up to the plate?

By 1977 Lee Philips was considered to be one of the top music industry attorneys in the U.S. The first time Gary and I met with him he was conversational, almost jovial at times. But my intuition told me that lurking beneath that friendly demeanor was a man with a killer instinct who would use his intellect and guts to bring home the best deal for his clients. Big time attorneys also carry a secret weapon called leverage. Since they represent other top selling acts across major labels they can play one label against another to get the job done. And they know the players. Yes, Lee was the man for Prince.

To be honest, I was shocked when Lee called and said that Warner's was willing to go to three albums — firm. I had pushed for it, spoken to Russ about, and even prayed for it. But the fact that Lee got it done was astonishing; it was an unheard of deal in those days for a new artist. With Lee's skilled nudging, Warner's proved they were the record label to develop Prince. And I knew from watching him make the demos in Minneapolis that Prince would reward them for it.

I flew out to LA for the final meeting with Warner's. In the meeting with Lee and WB business affairs the notion of Warner's involvement in partial ownership of Prince's publishing came up. Publishing concerns an artist's writing of songs and is not related to the release of their recorded product. During negotiations many labels twist the arm of the artist's lawyer by inferring that they might not make the record deal if they don't also own a portion of the artist's songwriting. I was horrified. Not because WB asked, but because I didn't understand publishing. I just wanted to bail from the meeting and get to a library and read up on the subject. If anyone in the room knew that as manager I didn't grasp that part of the biz I would have been replaced immediately. However, I had learned a nifty trick when you don't understand something in a business meeting; keep your mouth shut and let people think you're an idiot rather than opening it and letting them know you are.

"I'm not prepared to have this discussion," I said to the room's amazement. So instead of sounding like an idiot, I came off as super ballsy. My intent was to just buy time to get educated on the subject of music publishing. To my surprise, Lee picked up on my "balls out" approach, hammered home the point, and got Warner's to back off on ownership of Prince's songwriting. To be certain, Lee's brilliance got the job done — and it wouldn't have happened without him. But I like to think that I had a small part in Prince owning all of his songwriting because I didn't know what the fuck they were talking about.

Lee worked out the details of the final contract with David Berman, the head of Warner Bros business affairs department. A date was set to fly Prince out for the official signing. Warner's had also organized a company-wide luncheon after the signing at La Serre, a renowned restaurant in the San Fernando Valley populated by film and recording industry moguls.

Prince was not particularly comfortable with a luncheon held in his honor — especially when he knew that he'd have to gladhand, talk, and smile when he didn't feel like it. It wasn't his thing. David "Z" Rivkin suggested to Prince that perhaps he record a special song and play it at the luncheon. "Then your music can do the talking," he said. It was a stroke of brilliance and Prince loved the idea. Within a few hours Prince and David recorded "Me & WB" at Sound 80. "Now that I know your name and you know mine — we can make such beautiful music — together," went the lyrics. The unreleased song was an immediate hit with the WB staff.

Exhausted, and not quite ready to believe what had just happened to our lives, we returned to our rooms at the Sheraton Universal. The hotel was just down the road from Warner Bros Records — OUR NEW HOME. Almost immediately Prince came down to my room to tell me that he really disliked these luncheons and crowd gatherings. "It really makes me uncomfortable with all these people I don't know coming at me," he declared. "All I want to do is make music, Owen." I believe that any other manager would have told him that this was something he had to do to in the biz and to just suck it up. But after living and hanging with Prince daily for almost a year I had come to understand and respect his character. "I'll tell ya what, from now on we'll pick and choose who you need to meet with, and I'll try to keep it down to one-on one meetings — deal?" "Okay, please look out for me. I get super paranoid around people I don't know."

There was a knock on the door and Prince looked directly at me. This would be my first test at deflecting strangers. "Who is it? I'm resting!" I said to the door. "I have an envelope for a Mr. Owen Husney from Warner Bros Records." The man behind the door explained. A hand came in through the tiny crack in the door gave me a standard white envelope with the famed WB logo in the upper left corner. Inside was a check made payable to Prince Rogers Nelson and American Artists Management. It was for $80,000.00. The eighteen-year-old kid from the basement, over North Minneapolis, had just received an advance check for just over six months work. And within a few months he would receive a second payment of another $80,000.00. The total contract was worth well over a million dollars.

This was just the beginning.

Ready to Make an Album

I MAKE MUSIC FOR ALL PEOPLE:

The ink was hardly dry on the Warner's contract when Prince came to my house with an important announcement. "Owen, I will be producing my album. I do not want anyone else producing it." This was a pretty bold and ballsy statement for a 19 year old kid who had never recorded a full album. Nonetheless, after observing him for over a year I believed he could do it. So, with nothing more than my belief in hand I was charged with telling one of the largest record labels in the world that Prince would not only be playing all the instruments, writing everything, and singing all the parts, but he would also be producing his first album.

I decided that I'd first run the "Prince as Producer concept" by Barry Gross, our product manager at the label. If he didn't get it I'd move on to the President of WB, and if necessary, to the Chairman, industry legend, Mo Ostin. "I was just going to phone you," came Barry's breathless response. "We're all excited that Maurice White from Earth, Wind, and Fire has agreed in principle to produce Prince." Earth, Wind, and Fire were on the top of the charts and I understood their collective glee. "Well, Prince doesn't want anyone to produce him. He'll produce the album himself." There was silence on the other end and then a muffled laugh. "Sorry, Owen, that's not the way it works for an unknown making his first album." Prince and I huddled — and that night he dropped a note off at my house. In essence, it said that while he respects Maurice White he is totally against him producing his album. He went on to say that while Earth, Wind, and Fire's writing was new, he couldn't hear anything new to their sound and could pick it apart. Besides, he had picked all the parts for the album and there would be nothing a producer could add.

So, I came up with an idea and phoned Lenny Waronker — WB President, head of A&R, and a brilliant producer in his own right.

"Let's give Prince a test. We'll tell him that WB is giving him free studio time in LA for him to work out parts for the album. While he's recording you can arrange for any number of producers to come to the studio and watch him. If Prince passes the test he produces his own album." Lenny agreed to the plan. Prince and I boarded the plane to Los Angeles and what happened next was mind-blowing.

We didn't want to give Prince any indication this was a test. For all he knew the guys passing through the studio were maintenance men. In fact, they were the top producers in the world; Russ Titelman — producer for James Taylor, George Harrison, Randy Newman, Eric Clapton, and Chaka Khan — Teddy Templeman — producer for Carly Simon, Doobie Bros, Van Halen, Little Feat, Van Morrison, and Gary Katz   producer for Steely Dan. They watched, as a young man laid down a drum track in perfect time. Once complete, he added a bass guitar, then guitar, and keyboards. Prince was just getting ready to add vocals when Lenny pulled me into the hallway. "Okay, we get it. It's astounding; this kid who has never made an album has "record-sense." We'll agree to let him produce his album providing there's a recording engineer with gold and platinum on his walls to oversee the process. Tell Prince he doesn't have to record anymore today. He can be his own producer. I told Prince the good news and his answer was, "Okay but I want to finish my recording now. I never leave anything half done." When Lenny told Prince the news Prince's only reply was, "Don't make me black. I make music for all people."

OUR GOAL WAS COMPLETE CONTROL:

Our plan from the get-go was to stay in Minneapolis and record the album. The reasons were simple: my Ad agency, now billing in the millions, was fronting costs and artwork on behalf of Prince, Prince felt comfortable recording at Sound 80 where he recorded his demos, and we wanted to make the album with WB out of our hair. Besides, winter was coming, and what would be better than being forced to stay indoors and create your gift to the world. So now that Prince could be his own Producer my next call was to Warner's to tell them that we were staying put and recording the album in Minneapolis.

"You guys are killin' me!" Said our exasperated product manager. "We just got Tommy Vicari, an A-list recording engineer to agree to work with you." What makes you think he's gonna leave LA and move his ass to Siberia to make an album for an unknown artist?" I hung up from him and called Lenny Waronker. "Send me the specs on the studio and I'll speak with Tommy." I not only sent Lenny the specs for the studio, I met with the owners and negotiated reduced studio rates, and provided suggestions where Tommy could live in Minneapolis. Lenny replied that it was a go. Lenny Waronker, Russ Thyret, and Mo Ostin at Warner Bros Records were my heroes because they understood artists. Prince was excited to get to work. But then Tommy arrived in Minneapolis and things weren't so rosy.

A KINK IN THE PLANS:

"Owen, we've got a real problem here at the studio." Tommy sounded exasperated. "Huh? It's a world-class studio!" I said, feeling my heart sink with our glorious plans. "It is, but did you know they replaced the sound board a week before I got here?" "Isn't that a good thing?" "Absolutely not!" Tommy shot back. "It takes a good month or two to break in a new board and work out the kinks in the wiring. We don't have that luxury; Warner's expects us to deliver the album on time." "What problems could you possibly be having?" "To put it simply, when I press a button on the board, toast flies out of the toaster in the kitchen. We have to get out of here." Our plans to have full control of the process were fading and we were going to be toast.

I phoned our product manager, Barry Gross, with the problem. "Looks like you'll have to stick to our original plan and record here in LA." I could almost sense his snide grin over the phone. "We'll, not exactly." I said, cutting his grin short. "We're not recording in LA." Prince and I discussed the situation the night before. Prince didn't want Warner's people bopping in and out of the studio checking in on him. And I didn't want the wolves in LA stealing my artist. "You're fuckin' killin' me Husney! What's your fucking solution?" If he thought the guys from Minnesota were pushovers he was learning a big lesson; get out of our way and let us handle things. "I've discussed the situation with Tommy and Prince and we've come up with a solution. "I can't wait Husney, lay it on me." "We're going to record at the Record Plant in San Francisco." Barry shot back, "You guys want to move to San Francisco? Do you have any idea what that will cost? God, I hate working with amateurs." I shot back, "So do I. "Do you know what it would cost to record in San Francisco?" Yeah, I ran the numbers this morning and already cut a deal with the Record Plant. We can make everything work within the budget." I left for San Francisco on the next flight to find us a home.

The Record Plant was located in Sausalito, just north of the Golden Gate Bridge, and a minute from the bay. The vibe of the place was right on. The squat building's façade was covered in slanted barn wood, and there were animals playing instruments carved in the front door. The history of the studio was right too. It was the studio where two of Prince's formative artists, Sly Stone and Carlos Santana recorded. And best of all it was secluded — perfect for our merry band of Minneapolis transplants.

Warner's gave me a list of local home rental services. After viewing the second home I cut a great deal on the spot and rented it for eight hundred dollars a month. It was a furnished three level redwood home built into the side of "Little Tam" mountain in Corte Madera (Marin County). It too was secluded, and featured three redwood decks overlooking the bay. We weren't in Kansas anymore.

Back in Minneapolis Gary Levinson and I estimated all expenses and sent them off to WB. Within a week I received the approval, and the first part of the recording advance. These things happen when a label is excited about your artist. Gary sent a letter to the bank in Marin County and they opened a bank account in my name. We were in the business of helping Prince happen.

THE MERRY BAND BECOMES A FAMILY:

Prince wanted Andre Cymone to come with us to San Francisco. It made sense. I knew that Andre was more than just a pal to Prince; he was a fellow musician who spent countless hours writing, playing, and jamming while Prince was living in Andre's mother's basement. Additionally, I knew they were soul mates. From my experience as a musician and studio owner I knew about the intensity of the recording process. It could be brutal. And Andre was the perfect person to be at Prince's side. What I found remarkable was that here was Prince, a nineteen-year-old kid who was leaving his hometown to record his first album for Warner's Bros Records — a behemoth in the industry. He was going to write every song, play all the instruments, sing all the vocals, and produce the album — yet he never expressed any uncertainty about his ability to pull it off. He was beyond confident. And that's why I fought so hard for him.

Prince, Andre, and I jumped on a plane and headed to our new home in San Francisco. Within a few days our executive producer, Tommy Vicari, arrived from Los Angeles. Then, my wife Britt, and Shawna, our family dog showed up from Minneapolis. Inadvertently, we'd become one big family. Britt took care of the home front and provided needed companionship to Prince, I handled the day-to-day biz, Tommy engineered and executive produced the recording process, and Andre provided musical and moral support to Prince. The runner for my company, Bobby Z, was back in Minneapolis living and taking care of our house and

Gary was back there too keeping legal tabs on the entire process. It was time to make musical history.

One night, after the first week of recording, I came back to the house to see Tommy sitting on the couch with his head in his hands. Tommy is a slight Italian guy with puppy dog eyes and a dark fro. He had always been so confident and I knew that he had a stellar reputation in the business. He'd seen it all. "What's up Tommy? Are you feeling okay?" I said, ready to phone 911. "I can't get my head around it." "What?" What happened?" I said, thinking someone had been injured in the studio. "We've been recording all day and I still can't get my head around it. This kid is uncanny. He's not from this earth. I think it's Beatles time." I looked Tommy in the eye and said, "I know, I've been at his side for over a year. Why do you think I walked out of an eight million dollar a year business and moved half way across the country to stay with him and protect him?" We sat together on the couch without saying a word. We both knew this wasn't just another project. It was a mission.

Prince and Tommy continued to work away in the studio, sometimes late into the night. I could see the process was beginning to take its toll on all involved because Prince was a perfectionist. If he was scared or self-doubting he never showed it. He had everything planned in his head and if he found himself in a tough creative spot he just plowed through it in an exacting method and made it better. But it was driving everyone mad. "Owen, I want to make sure the vocals are perfect. Could you please fly David Z (Rivkin) out here?" David was known for having perfect pitch, and Prince appreciated the job David did engineering the original demos. Prince wanted perfection. I submitted a budget for David's services to Warner's and within a week David was on a plane from Minneapolis. His presence at the house was a welcome icebreaker — not just because of his talent, but because David and I had a history of playing practical jokes when we were in a band together. It was too bad that Tommy would be our first victim.

"Tommy, we're taking time off to go to the movies. Wanna join us?" Prince asked. "Sorry guys, think I'll just hang out in San Francisco for the day." Tommy left, and that was our cue. David and I told Prince of the plan that would be played on Tommy. He was all for it. We just didn't know the extent to which Prince would go to improve it.

"See, you take your clothes and stuff them with your clothes." I uttered standing at the end of Tommy's bed. "Now watch," I instructed, like a surgeon showing students how to perform brain surgery. "I take my pants and stuff them with shirts, underwear, socks, anything that fills them out." My trousers swiftly took on human form. "Now, you button a shirt up and stuff it with clothes too. See, it fills out and looks real." "Stuff a little more near the waist!" Prince insisted. He was all in now. Andre looked on like a skeptical parent. "Now, you put the top and bottom half together and push them a bit under Tommy's bed so you can't tell if there's a head. Then, I put my sneakers at the end of the pant legs." We stood back and began giggling in unison. It looked like I had passed out under Tommy's bed. Then, Prince hatched the ultimate plan. He ran to the kitchen and returned a long knife and a bottle of ketchup. "If you're going to do something don't half-step." He said, plunging the knife deep into "my" back. He poured ketchup around the knife wound until the "dead body" looked so real we all gasped. "When it dries it will be the perfect effect," Prince said, taking ownership of the prank. It was all great fun until I realized the shirt was one of my favorites.

When we returned from the movie around 8 p.m. we saw Tommy's car in the driveway but all the lights were off in the house. "I'll bet he's got something special planned for us in retaliation." Britt said. "Be careful when you open the door. He'll probably try to scare us." Prince told me to go in first — gee thanks Prince. I opened the door ever so slowly and tiptoed down the hallway looking into every room to see what Tommy had in store for us. "Tommy!" I shouted to an empty house.

"Tommy, are you in here?" In the dark, I saw an outline of some-one sitting upright in the living room chair. "Tommy?" There was no answer. "Tommy, you okay?" He looked lifeless as he stared straight ahead. "Owen…I…thought…they…killed…you. I…came home…went to my room…and…you were stabbed and bleeding…you were…DEAD!" Yep, the practical joke had gone too far. It took another day for poor Tommy to come around. I couldn't apologize enough.

The next morning Prince was all business. He had worked out the credits for the album late into the night. He hand printed them in pencil exactly the way he wanted them to appear on the album and asked me to type them up and send them to Warner Bros immediately. He then insisted that Tommy and Andre get up and, "Get to the studio." He had also written a new song that he wanted to record immediately. Yep, Prince was in action.

The next weekend I dropped Prince and Andre off at a mu-sical instrument store in San Francisco. It was part of my new plan to keep the recording process from becoming too tense. Prince would record around the clock if he could but people needed a break. The two nineteen year olds loved to show up and jam away on different instruments; Prince on guitar and Andre on bass. It was another way to break the intensity of recording. After I picked them up and returned to the house I received a call from an excited dude. "We just met these two guys jamming at the music store and they blew us away. We'd like to come by the house and hang." The last thing we needed was a stray San Francisco band showing up at the door and turning our house into party house. "I'm really sorry but we're only here for a few months recording an album. Everyone is pretty tied up. "Well we thought Prince might want to come by and jam with our band." "Okay I'll let him know," I said, buying off on the call. "What's the name of your band?" "Oh, sorry, it's Santana. We also told Carlos about this Prince guy and he'd like to meet him."

Following Carlos's directions, Prince and I drove straight up Mt. Tamalpais to a beautiful all white semi-contemporary home.

The routine fog was setting in and everything was fresh with dampness. Carlos met us at the door wearing white pants, a silky white knee-length shirt, and white socks. He politely asked us to remove our shoes in a hushed voice. Peering into the house I could see that everything was all white; the furniture, lamps, and drapes as well as the beautiful handmade rug that stretched throughout the house. The whole setting had a spiritual vibe. Earlier, I suggested to Prince that he should meet with Carlos one on one, as I'd just get in the way of the two musicians. I'd wait outside or in another room. As Carlos motioned for Prince to follow him, Prince caught me by the arm and whispered, "I don't remove my shoes for nobody." They turned and walked into another room I noticed that Prince's muddy boots were leaving a trail across the all-white "spiritual" carpeting. I was in shock and thought quickly. Wearing only my socks I removed them, got on my knees, and scraped away at the muddied carpet removing the footprints. I was now on the floor of my idol, Carlos Santana, cleaning his carpet. I must have done a good job as no one was any the wiser. I guess my protector and manager's job description now includes carpet cleaning to the stars.

Either late at night or when Prince awoke in the morning he'd play me the latest rough recording. It seemed like everything he recorded, although rough and unfinished, was remarkable. The exactness to which he attended to his vocals and instrumentation was downright scary. Each vocal track was precisely layered over the other and the harmonies rich and full. What seemed uncanny was that neither the vocals nor the instruments felt like it was one person doing it all. To me, it felt as if he hired a whole chorus of singers and brought in an entire band to play on the album. It was enough to give me the shivers. How could Prince have learned and grown so exponentially in a year? And how many different personalities were in there?

The honchos at Warner's hadn't heard anything yet because I'd made sure they left us to our own devices some five hundred miles away. I knew they'd love it and I knew that everyone of us on team Prince loved what they were hearing. But one thought kept haunting me: would the DJ's love it? And would audiences love it? I'd seen projects where a record label had bet the farm on an act only to lose the farm in a fire sale. I know how fickle DJ's and audiences can be. I know, because I've seen the floors of distributor warehouses piled high with palettes of useless cassettes and vinyl albums; every album sitting on those palettes representing a failed reach for the Holy Grail. One bad review and it could all be over. And then, Prince would play me a rough of, "My Love is Forever," or a newly minted, "In Love," and I know what I'd have to do — keep this thing together, keep kicking fucking ass, and keep Warner's away, at least for a while.

Prince returned from the studio and was standing in the dark at our bedroom door. "Owen, you up?" "No Prince, its 3 a.m. and Britt and I are sound asleep." "You're not going to believe this, but Chaka Kahn came to the studio tonight!" I'd never seen Prince so excited. "Was she recording?" "No, she called the studio around midnight looking for Sly Stone and I answered the phone. She said, "Is this Sly?" and I said, "Yeah, baby, what's up?" She asked if she could come down to the studio." "No, Prince, you didn't…" "Yeah, I told her to c'mon down and bring another chick with her. About a half hour later they show up and I answer the door." "Did you invite her in?" "No, she just stood at the door and said, "Who the fuck are you!" and then she cussed my ass out and left." "So, how you gonna clean this up before word gets back?" Prince looked at me and said, "I'll write her a hit some day."

The gorgeous California sun rose and set over the picturesque San Francisco Bay as the days wore on — but no one was paying attention. Prince's increasing intensity to get things right was taking a toll on everyone, and tension was on the rise. Further, he insisted that everyone stay up deep into the night to get just the right take. I noticed that Tommy and the Record Plant staff began to look like zombies from sitting 24/7 in the darkened studio. My phone began to ring with desperate calls of, "We just can't take it anymore." My response was always the same, "Stay with it, you're creating history." Despite the tension, Prince delivered. It was one thing to be a demanding jerk and fail, and another to be demanding and have everyone gasp in amazement with your creation. That's why we all stayed with him.

More than half way through the recording process Prince came to me and said he wanted Tommy to return to Los Angeles. "I don't need him anymore," came his directive. I knew from experience that the intensity of recording day after day and arguing over every detail of what goes down on tape extracts a heavy toll. I'd even seen fistfights and worse breakout. Tommy was there to engineer and watch over every aspect of the process because Prince was allowed to be his own producer — something that was never granted to a first time artist, let alone a nineteen year old kid. Tommy was there because he had a history of success backed up with gold and platinum records on his walls. He was well respected in the biz and a decent guy. But that didn't matter to Prince. I'd seen it before while recording the demos. Prince would absorb every detail of the process like a crazy sponge and then he'd have no use for you. Nothing personal. However, this time it mattered. A major record label had spent a whole bunch of money and effort and given Prince the keys to the kingdom. If Tommy were let go they'd say it was because I had no control over my artist — and worse, that Prince was an out of control artist. It would be a lose-lose situation. But it didn't matter because Prince wanted him gone. I figured in this case it was better to ask for forgiveness than ask for permission so I drove Tommy to the airport. It was a sad day. Prince didn't miss a beat; he returned to the studio and threw himself even deeper into the process.

When Warner's caught word of what happened they sent their A&R execs up to San Francisco. "We'd just like to pop by the studio and see how things are going," they said, like parents visiting a kid at camp. That night I brought them into the studio. Prince was laying down tracks for "Crazy You," a gorgeous down tempo song. Prince was more than accommodating, and even prepared a "rough mix" of the track for the powers at WB. We sat in the darkened studio and listened. During the playback, one of the WB honchos said, "Unbelievable, this song will be great once a bass guitar is added." Prince turned and faced them; "There is no bass on this song, that's the way I planned it! Now get out of my studio, get out!" The honchos scrambled out like scared puppies as I watched in horror. Prince went back to work as if nothing had happened while I went out to face them. I stepped into the hallway, and before I could say a word the head of A&R raised his hand, "He's incredible, just let him finish his album." I was reaffirmed on two levels; Warner's was the absolute correct choice of label to develop young Prince, and my initial belief in him, and willingness to protect him were justified.

Prince wrapped up the track recording for his album and sadly; it was time to leave San Francisco. Next stop, Los Angeles, where Prince would mix and master the album, deliver it to Warner's, and eventually the world. I flew down to LA a few weeks before and cut a great deal to rent a furnished house at the top of Mulholland for our family. It was really tough to say goodbye to the believers who helped us through our brand new adventure. So, to repay them we threw a huge party at the house for everyone, including the Santana band members. The next morning as we were preparing to leave Andre pulled me aside. "I just want you to know that living with you and Britt and your dog is probably the first sense of a real family that Prince and I have ever had — and you're white folks!" I laughed out loud as Andre continued, "One more thing, I think it's also the first time Prince and I ever had salad before dinner!" I shot back, "You know Andre, you really get to know someone on a whole other level after you've lived with them and washed their underwear!" We laughed again and hugged. I truly loved both these guys and knew it would be hard when we weren't all living together. And I couldn't help but feel that the "family" had fulfilled a need in all of us. Prince, Andre, Britt, and myself had all been abandoned in childhood, either physically, emotionally, or both. We understood the dark and silent loneliness that tags along with the gift of abandonment. In our individual ways we learned to cope and survive, and now, here we were, randomly thrown together helping to create history. We loaded up the car and the family headed for the entertainment capitol of the world; our initial dreams accomplished, our future dreams just down the road.

T. Marvin Hatley: Hollywood Hills — 1978

Visiting Hollywood for business or vacation is like watching television. You can turn it off, or change the channel whenever you like. Living and working there is another story — the real one.

WELCOME TO THE HOLLYWOOD HILLS:

The iconic Hollywood sign sits high atop Mt. Lee in Los Angeles and proclaims its existence throughout the city. Below its fifty-foot letters is an area of eight square miles known as the Hollywood Hills. It's where professionals, those in the entertainment biz, and too many scoundrels call home. The string of unity that binds them all is a searing passion for their craft — with either fortune, or fame and fortune as the prize.

But for every palm tree and sparkling pool in the hills there are a hundred stories of fortunes lost. Some have squandered their golden opportunity and pray daily to the god of "one more lucky break." Others have been swallowed whole by the passage of time; a glorious heyday left in their rear view mirror. An incredulous student, I'd soon learn that two of these one-time greats managed to cling to their crumbling castle in the hills. They await a ghost of a dream that will never materialize. And these days, the only agents who show up at the door are those who collect money for debts. We crossed paths in 1978; they left an indelible mark on my life.

FEBRUARY 1978:

I negotiated an incredible deal to rent a three level home for our "family" in the Hollywood Hills. Renting a furnished home for almost three months is far cheaper than a hotel. And, it gives our family a sense of home base during the demanding process of making a first album. Our house is perched on stilts along the top of the Hills. The daytime view offers the endless San Fernando Valley below, and the expanse of the Santa Monica Mountains in the distance. At dusk, the twinkling suburban lights from homes in the Valley appear one by one like stars — a breathtaking mirror of the nighttime sky. Not bad for a bunch of foreigners from the flat farmlands of Minnesota with the names Nelson, Anderson, and Husney.

After lunch and chores it was time to drive "the kids" down to Sound Labs Recording Studios located along the noisy and bustling streets of Hollywood. Prince, with the support of Andre, will work all night if necessary to prepare his album for release to the world.

Once Prince and Andre were safely tucked inside the studio, I'd rush back up the hill and attend to business. At the end of the day I'd stick a joint in my mouth and take my dog Shawna for the usual walk along the verge of the legendary hills. On this day I decided to change things up. Instead, we took a new route and circled our neighbor's sprawling driveway at Rue de Vallee. It was the magnificent estate of Rudy Vallee, the iconic 1930's megaphone-carrying crooner of stage and screen. His signature megaphone, seen countless times in his films from the thirties, was now a loyal mailbox. We ambled down to Woodrow Wilson Dr., the connector to Mulholland Dr., and strolled along the edge of the hills.

Shawna and I wandered into an area of homes that made me so envious I wanted to turn around and walk back. On either side were staid Tudor mansions, modern and ultra-modern architectural dream homes, and ranch homes that seemed to stretch on for a city block. The visible property in front of each home was manicured to perfection; some had fruit trees of orange or lemon, others with swaying palm trees, large-leaf banana palms, and deep purple or red bougainvillea. I knew it was still winter back in Minnesota and soon we'd return to snow and to folks who'd rather die than take down their fading holiday lights. The thought saddened me. I passed an elderly woman collecting mail from the box in front of her house. The sprawling ranch-style house behind her had seen better days. Tiles were missing from the roof, and the paint around the windows was peeling off, leaving scattered white chips on the yellowed lawn. Most of the foliage was drying or dead. Our eyes locked for an instant and I moved on.

"Young man, young man!" Came the urgent voice from the woman at the mailbox. I turned around to see if she needed help. "You mean me?" I said. "Yes, my husband asked to meet you. Would you like to come in?" I had no idea who she was let alone her husband. "Does he need help with something?" "No, he'd just like to meet you."

I secured Shawna's leash to the mailbox and entered the home of two people who, I would learn, were bonded forever — one by fearlessness, and the other by genius. Together, they fought their way to the top during Hollywood's golden era. And together they struggled to stay alive as both the gold and the passage of time slipped through their fingers.

The woman led me through a splintered front door and called out, "Marvin, Marvin, someone asked to meet with you." Okay, I didn't ask to meet Marvin but this was getting damn interesting. As the woman disappeared down a hallway to fetch Marvin my eyes adjusted to the darkened room. I noticed there was a concrete floor throughout the house. Not the trendy concrete floor of fashionable LA Lofts and restaurants — just a cracked concrete floor. The carpeting had been pulled up long ago and large bits of it still clung to the sideboards like a balding man in denial. Sun-yellowed bed sheets covered all the windows. The furniture was covered with old bed sheets too. I thought to myself how Miss Havisham would feel right at home here. To the rear of the living room was a sliding glass door that must have locked up years ago. It too was covered with two yellowed bed sheets strung side by side. Through a large space between the sheets I could make out an Olympic size swimming pool in the backyard. No longer useful, it too was chipped and peeling with just enough winter rainwater to form a thick coating of greenish sludge at the bottom. Beyond the pool was one of the most dramatic views of the San Fernando Valley I'd ever seen. It encompassed the expanse from Burbank on the east to the far stretches of the Valley on the west. This must have been some place back in the day.

Startled, I turned to face the click and clomp of footsteps on concrete coming down the hallway. It was mysterious Marvin rounding the corner. He strode in with great intent like an orchestra leader approaching the podium. His face was thin, wrinkled and stern. Neatly trimmed white hair streamed forth from under a brown beret. The beret was carefully slanted to the left for effect. His jacket was a brown military-style cloak. It was impeccably pressed with a matching brown sash to keep it closed. His pants were brown riding jodhpurs, each pant leg carefully tucked into shiny black riding boots. Holy shit, it was the uniform of movie directors from the twenties and thirties! Did he change into this guise just for me? Is that why it took so long for him to appear? As he approached he raised his right hand. I assumed was going to shake my hand. Instead, he brought an unlit cigarette stuffed in a black mouthpiece to his lips. He grasped the holder from the underside like Adolph Menjou in "Gentleman of Paris," and puffed at nothingness. Behind him, looking more like an anxious stage mother was his wife. All I could think of was that no one is ever going to believe this, and how great is it to be stoned here at "Grey Gardens."

"Nice to make your acquaintance, Mr.?" "Husney," I said. "Thank you for wanting to meet with me." He took another smokeless drag. "You're welcome, the pleasure is all mine." I began to sense what was going on here and thought I'd play along. Being stoned helped.

"Marvin, why don't you take Mr. Husney to the music room? The two of you can talk there," his wife directed. I followed Marvin down a long hallway past rooms with closed doors. On the walls were silhouetted shapes of oval, round, and square outlines where pictures once hung. Okay, this is eerie. Should I even be here?

As we entered the music room a splash of red hit me mid-chest and I stopped dead in my tracks. Marvin cracked a thin smile. Looking up I saw a stream of yellow shoot across the room and spread out on the wall behind me. Streaming into the space in every direction were random bolts of reds, blues, and greens. The colors leapt from wall to wall sometimes redirected by floating specks of dust in the unventilated air. The area was at least forty feet by forty feet with a soaring twenty-foot vaulted wood ceiling. I searched everywhere for the origin of color. Marvin pointed his cigarette holder to the west wall. Near the ceiling was a single glass prism positioned strategically in an opening to the outside. The intense rainbow was born from the setting sun through its individual facets of glass. It was the only source of light in the otherwise semi-dark room.

Dangling on the walls were ancient banjos, dented horned instruments, and guitars without strings. And in the middle of the room was a tired organ from a bygone era. I stood transfixed.

"Mr. Husney, do you like my music room?" "It's a magical sanctuary." I replied, partially appeasing old Marvin, yet not wanting this moment to end. "Thank you. They said I couldn't do it." "Do what?" "I built this room with my own two hands in the forties. My wife encouraged me to do it. She was the only one who believed in me." He said, exhaling another imaginary drag from his cigarette holder. "Would you like to hear an original song?" I knew this would be another moment. "Of course." I replied, as Marvin sat down at the old wooden organ.

Marvin sprang to life and became a fucking one-man band. His left hand whizzed along the organ keyboard making sense of the black and white keys. His right hand held an old trumpet to his mouth — fingers in motion. His feet traversed the giant bass keys below while a left elbow simultaneously pushed a device that kept time on a snare drum contraption. I listened as one original song after another — obviously written in a bygone era — were once again brought to life by their creator.

When old Marvin began the third song my ears sprang up like a dog hearing his master's voice. I knew this song. It was from my childhood, and as familiar to me as my own name, but I never knew the title. "Is that yours too?" I asked. "Yes, I wrote it in 1933 as a musical cuckoo clock for a radio station I worked at. It's called "The Dance of the Ku Ku's." Stan Laurel loved the song so much he bought it from me for twenty-five bucks." So Marvin wrote the fucking Laurel and Hardy theme song! I grew up listening to this song sitting in front of the TV every freezing day of my life in Minneapolis. Now, here I was with its author; my new neighbor in the Hollywood Hills. I wanted to hug him but Marvin was too stoic a man and I knew better.

Marvin told me he was the Musical Director for Hal Roach Studios, one of the early film studios to put Hollywood on the map. He not only wrote most of the music for the Laurel and Hardy series, but almost all the music for The Little Rascals, aka The Our Gang comedies.

"You know son, I was nominated for three Academy Awards in the thirties for scoring the music for the films "Way Out West," "Blockheads," and "There Goes My Heart." He then played me "Honolulu Baby," another ditty that was etched in my mind. As the setting sun dimmed the room I reimagined a young Marvin in the shadows, so passionate, so determined to make it into the big time. "I made great money in the thirties and forties but it was all Work For Hire," Marvin explained. When the work stopped coming in I was forced to become a lounge act with my one man band." I knew what Work for Hire meant. Creative people who worked at movie studios in that era were paid a handsome fee for writing music. Once they turned in their creative work the studio maintained ownership and there were no on-going royalties. Although Work For Hire still exists, the copyright laws have changed dramatically. Important composers are now able to negotiate continuing royalties and own greater portions of their works. Many distinguished songwriters of the twenties and thirties became impoverished when their work dried up and they had no residuals. Marvin was the poster boy.

"I thank my wife for everything," Marvin continued. "Without her I would never have had the determination to drive to Los Angeles from our hometown in Oklahoma. "So was she your agent at the time?" I said, angling for more. "No, we were a team from the beginning. The day we arrived in Hollywood she drove me directly to Hal Roach's mansion in Hancock Park and knocked on his door." I was a geek on all things Hollywood and knew that Hal Roach was the famed producer and Studio owner. He gave us the likes of Harold Lloyd, Laurel and Hardy, and the Our Gang comedies. "Was he home?" "Yes, and he threatened to call the police, but my wife insisted that I come in and play the piano for him." "Did he throw you out?" "No. He invited us in, I played my heart out, and he hired me on the spot." I was the musical director for Hal Roach Studios for over a decade."

Marvin's wife appeared at the doorway of the music room. "Exactly what is it that you do Mr. Husney?" She said, again sounding more like agent than wife. "I manage a young artist who just signed to Warner Bros. Records. In fact, I have to leave to pick him up from the recording studio in a few minutes" "Did you hear that Marvin?" She said, looking directly at him. "Young man, please come in the kitchen for a minute."

Marvin and I followed her orders and we all wound up sitting at a table that had three and a half legs and a brick. Stuck in the walls with push-pins were yellowed and tattered photos. They were the only pictures in the house. The tired images were of Laurel and Hardy, glamorous stars and starlets, the Our Gang kids — Alfalfa and Spanky, Marvin and his wife, and the man himself — Hal Roach. They were frolicking in the California sun while being served drinks poolside by attendants. Then, it hit me, this was their pool, and their home in better days. My heart sank and I could hardly utter a word.

"Young man, you can see how talented Marvin is and I'm sure you can use his services. Perhaps your artist could use him on some of his sessions. Marvin is ready for his return." I stood up ready to leave and she said, "Marvin, be sure to get his number." I gave out my number as I headed for the door and noticed that Marvin was writing it on the palm of his hand.

Marvin and his wife were still working as a team after all these years. His passion was music. Her passion was an undying belief in Marvin's talent. And they were still at it. Like with Hal Roach back in the day, she got me in the door to listen to her talented husband and I was knocked out. For them, it was another day and another possibility.

As I untied Shawna's leash from the mailbox I thought of the irony of the situation. Prince was a young prodigy and so was Marvin in his time. And both were considered a one-man-band because they played all the instruments. Their only need was someone to get them in the door.

I felt a strange brew of inspiration and melancholy as I said goodbye to old Marvin and his wife that evening. I knew I'd never see them again.

A nagging question haunted me for months after meeting Marvin and his wife. Where would I be in forty years? Sitting at a broken kitchen table with pictures of Prince pinned to the walls? Where would Prince be in forty years? Would he be become a flash in the pan, or an enduring artist? Marvin and his wife inspired me to trust my instincts and never give up my core belief in Prince's talent. I also learned how important it is to have someone believe in you — and for you to have someone to believe in. To me, Marvin and his wife were far ahead of all the wealth in that ritzy neighborhood.

Shawna and I then headed home east along Mulholland as the California sun sank behind us in the Hollywood Hills.

Back Home

I couldn't help but notice the up-tick in Prince's appearance when he walked into my office. Gone were the days of showing up in a t-shirt, cutoff jeans, calf-high white socks, and sneakers. I used to joke about his fro, and call it a J-7, as opposed to Michael Jackson's coiffed J-5. Now, his emerging look was less casual, augmented by a trimmed fro; black leather jacket, a pullover white V-neck linen shirt, dress pants, and high-heeled boots. The teen acne that had plagued him during the first photo shoots had all but disappeared. Now that the album was recorded Prince was turning his attention upgrading his appearance.

I was opening a square box that was just delivered via UPS. It had a big WB logo on the side and was marked in block letters, "Promo Copy — Not For Sale BSK-3150." "Do you want the honors?" I said, as soon as the box was pried open. "Sure," came Prince's one word reply. He reached in and produced a single vinyl album from the box of twenty-five. On the top it said, "PRINCE-FOR YOU." Beneath the title was a photo of Prince, streaks of color fading off from his face to the left side of the album; a single white streak emanating from his eye. Prince then reached in the album jacket and pulled out the dust cover. "Lets see if they got it right." He said, examining the superimposed shot of him naked on a bed, a guitar covering his private parts. "It's perfect." Prince was so proud of his concept that he made sure that the liner notes read: Dust cover concept: Prince.

Prince had the idea for the dust cover before we left to record in San Francisco. "What if I'm naked, playing guitar on a bed? We'll superimpose the shots so I'm on the edge of the bed facing the camera, and a then a shot of me to either side of the bed." The idea would be controversial at best. I liked it because I was a student of P.T. Barnum. P.T. knew the value of controversy. When the bearded lady was displayed as a "Freak of Nature" in a tent he sent shills outside; some to say she was real, others to claim she was a fake. The end result: everyone had to pay a nickel to find out for themselves. Also, being a student of Colonel Tom Parker, Elvis's manager, I told Prince about the first time Elvis appeared on The Ed Sullivan Show. He swayed his hips in such an overt sexual manner that the second time he appeared Ed would only allow him to be shot from the waist up. The end result was massive ratings for his second appearance. The same with the Beatles: the first time they played Ed Sullivan people could not believe the length of their hair. The next day that's all anyone was talking about. Controversy creates awareness, and awareness begets money. However, you better have the ultimate talent to back it up otherwise you're merely an oddity in a freak show.

To make sure the naked bed bit was going to work my art director, Jeff Framakes, suggested we try another local photographer, Joe Gianetti. Joe came over to my house and shot Polaroid's as Prince stripped to his skivvies, and positioned himself on our bed. Holding a guitar he took one photo head on, and two more sitting on each side of the bed. Joe somehow superimposed the Polaroid's together and there it was: three naked Princes on my bed, each holding a guitar. Once we were in San Francisco, I talked Macy's department store into opening for us on a holiday and flew Joe out. Alone in the giant store we tried all the bed displays until we found just the right one; a queen sized bed with an arched window behind it. Joe shot away and returned to Minneapolis the next day. Jeff completed the superimposition of the three Princes, and sent the elements to Warner's. Prince was so impressed that he asked Joe to shoot the album cover — no help from WB was necessary.

The finished product in my office had been the end of a long hard-fought process. We demanded full control almost every step of the way: recording, where we recorded, who recorded Prince, and even the album artwork. And for the most part

Warner's had given it to us. Most new artists were thrilled to take direction from their label, but Prince saw it as an impediment to his vision. Lucky for Prince, he had a manager who believed in him and was willing to fight for him. Even luckier, he had a record label that understood his ultimate talent. They knew that letting Prince have his way might cost them sales on the first, and possibly the second album. But they were willing to roll the dice in hopes that Prince would deliver in a big way in the future. But I wondered if there was also a flip side; would we also be contributing to the making of a prima donna, or worse yet, a monster of control that would harm his career? I knew if the album didn't sell Warner's would rein us in like runaway horses. And knowing Prince, he'd demand to be let out of his contract and a major war would ensue. However, Prince is one smart, talented, super confident guy, and I'm a believer and a gambler — so lets roll the fucking dice.

I observed the kid from the basement holding his finished product. He had a new album, a new car, new clothes, a more focused look, and advance money in his bank account. It was less than a year and a half since I first grabbed the phone from Chris Moon in this same office and promised to protect young Prince. Now, we were signed to Warner Bros Records after making the biggest deal in the history of the biz for a new artist. In addition, the eighteen-year-old artist was given full control over his recording — unheard of at the time.

Prince left my office with the box of albums under his arm. I couldn't help but stare through the window as he climbed into his new Datsun and drove off. There had been no time during the lightning-speed process to take in what we'd just accomplished. It was then that it all hit me — our team had just made the impossible dream possible.

Once Prince was gone I flipped my copy of the album over to look at the liner notes and "Thank Yours." It read: "Special thanks to God, Owen, Britt, Bernadette, My Father and Mother, Russ Thyret, Gary, David Rivkin / Sound 80 Studios, C. Moon,

Eddie, Sharon and Eleanor, L. Phillips, Bobby "Z" Rivkin, Tom Coster, Graham Lear, Joe Giannetti, Patrice Rushen, Charles Veal, Jr., Shirley Walker, Knut Koupee Music, Chuck Orr, Lisa H., and You!" Damn, I was second to God — but this was no time to gloat, or exhale.

4 A.M.

"You and I"

September 1978: four in the morning, a $35 motel room somewhere between Fresno and San Francisco. After yet another grueling day on the road a just-turned 19 year-old Prince Rogers Nelson collapsed in exhaustion and was sound asleep in the bed next to me. I was wide-awake.

We were on the twelfth day of a promotional tour for the first album, "For You," and the newly released single, "Soft and Wet." Shipped out on a shoestring by Warner Bros Records our job was to gin up support from local radio stations, small retailors, and locally owned one-stop distributors across the country. "Smile, and shake as many hands as you can." The heads of radio promotion and sales said in unison. "Promotional tours are key to the early success of an artist's first release."

Not surprising, hardly anyone knew of Prince. We got a lot of gratuitous, "We'll add the record to our playlist" from small-time radio stations, and "Yeah, we'll call WB and order a few copies for our store." But we never truly believed they'd follow through. Truth be told, we couldn't wait to get the hell out of these places and back to our cut-rate room.

Tonight, our motel room in Fresno was especially dank, with the sour smell of too many prior occupants. Fearing for my life I kept the yellowed sheets at a nontoxic distance from my face. My bedspread, smudged with enough DNA to keep the FBI busy for a year, was safely hurled across the room. I was freezing and wide-awake as I had been for the previous eleven nights in seemingly the same room, different city.

Per Prince's strict orders tonight, as every night, the clock radio on the laminated nightstand between our two beds would blast one song after another at full volume, it was the only way he could sleep. Tonight it was Rick James — "You and I," Funkadelic — "One Nation Under a Groove," Donna Summer — "Last Dance" — they all poured forth from the tiny speaker — now an open spigot of flooding funkiness. No sleep for me again tonight I thought as I stared at the parking lot lights through the sun-shredded curtains.

But tonight was going to be different. Tonight was the night that I would dare to reach over, hit that off button on the clock radio, stop the music, and enjoy a few hours of uninterrupted sleep before the next town and the endless radio stations and record store stops. I cautiously leaned over and could hear Prince breathing deeply, a sure sign of his peaceful slumber. Ever so carefully my hand reached for the off button and I pressed it — without a sound. Mission accomplished. A warm, silent calm you could bathe in suddenly filled the room.

As I laid my heavy head back down on the pillow and drifted off Prince immediately sprang up. "Owen, wake up!" He demanded. I looked up. His large almond-shaped eyes stared at me with the kind of restrained intensity that people use when they are pissed as hell but trying to maintain their cool. "Do not ever do that again, do you understand?" His voice then ticked up a notch and he growled, "Music soothes the savage beast!" Prince slammed the on button, laid his sleep-flattened fro back down on the pillow, and instantly fell back into his peaceful slumber while The TRAMMPS — "Disco Inferno" urgently bounced off the walls of that dingy motel room. If I were lucky I would get maybe three and a half hours sleep, again.

In the morning a bright-eyed Prince and bleary-eyed Owen set off in a limousine, compliments of Warner Bros. It would be three-hour drive to Unique Records, a small Ma & Pa operation near South Los Angeles. "Soft and Wet" was getting some minimal airplay and this was to be our first "in-store" record-signing event. The limousine was intended to make us look like stars when we pulled up. From my past experience I counseled Prince that there might only be only three to four people in the store asking for autographs and they would probably be relatives of the owner. "Let's keep our expectations low," I said with authority.

The drive found us in the middle of a huge sale at the local supermarket in the same nondescript strip mall as Unique Records. As we drew closer Prince turned to me and said, "They must be giving food away for free, look at the people lined up all the way down the street. Let's stop by after the in-store and pick up some snacks for the rest of the trip".

Our limo rounded the corner and pulled into the parking lot. The crowd, some three to four hundred strong suddenly turned — and surged towards us! They were shrieking, "It's him! Prince…Prince! Oh my God he's really here! It's Prince!" I shouted to the driver to roll up the windows. As the tinted windows went up the mob converged on the limo pounding on them until I thought they would shatter. The crowd began rocking the limo back and forth to the point where we were sure they would push the vehicle over on it's side.

Prince grabbed my arm in terror but there was no escape. Not even a good manager like me could get us out of this one I thought. Pubescent girls pressed upon the car so hard their mascara left black rivers of tears running down the windows as they cried hysterically. Others, just simply flashed their breasts at us. The boys, curiously oblivious to the display of youthful tits, propelled the girls away so they could snap Instamatic photos — the flashes off the windows only reflecting back in their own faces.

I screamed to the driver to pull the car around to the back alley where we could be sheltered from the onslaught and possibly gain a more secure entrance to the store. If not, we would be forced to flee the scene like little sissies, not badass funksters. I was concerned. Prince is a slight guy with a delicate frame and the zombies would eat him alive if given the chance.

But Prince knew better. He calculated that if we could some-how make it in the store there would be tons of publicity to be had. I agreed. "Owen, you got your camera?" "Yup," I said with a gulp. "Then get ready to start snapping pictures." I instructed the driver to make it look like we were leaving but to pull around back into the alley. I figured we had a fifty-fifty chance if we made a break for it in to the store. This was our *Night of The Living Dead*.

We bolted from the safety of the limo while the car was still moving and raced into the back entrance of the tiny store. Once the old metal door was safely shut and bolted behind us, it hit me. If we live, this shit is gonna be fucking huge!

Phoning a skeptical Warner Bros from the record store I explained how we almost died, and demanded security, and at least a WB local promotion man for every future city. They only laughed, thinking we had become premature prima donnas and told us to calm down and just do our job. But after reports of the same reaction in Chicago, Detroit, Atlanta, Charlotte, Dallas, and Houston they had to agree, this shit was gonna be fucking huge!

The next stop on the schedule was Washington D.C. Warner Bros now realized they had an investment to protect so Prince and I were given separate rooms in a swanky hotel. But even so, as I was falling asleep I could still make out the ever so faint pounding of funk coming from Prince's room down the hall. It was then that I came to understand the true depth of his musical soul; he couldn't stop the music in his own head let alone the radio. He created music, played music, recorded music, and slept to music.

I lay in bed that night in my swanky hotel room thinking of the impact his gift would have once unleashed and released to the world.

That lone thought kept me wide-awake. Yes, another sleep-less night for me.

"Music soothes the savage beast."

Crossroads

P rince walked into my office a day after the grueling three-week promotional tour concluded. I was still in recovery from no sleep and having trouble focusing. Prince was heavy-eyed too, but that didn't seem to matter. I could tell that he'd been working on his appearance. His everyday clothes were taking on an even more stage-like expression. Dress pants, a black jacket with a flowing scarf, and black boots replaced the usual Minnesotan jeans, turtleneck sweaters, and sneakers. His fro was now trimmer and back to a J-4. Does this guy ever sleep?

"Owen, I'm getting a band together. No more jamming at your office, it's time to get serious and tour." Prince said, energized, on a mission, and serious as a heart attack.

THEN, HE LOOKED ME DIRECTLY IN THE EYES:

"And let Warner Bros know I won't be an opening act for anyone."

Wow. This was so naive. I tried to bring some reality to the situation.

"Prince, the album hasn't been released yet. There's a process to all this. Plus, it's not in your best interest to headline out of the box."

I needed to buy some time. Any further lecture on my part would only fall on deaf ears.

"Have you thought about who you want in the band?"

"Yeah, we'll audition people. Just get your part done."

Prince had it all planned out in his mind, and that was a good thing. It's just that his timing was off. It was my job as manager to explain that to him. I could sense storm clouds forming on the horizon.

There are two types of bands who tour: singers with no dedicated band members — just hired hands. Then, there are self-contained road-dog bands like The Allman Bros. Bands like the Allman Bros played every nook and cranny for years before getting signed. Putting road-dog bands out to support a new album is relatively simple and cheap. They usually have a following of dedicated fans, and relationships with clubs and small venues. They have their own van, and are used to starving on the road. Prince was the former, but even more complex — he played every instrument and sang all the vocals on the album! Putting a band together from scratch would be costly; the new band would have to learn every song exactly as Prince recorded it — down to every nuance of the background vocals. The band members would need to be salaried while rehearsing and touring, and the cost of gear and a rehearsal space would be astronomical. Additionally, you have to take into account the actual cost of on the road expenses. Untested bands make little to no money on the road.

I also knew that Warner's would have to foot the bill in a form of loan called, "recoupable tour support." That means you'd have to pay 'em back before you get a dime of royalties. Warner's would also want to see proof of serious chart activity, and a "tight" band before they'd write a check. I knew this, Prince didn't. Prince had gone over budget recording the album. In a private moment he even admitted to me that perhaps he had over-produced the album in an attempt to make it perfect. I was concerned that he'd get into too much debt with the label — even with a major hit record. And that would give the label control over him.

Even if the label agreed to everything we'd need a major booking agency to arrange the dates. Simply put, Prince was a newbie act with no road experience.

And he didn't want to be an opening act?

Needing to lower expectations, I said, "Okay, put together a list of possible band members and we'll audition them here at the office."

"Cool, just get it done," came Prince's response again as he headed for the door.

What was this new shift of character and attitude I was witnessing?

Halfway to the door he turned around and said, "Owen, my bathroom plumbing needs fixing. Go over there and fix it."

"Me?"

"Yes, just go over there now."

It was a demand. Prince walked out and closed the door. Huh? Was he serious? I'd seen this attitude shift before in other artists; it's usually when someone with no practical knowledge of the music business starts whispering in their ear. But who was it?

My brand new stereo boom box was whirring away, recording cassette after cassette, as a trail of local Minneapolis musicians stopped by my Loring Park office to jam and audition with Prince. My employee and friend, Bobby Rivkin, was now a staple on drums. He and Prince had really hit it off while Bobby was driving him around town for me. Bobby was a funky-ass drummer and Prince knew it. Of course, Andre was on bass. Prince played a guitar, loosely slung across his shoulder, so he could swing it around and transition to keyboards. Bobby's cousin Robbie Paster stopped by to join in on bass, as did local greats Bruce Kurnow on harmonica, Bobby Schnitzer on guitar, and prized Peterson musical-family member, Ricky, who was a killer on keyboards. With the exception of Bobby and Andre, Prince wasn't feelin' it. He was going after a very specific sound and look — a band he could mold in his own image.

"Lets see what LA has to offer," I offered, my ears burning after nights of endless jamming. "We could hold an audition there with the help of Warner's."

"Okay, get it set up now." Prince demanded.

I pulled Bobby aside, "Are you noticing a shift in Prince's attitude?"

After a brief discussion, we agreed that the pressure on nineteen-year-old Prince to deliver was immense. He wasn't alone in this, but he probably felt that way. In addition, we agreed that his biggest fear was standing still. In his mind, if he wasn't moving forward at lightning speed he was dying. All we could do was support him. But I knew it was a double-edged sword; say yes to everything and create a monster, or say no — and risk the wrath of your artist. To an inexperienced artist the word "no" sometimes equates to not believing in them, when in fact, the opposite is true. Once an artist hits the big time everyone in his or her proximity is on payroll. And hired hands always say "yes," or they get fired.

Prince, Andre, Bobby Z, and I flew out to Los Angeles with great hopes of auditioning musicians. The WB product manager secured rehearsal space at S.I.R. on Sunset Blvd and advertised in the local music rags; "Warner Bros artist seeks auditions for band members: Wednesday, between 1pm and 5pm, Studio Instrument Rentals, Sunset Blvd."

We arrived early and set up in anticipation of auditioning hundreds of musicians and singers. We knew the level of musicianship would be awesome because this was Los Angeles. By 4pm, only five people showed. Three of them looked and sounded like they had just been released from a secure facility for doing something very nasty. We returned to Minneapolis deflated. Prince was now more determined than ever to get a band together. I knew we had time because the first single from the album, "Soft and Wet," was in the early stages of being serviced to radio. It would be a long time before we'd even be close to touring. I just didn't want Prince to tour too early. When you're in the creative business, you're better off being two days late and having your shit together than a day early and having it suck.

Prince was picking up on my reticence. He may have thought I was half-stepping, but I knew I had to hold my ground. I didn't want to keep borrowing money from Warner's in the form of advances. The more you borrow, the longer it takes to pay the piper from your royalties. One of the toughest jobs a manager-protector has early on is shooing away outsiders with selfish motives. Those are the ones who whisper, "Yes" behind your back.

Prince is a true blue Minneapolis guy. Like all of us working on this project Minneapolis is our home and our cocoon. The Hollywood experience left us feeling like we were auditioning mercenary soldiers to fight in a land they had never heard of before. There was geographical prejudice too.

One dude, who thought he was Jimmy Hendrix, said to me, "What goes on in that stupid frozen place, the Pillsbury Doughboy? Isn't he the biggest star to come out of there?"

He laughed as I opened the door and sent him packing into the California sun. Prince wanted his band to be a family. For many reasons he needed a family. And he had the beginnings with Andre and Bobby Z. Now, it was time to return home and dive deeper into the Twin Cities musician pool. First, I had to find a suitable rehearsal space. My Ad Company could no longer sustain the late night comings and goings of so many people auditioning.

Eager to find a cost effective rehearsal space I started contacting music instrument stores.

"You only need to contact one person," Carl from Knut Koupee music said.

"Who's that??"

"Steve Raitt."

"He uses a facility near Seven Corners by the U of M. It's an old tire warehouse called Del's Tire Mart. He does some recording there and stores sound equipment in the space. I'm sure he'll sublet it to you for a while."

In the early 1970's Bonnie Raitt recorded her first album in Minneapolis. It was recorded on Lake Minnetonka's Enchanted Island — a forty-minute drive west of downtown. Formerly an old summer camp, it reminded her of a camp where she performed as a kid in upstate New York. Initially, master musicians Willie Murphy and John Koerner attracted Raitt to Minneapolis. She was so impressed with the level of multi-racial musicianship that she used almost exclusively Twin City musicians and producers for her album. A few years later, I booked Bonnie Raitt into my Marigold Ballroom. The show proved to be her first sold out performance. Around the same time, Bonnie's brother Steve took a liking to the Twin Cities, and made it his home. He became a respected fixture on the scene, not only as a musician, but also for his first love as a sound engineer.

Steve and I sat in the warehouse and discussed rental rates while the twang of old rubber permeated the dingy space. It was definitely big enough to facilitate a growing band. Even better, there was an adjacent parking lot to accommodate band members, those auditioning, and hangers-on. The timing was perfect. Winter would be upon us before we knew it so it was good time to get a band together and rehearse 24/7.

Prince came by the space, looked in the door and said, "This will work."

Two days later the lease was signed. Prince grabbed the keys from me, muttered something indistinguishable, and drove off. The kid from the basement had a brand new album, his own rehearsal space, a new car, and a new furnished home on France Ave. in Edina, Minnesota. The band would be the last step on the way to bringing Prince to the world. But there was trouble brewing in River City.

Back in my office my work was just beginning. The next step was to place an ad in the local music publications to look for musicians. I wanted the ad to be short and simple; it read: "Warner Brothers recording artist seeks guitar and keyboard player for national tour. Phone American Artists, 612-871-6200 to schedule an audition."

Within days, calls were streaming in and auditions were being scheduled at the rehearsal space. Prince wanted to get a band together and tour; that meant gaining the interest of a major talent-booking agency. He didn't have a band so this would be tricky. I'd have to use the same technique selling him to the booking agency as I did in selling him to the major labels. That meant selling futures. I'd have to convince them that they'd be losing out big time if they passed on representing an unknown genius — with an incredible band that didn't exist yet. I had three original press kits left over from the label pitching days for presentations to the agencies. And now I'd have real album tracks and updated pictures from the album shoot. Soon, I'd be on a plane pitching again.

"Hello, is this Mr. Husney?" Came a voice on the other end that sounded more like a radio announcer.

"My name is Dez Dickerson. I saw your ad for auditions. I'm a guitar player in a local rock band."

I liked the sound of a rock guitar player. Of course, it would be up to Prince, but I liked the option of a rock player over a blues or proficient jazz guitarist. Although scarcely able to keep up I knew from jamming with Prince myself that he had a strong rock edge. He could easily play a lead riff that would impress the current rock gods.

"Okay, can you make it tomorrow? I'll schedule you in."

"Yeah, but it will have to be quick I have a gig out of town."

I learned from my band days that hiring a working musician was always a good sign.

"Mr. Husney, what is the name of the artist?"

"Oh, sorry Dez, it's Prince."

"That's what I thought. No one around here has actually met him, but he's already a legend."

Dez showed up the next day and jammed with Prince, Andre, and Bobby. Prince called me that night and said he wanted Dez in the band but wanted to get to know him first. He was particular about his family.

Everyone brought their own gear down to Del's Tire Mart and the jamming, rehearsal, and auditions began to take on a very serious tone. Prince, driven by a work ethic, focus, and sense of direction years beyond his physical age, was taking the reins and becoming the CEO of his organization.

I'd get calls late at night from Prince demanding something or another, and from the new band members complaining that they were being worked to death. All I could say to the band members was, "I understand, but stay with it. You've seen how far we've come in a short time — just imagine where we're headed."

Behind the scenes however, I was still concerned that we'd burn through too much money and have to relinquish too much control to the label. Additionally, I was very concerned that Prince was serious about headlining out of the gate. That would negate any possibility of doing small gigs to warm up the band and gain audience reaction and feedback — so essential to success. The Beatles in their early career played relentlessly in small clubs in Hamburg. The Stones once played a small dancehall outside of Minneapolis and were booed early on during their first US tour. Both Bonnie Raitt and Billy Joel played at my tiny Marigold Ballroom at the beginning of their careers.

People, eager to get close to the Minneapolis wunderkind, would tell him anything to gain access inside his realm. Though I trusted Prince to know the difference — he always relied on my word and trusted me — I knew the chatter chipping away would have a harmful effect, not only on Prince's future, but also on our relationship.

The call came in at 11pm on a Wednesday night.

"Owen, I'm calling the band members but they're not picking up so I though I'd ask you." It was Prince's cousin, Chazz Smith.

"It's a little late, what's up?"

"I didn't know you guys were leaving out on tour," Chazz said.

"No one is going anywhere," I yelled. "What the fuck do you mean?"

"Well, I dropped by the rehearsal space and all the gear was gone."

"Huh?"

"Yeah, this dude said the band boys came by with a truck and loaded all the band gear in and left."

We didn't have any band boys.

"Thanks Chazz, I'll get back to you."

I was in shock. I called Prince and there was no answer so I jumped in my car and sped to Del's. When I got there the door was wide open and the gear was gone — all of it. Prince pulled up and we walked around the empty space in disbelief. Whoever it was didn't even leave a guitar chord or mike stand.

"When did you guys finish rehearsal?"

"Around 8pm I guess," Prince said in a hushed tone.

Some hangers-on must have come by the space to hear the rehearsal. What they found was no one home and a wide open door. Worse yet, the band members owned the stuff that was stolen. It was their gear. I didn't push it any further. What would be the use? There was only one key and it was always in Prince's possession.

I was back on the phone with our WB product manager.

"Why the hell are you guys rehearsing anyway? There's no tour, and no chart activity!"

I knew he was right. And I didn't dare mention that Prince wanted to headline. He would have flown to Minneapolis and had me committed.

"Because it'll take months of rehearsal to whip the band in shape. Prince is a serious dude," I shot back.

"He should be writing new songs," the product manager fired back.

I was getting pissed.

"Look, he probably has the second album written already but we've got a serious problem here," I declared, ready to deliver the next punch to his gut.

"I can't wait."

"All the gear was stolen from our rehearsal space and it needs to be replaced."

"You guys are really fuckin' killing me. Get your fucking artist under control!"

"Or what!" I demanded.

I didn't wait for his answer. I hung up and started calling up the line of command. I phoned Russ Thyret, VP of promotion, my friend and main reason Prince was at Warner's.

"I'll bring the situation up in our meeting tomorrow and get back to you."

We may have just dodged a bullet. The problem is that the day will come when Prince will have to pay the piper. The advance check from Warner's to replace the stolen gear arrived in the mail within days. Soon, Prince was back in business again with brand new gear — and this time he owned all of it. We didn't want to return to Del's. It didn't feel right after what happened. In addition, Warner's wasn't giving us money any time soon.

* * * *

I first met Pepe Willie in 1977 when Prince was recording his demos at Sound 80. Pepe knew Prince from the early seventies when he moved from New York to Minneapolis, and was briefly married to Prince's cousin. A musician and singer, Pepe formed the band, "94 East." Coincidently, Bobby Rivkin answered an ad and was 94 East's drummer for a time. Pepe eventually hustled a "demo deal" from Polydor Records. He was given a budget to record a few sides at Sound 80; if the label liked what they heard they'd sign the band to a recording contract.

"Owen, Pepe wants me to play a few parts on his 94 East sessions. Do you think it's okay?" Prince said to me on the other end of the line.

"As long as you keep it to just instruments, no step-out vocal performances," I said, knowing that his vocals would be a defining factor and needed to be protected for his career.

That was the first time I met Pepe Willie, and our relationship grew over the following months. We even drove to Chicago, and worked the Ma and Pa record stores on Southside to help promote the new album. When the rehearsal space was robbed Pepe generously offered his house to the band. A few weeks later we moved into Pepe's basement and rehearsals began in earnest. I left on a plane to New York. The William Morris agency answered my calls and listened to the album. They wanted to begin talks ASAP about representing Prince on the road.

While I was in New York, Prince's cousin Chazz asked Prince if he would audition Gayle Chapman, a keyboard player living near him in North Minneapolis. After her audition at his house Prince was all for it. I called him from the hotel to check in and tell him I had great meeting with William Morris.

"Good," came his newly familiar, unthankful response.

Then, with renewed animation he said, "I auditioned this bad-ass girl keyboard player." He described her as super-sexy, with peach colored skin and beautiful curls of red hair flowing to her shoulders.

"But she'll have to stand in the back. She's taller than me."

Gayle fit perfectly into Prince's vision for a multi-racial/multi-gender band. The "rainbow" family was coming together.

"When are you coming back?"

"I'm on a flight in the morning," I responded enthusiastically.

"Good, you need to get back to work."

Jesus, what did Prince think I was doing? The comment sucked and seemed so out of character. Was it because he knew I felt it was too early for a tour and he resented me for it? I was willing to support his vision — as long as we didn't burn up too much money. Saying no is a necessary and dangerous path to go down for a manager. It opens the door for a young, inexperienced artist to think you don't believe in them — when actually the opposite true.

I sat in my office, inspired after having returned victorious from New York. William Morris agreed to represent Prince, and even agreed to a set up a small tour providing Warner's supported the idea.

My secretary buzzed through: "A guy named Matt is on the phone, says he's a friend of Bobby Rivkin's."

"Is this Mr. Husney?"

"Yes, you're a friend of Bobby's?"

"Yeah, we went to school together in St. Louis Park. I'm a keyboard player."

"Damn, my old alma mater seems to be ruling the music scene these days. What can I do for you?"

"Well, I've been bugging Bobby because I heard Prince is looking for a keyboard player. I guess I bugged him too many times because he got mad and said to call you. Maybe you could put in a good word with Prince."

I hung up and called Bobby.

"Do you know this guy Matt Fink?"

"Yeah, I know him from high school. He's been bugging me to audition so I told him to call you."

"Gee, thanks. Is he any good?"

"He's pretty damn good. People made fun of him in school and then he emerged as this monster keyboard player and blew everyone away."

I knew the feeling.

There was no time to waste. I hung up from Bobby and started to call Matt when my phone rang again.

"Owen, this is Matt Fink. Sorry to bug you. Did you talk to Bobby?"

I was beginning to get the picture.

"Yes, Matt. Since Bobby is your friend I think we should let him mention you to Prince. If he's open to it I'll back you up."

Two days later Prince called and asked if I knew someone named Matt Fink.

"He's a friend of Bobby's from St. Louis Park."

"Damn, you St. Louis Park guys sure stick together.

Matt auditioned and got the gig. The band was now complete: Andre on bass, Bobby on drums, Gayle and Matt on keys, Dez on guitar, and Prince on any instrument he chose to play in the moment.

Rehearsals continued 24/7 in Pepe's basement as winter made its first snowy attempt. I was now getting calls on a daily basis from band members:

"He's working us to death," was the usual mantra.

"We show up in the morning, jam for hours, learn songs from the album, and then jam for hours. We hardly have any time to eat lunch, dinner, or even go to the bathroom. The breaks are few and far between. Owen, please, talk to Prince about this."

I was conflicted. Having been around superstar bands I knew that in addition to pure talent, a fierce work ethic was mandatory. Prince seemed to be the poster boy for work ethic. I never saw him do drugs, or even drink alcohol   although the band and I were beginning to wish he did. A little relaxation would do wonders for everyone.

$$* * * *$$

Early on, I took various trips around the country, without Prince, to specific markets like Chicago, Detroit, D.C., Atlanta, and Dallas —bankrolling quite a bit of the trips myself. I did it independently to make personal relationships at black radio, and ma and pa record stores, so strategic to breaking an artist.

I traveled to Detroit and met with "The Electrifying Mojo." Mojo was a force in Detroit radio. His mysterious show was an eclectic blend of mainstream R&B (WGPR was an R&B station). But Mojo was doing something unique: he was introducing stone-white groups like Devo and the Romantics to Black audiences. He was a forecaster and a tastemaker — and that meant if he gave the record a spin other stations around the country would follow suit.

I walked into Mojo's darkened studio, lit only by candles. I didn't know if I should shake his hand, bow down, or kiss the ring. I immediately felt that I was in the presence of someone who had broken the mold of the standard disc jockey and deserved respect. While records were spinning I presented him with one of the rare fifteen press kits we made to accompany the original demo tapes. Mojo thanked me, and said the kid from Minneapolis was already on his radar.

The real job of getting "Soft and Wet" on air would be up to Warner Bros Black promotion department. They would have the tough gig of actually getting the record played by hook or by crook. And I knew because of Prince's talent and their belief in him the Warner's crack radio promotion machine would get the job done.

So when I got word from Warner's promotion department that "Soft and Wet," was beginning to show signs of life I was elated. "The Electrifying Mojo", had become one of Prince's earliest fans. He added the single to his playlist and that meant other stations around the country would be playing it as well.

"Soft and Wet" began to climb the charts, and that put a lot of pressure on everyone. Although elated, I knew Prince wanted to get out and start touring sooner than later. I still never thought the time was right for doing that. His band was just getting to know each other let alone learn the songs. I also knew from experience that the band should warm up at small clubs and out of the way venues. This would be abhorrent to Prince, but so necessary to learning early on about audience feedback; what audiences like and don't like about your songs and performance so you can adjust and move on to bigger and better venues.

The single climbed the *Billboard* Urban charts but stalled at #12. Although respectable for a first time artist we were all expecting #1. I could sense that Prince was disappointed. I was concerned that blame would be fired in all directions, whether it was with Warner Bros., the WB promotion department, or me. Going backwards was not something that was in Prince's mindset.

I also knew from being in the business that like most first-time authors who have bestsellers, or young filmmakers with a hit out of the box, it's probably the worst thing that could happen to their career. It's like cocaine: you spend the rest of your life trying to get back to the thrill of when you first did it, but it was never going to be the same again. For me, the slow build on a firm trajectory was the way to go.

The album hit #92 on the *Billboard* Hot 100, then dropped. We were all disappointed. For Prince, disappointment is met only with increased drive. No resignation — just an amplified desire to succeed. And my love and respect for him meant that I would never want him to look at me with dissatisfaction in his eyes. We had worked side by side since the minute we met when I gave him the keys to my house and he put his trust in me. But Prince was different now, and I didn't want to be perceived, whether real or imagined, as a roadblock to him on the way to achieving success.

Prince was gifted with the ability to see down the tunnel of his own success, which is really, really unusual. He understood how exceptional he was, where he was going, and he knew where he was gonna wind up. However my caring for him would not allow me to "yes" him either; I would treat a child of mine the same if they were exposed to danger.

But Prince's demands on me were growing by the minute. It wasn't so much that he was asking for things to be done — that was my role as manager — it was the way he was demanding things get done. Privately, the band and I joked that, just like the Robert Johnson song, Prince had gone "Down to the Crossroads and signed that deal with the devil. We weren't serious; it was just a way of relieving the stress.

Weeks later, I was sitting in my office, waiting for one of the more strategic calls of Prince's career. William Morris was actually calling to go over a listing of cities for a small tour. They wanted me on a conference call at 3pm Minneapolis time. I would still have to convince Prince to do a bunch of tactical smaller shows, but even that would be better for him than headlining or even being an opening act for a major group.

My secretary buzzed in. I thought it was the William Morris call, but it was one of Prince's band members calling from rehearsal.

"Hey, Owen. Prince wanted me to call you and tell you that it's fucking cold here in the basement at Pepe's, and he needs you to bring us a space heater now."

I explained that I was waiting for a very important conference call with William Morris.

"Pepe's right there. Perhaps he can go get it. I'll drop by the house and reimburse him after the call."

The band member agreed and hung up.

Two minutes later, Prince is on the phone.

"Owen. I need you to bring the space heater."

"I can't right now, Prince. I'm waiting for the conference call from William Morris."

"Well, if you don't bring the space heater, I'll find a manager who will."

I don't know why — this self-preservation just kicked in. My mindset was, I don't want anyone to ever talk to me like that, ever.

So I very calmly said to Prince, "Well, then find another manager." And I hung up.

I told my secretary that if William Morris called, to tell them I'd gone home ill, because I just didn't want to deal with it.

I was resigned, at the time, that I just didn't want to be the youngest, richest manager in the graveyard. And so, in my mind, it was over. And I never reached out to Prince.

Three days later, someone drops off an envelope at my house. Inside the envelope was a letter from Prince, to me. I thought, this is interesting.

The letter was written on three white inner sleeves from vinyl album jackets.

In the letter, Prince explained himself to me. And I don't wanna go into detail on that, because it's no one's fucking business. But he wrote the letter because it was the only way he could express himself to me, and get everything down, without just having a conversation.

First of all, he let me know that I led him to believe that he was going to be worth a great deal of money, because he's gonna be around for a long time. And I knew it! But as I read the letter, I still felt that I didn't want someone to treat me like that.

But what it came down to was this:

He didn't want to come off as a prima donna. But he absolutely did not want to be responsible for anything "normal," because he hated "normal," and past that, he just wasn't good at "normal." He couldn't go to the drug store, because Prince couldn't be seen at a drug store. And he couldn't be taking 45 minutes away from rehearsal for guitar strings, or space heaters, or anything, because those were 45 minutes he could be teaching the band arrangements, or dreaming up the next essential piece of music.

I'd been great for him all through the making of the album, but now he needed to be ready at all times. His hair had to be just right. His complexion had to be just right. All the visual details and design elements and musical elements had to be perfect, and he didn't have time to think about anything else.

While I was reading the letter I kept thinking, he's exactly right, it just isn't the time to be making these types of demands yet.

He told me he loved me, and respected me, and if there were anyone better at being his manager, he would have found them. But he needed me there 100%, for all of his needs, whenever he needed it, and this was not negotiable.

There was more, of course. But that was the gist.

I never responded to that letter.

* * * *

I never responded to the letter because I knew that someone was whispering in his ear — someone with an ulterior motive and obviously no real experience in the music business. Whoever it was had convinced Prince that he needed me one hundred percent of the time and should be demanding of me to get his way.

I got a phone call at the time from a mutual friend who knew what was going on.

"This dude has been telling Prince that you need to walk out of your Ad agency."

"But my agency funded Prince from the start. Additionally, he has a full art department at his disposal. We've done all his artwork from his press kit, to his demo reels, to his album cover and beyond. He has three secretaries at his disposal for anything he needs done, and I have a staff that will get him anything he needs."

"Owen, the dude convinced Prince that YOU should be doing all this."

"If I become Prince's personal gopher then who will handle the record label on a day to day basis and make sure they pay attention to Prince over their other acts? Who'll kick ass on marketing, promotion, and radio promotion from our side? Who will plan the tour and ride herd over the booking agency? Who will make accurate financial projections and watch over the money?"

In that moment I realized what was happening and why it would be pointless for me to answer the letter. The fool who was whispering in Prince's ear was probably a failed musician who was projecting his hopes and dreams on Prince's rising star. Prince was too young and inexperienced to figure it out. Any attempt I made to explain the business to him would probably fall on ears of mistrust.

But Prince was no prima donna. If anything, he was brilliant and driven. I was sure that while we were all sleeping he was up planning and creating his next move. I believed him when he told me he didn't like anything "norm." I knew he had trouble in social situations. He'd be more comfortable on stage in front of ten thousand strangers than in a room with five people. That's why I also saw the letter as a veiled cry for help. Perhaps he wanted to be more outgoing like everyone around him, but that wasn't the way he was wired. When you can't stop the music in your head — then that's where you live — 24/7. And functioning in the "real" world is painful, if not, next to impossible. Prince spoke through his music, and that's all he ever really cared about. I was worried that when success came he could wind up rich, alone, and isolated. I didn't want that for my friend, but maybe I was just too naive.

I never answered the letter because I knew it was time for Prince to move on, even if he didn't. He was moving into the next phase of his career — at lightning speed. Even though I felt it wasn't time to tour he would never hear it, especially if people were whispering in his ear. Let the whisperers promote a live show for him and see how that goes was my thinking. It's like a child you love dearly and telling them not to drink and drive with their friends. They think your full of shit until they hit a phone poll and learn for themselves.

Prince's brilliant mind was growing exponentially in terms of his ability to make music, record music, and see the world, not as a bystander recording events, but as a visionary changing events.

There was a recent time when his new car got stuck in the snow in the middle of the street. He phoned me and demanded that I come by immediately with battery jumper cables. I arrived shortly and began to attach the cables from my car battery to his battery. Suddenly, and without warning, Prince bolted off down the street into the winter cold leaving me with two cars, holding a set of jumper cables. As he was running away he shouted, "What if my fans see me!" Interesting, this was before his first album or single had come out. Was this a prima donna move? No, I understood it. Prince absolutely knew he was the real deal. His mind had already calculated where he'd be three years down the road from that very moment — because that's where he lived. And standing in the middle of the street like a nebbish didn't fit into the persona he was creating.

And I was perceptive enough to know where I fit in with regard to Prince's career. I had even discussed it with Warner Bros. At the point I received the letter I knew what my calling had been. I was called upon to protect a young vulnerable kid living in Andre's basement, mentor him and shield him from the wolves. My calling was to garner an historic record deal, give Prince a home with my family in Minneapolis, San Francisco, and Los Angeles, and establish early control for him in a budding career. My job was now complete. Prince was free to move on to his next phase.

We parted ways without fistfights, shouting matches, or lawsuits. I wanted it that way — even though I had an ironclad contract with him. I believed too much in Prince to want to harm his career by tying him up in court. Nor did I believe that my management career would survive if I were known as the guy who held up and ruined the career of a budding superstar. Even though I made no money (Prince was not an earning artist yet) I was happy knowing that my role in building his foundation would be written into the books. And I knew that I could move on with my career because label folks on the coasts trusted my "ears" in being able to hear true talent.

POSTSCRIPT:

Within months of our breakup I heard that Prince was planning three shows in January at the Capri Theater on the near north side of Minneapolis. The whisperers were organizing the event. It would be the debut performance of Prince and his band for the entire world to see — and a showcase for Warner's execs. They would fly in to determine if the company would finance a tour behind the first album. From what I heard, the band had only rehearsed for the performance; they never played a single warm up gig in front of a live audience before climbing on stage.

Although it would have been awkward for me to attend the performance it didn't stop my phone from ringing off the hook the morning after the second show. Demoralized band members and Warner's execs called to express their dismay.

"Their equipment didn't work, and we had to wait outside in ten-fucking-below-zero weather!" Said one WB promo man.

"He didn't even face the audience," said an angry WB VP. "We're not putting our money behind this. He'll have to wait and we'll see how the next album does."

"Owen, it was dismal," said a band member. "It felt like amateur night at high school. We should have gone out and played a bunch of gigs for free before the show. What were we thinking?"

But one reporter had it right.

"Owen, maybe Prince isn't ready to perform on tour yet but I caught glimpses of true genius last night. He'll get it together.

Those were the words I wanted to hear.

Crash, Burn, The Resurrection, and a Shocking Record Deal

"You never know what you're made of until you stare into the abyss"
— Norton Gray — *my brother-in-law*

PART I: CRASH:

By 1983, everything was screaming along. Our advertising agency, The Ad Company, was billing in the millions. American Artists, my artist management company, was signing artists to major labels, and our new 24-track recording studio was up and running. The studio was actively recording our management clients, local artists, and even parts of Private Dancer, Tina Turner's comeback album. With the addition of the studio, and the growth of the businesses, we went from a single office, to occupying the entire first floor of the large beauxarts office building at 430 Oak Grove. Britt and I had moved into a beautiful home twenty-two miles out of the city overlooking Lake Minnetonka. Our first born son, Jordan, now three years old, was amazing everyone with his ability to program my Apple II computer in Apple-Basic. Life was good.

I signed Sue Ann to Warner's, Andre Cymone to Columbia, and The Girlz, an act formed, written for, and produced by Andre to Columbia. I could get any label head or A&R person on the phone. In fact, they would routinely call me to see what I had next. I was able to float free, travel, build studios, and sign acts because my partner, DJ Rosenberg, was my rock. At thirty-seven, DJ was four years older than me. He was tall and lean, with a dark "Jew-fro," beard, and thick trendy glasses. I called him "the hippest CPA," though he was much more than that. DJ made sense of my deal making; he kept the books, met with the accountants, and handled 90% of the paperwork that flowed through the office. He kept track of The Ad Company, American Artists Management, and American Artists Studios. We were over twenty employees now and DJ oversaw their activities, and payroll, etc. while I oversaw the creative flow of the company. Together, we met with advertising clients and tried our best to keep them happy. But DJ was the man who held it all together — until…

"Owen, I've been so tired lately. I can hardly drag myself into the office." Well, that's understandable," I said, knowing what the problem was. "We've worked side by side for the last ten years building our companies. You're just burned out from 12-hour days and no let up on the weekends. And, you're not married with someone begging you to come home once in a while. Why don't you check-in with a therapist? Maybe it's time to start pacing yourself." DJ agreed, "Great idea, I'll do it."

A few weeks later DJ asked if I would come down to his office. "How's the shrink?" I asked. "Well, the shrink doesn't think I'm burned out but something funny happened last night." "Go on," I said, not liking the sound of this. "I got up to go to the bathroom and I think I passed out. I woke up on the bathroom floor and went back to bed and slept it off." "Shit. Have you noticed anything else?" "Yeah, when I took a shower this morning I passed out again." I took DJ by the arm and physically threw him out the back door of the office. "You are not allowed back in this building until you go to a doctor," I demanded. "And I'm not fucking around!"

DJ called the next day and thanked me profusely. "Just want to say thanks. The doc says I have a massive infection but we caught it early. Thanks for throwing my ass out the door. I never would have gone." "Whew, we dodged a bullet." I said. "How's he gonna treat it?" "He thinks he can get it with large doses of antibiotics since my white cell count is so high." "Let's thank our lucky stars. Do what you have to and I'll cover for you."

I was relaxing after work with a drink on my deck overlooking the lake when Britt handed me the cordless phone. "Owen, it's DJ. He needs to speak with you now." "What's up? How ya feelin'?" I said, grabbing the phone. "The antibiotic didn't seem to be working so they ran some more tests." "Uh huh." "And the doc says I have a violent form of leukemia called CML. He says I have nine months to live — max." We talked for another hour, and after we hung up I sat motionless on my deck until two in the morning.

DJ and I agreed not to tell the staff for weeks while he put his affairs in order and started chemo. But word got out and there was understandable employee anger and sadness that a member of our family was dying. I had to stay strong — this was no time to crumble. I sought the advice of attorneys and mentors. They all told me the same thing; replace DJ immediately and bring in someone to handle his duties. But I couldn't do it. I couldn't tell someone I had seen more hours a day than my wife that he was being taken off salary, replaced, and now he must go home and die alone. So I simply told him, "Come into the office when you feel up to it." That single decision would prove to be the downfall of everything we had built.

Once DJ's clients heard he was dying they scrambled for the hills and within four months we had lost more than half our billings. The staff, overcome with grief, became angry that our little world had been so violently rocked. Unable to contain their feelings the anger came in my direction as they put their résumés together. And then, the bombshell hit.

"Owen, I couldn't deal with my own death and concentrate on the company books at the same time." DJ said, looking gaunt, his fingernails turning black from the chemo. "Ok, we'll bring in someone to handle our internal accounting." I said, holding back the tears. "You don't understand. The company is in serious debt and we have no way to pay our bills. I'm so sorry I did this to you. I've been keeping this from everyone. Our creditors are sending notice that if we don't pay up they'll force us into bankruptcy." I drove DJ home, gave him a big hug, and headed out to my home at the lake. When I walked in there was a burly man playing with my son on the living room floor. "Excuse me, who are you?" "Your wife said it was okay to wait for you." With that he got up, served me legal papers, and left. It was a demand for a hundred and fifty thousand dollars from one of our vendors. It would be the first of many demands to come my way.

I sought the advice of a bankruptcy attorney. He had an office chair that reclined the more he leaned back. By the time I finished my story he was completely horizontal and I was staring at the soles of his shoes. "Owen, I have one piece of counsel for you. Go bankrupt." "I can't, most of these creditors are long standing friends that DJ and I built through the years." I said, the gravity of my situation sinking in. "Okay, here's your choice: you're young, so use the law, go bankrupt, and rebuild your life starting tomorrow — or spend the next twenty years working three jobs to try and pay off your creditors." I made the decision; Christmas was coming, I'd call up every marker, limp through one more payroll, and then close my companies after the first of the year.

On the evening I let my staff go I cleaned out their offices and desks myself. Maybe it was shame, maybe it was foolish pride, but I could not ask anyone for help. I had to go it alone. It took until five in the morning but I did it. When I was finished I sat alone in the dark surrounded by the ghosts of my successes and stared deep into the dark abyss. My partner was buried that same week.

PART II: THE BURN

The principle of a moderately successful Minneapolis based booking agency heard of my demise and hatched a scheme. The agency was best known for booking small to midline cover bands into clubs throughout the Midwest. He sensed an opportunity to expand into my area of recording and signing acts to major labels by taking advantage of my circumstances. He figured he could "own" me. And I was a vulnerable and willing victim.

"Owen, we'd like to buy out your assets, especially the studio." Came the lifesaver phone call. "The money can then be used to have the bankruptcy court settle in part with your creditors. When that's concluded we'll hire you and put you on salary." They bought me out for pennies on the dollar. I didn't want to take a job at Burger King and I was too young to be a greeter at Target so I accepted the offer. A life raft is a life raft — even if it's wobbly.

The first sign of a small hole in the life raft came when they asked me to hear Chameleon, a local act they were pushing. We drove about an hour out of Minneapolis to a small club to hear the group. They were decent enough. The lead singer/guitar player was actually good. A heavy Hendrix-like presence, he was rock star cool: tall with a low biting voice, and a mofo of a guitar player. The keyboard player, with his long black hair and groovy mustache, was super good looking and talented. But he seemed to be his own man and not part of the group. The drummer was off the charts good. In fact, the whole band was good and their followers loved them. But there was one problem: I didn't hear any hits. "What did you think of the band, Owen?" "They're great musicians but there's no hits. They sound like hits — but there aren't any." My new "boss" looked quite disappointed with me as the set ended. I was hired to make them stars.

After the show we went back to the group's trailer and introductions were made. On the way out a sharp piece of loose metal on the trailer door sliced through my shirt and deep into my skin near my waist. I didn't notice that I was badly cut and probably needed stiches. Riding in the back of my "boss'" car for the long ride home I felt faint and noticed that I was losing blood. I told my "boss" what was happening and that I was cut pretty bad. He looked over and said, "Hold on, I'll stop at the first gas station we see!" When we got to the station he jumped out of his car and ran inside returning in a second with paper towels.

Okay, he has a heart I thought. "Get out Owen, get out of the car!" Holding my side I jumped out ready to be helped. Instead, he pushed me aside and pulled out a bottle of 409, scrambled into the back seat, and began cleaning the seat. "Go get yourself cleaned up. You ruined my car!" I stuffed the paper towels deep into my gash for the ride home and thought; I'm gonna fuck this fool the first opportunity I get.

It didn't take long for that opportunity to arise. A few weeks later I started getting calls from my A&R friends at the major labels in Los Angeles and New York. "Owen, are you managing a group named Chameleon? Why would you send us this?" I had no idea what they were talking about. "I don't understand. What did I send you?" "We received a letter from you saying you were now managing this group Chameleon. And the group's demo tape was wrapped in a woman's crotch-less underwear."

It took me seven seconds to make the drive across town to my boss' office.

"Well, Owen, we own you now, and as our employee we have the right to your contacts." "You don't have the right to shit, motherfucker! So, your plan all along was to use me, and my reputation for your personal gain? Kiss my everlovin' fuckin' ass!" I stomped out of his office closing the door so hard that I could hear pictures falling off the walls inside. Even though I was practically broke I returned to my office and made a deal with the building manager to rent the office across the hall. By the end of the day I had moved everything from my old office, contacts and all master recordings, into my new office and set up phone lines. For better or worse I was back in my own business and relishing the opportunity to be in competition with my old "boss."

PART III: RESURRECTION

Within a week I got a call from Jesse Johnson. Jesse had recently quit The Time, one of the more successful acts under Prince's tutelage. Jesse wrote two giant hits for the group: "The

Bird" and "Jungle Love," and was ready to move on and go solo. We sat in his car outside my office and listened to demos of his new songs. There was no doubt in my mind that I could get Jesse a recording contract with a major label. Jesse knew how to construct a hit song. He was one of the best guitar players I'd ever heard, and had a voice that would break through the muddle of the airwaves. Did I mention that he was cute as hell — and funky as hell? He was that good. "Why didn't you go to Prince's management? They'd get you a deal." I said. Jesse was direct in his answer. "Because their only interest is in Prince. Where would I fit in? And besides, Prince is super competitive so I need to break free. And Owen, in all my conversations with Prince he always said he trusted you." I agreed to manage him on the spot. The Phoenix was about to rise.

I needed a partner, someone like DJ to handle the biz so I could float free again and nurture talent. I'd learned my lesson though. Pay attention to the business side and stay close to the books of the company. Even though you trust, read every statement, every balance sheet, and know every nuance of the biz side.

In a phone conversation with my father he reminded me of someone I used to babysit. "Remember Ron who lived behind us? I spoke with his uncle the other day and he graduated UCLA at the top of his class. He's a lawyer now and moved back to Minneapolis. His uncle says he likes the entertainment side of the biz and loves film making."

Ron and I had just three meetings before we shook hands and agreed to go into business. "I can get financing too," he added after the third meeting. Ron also had a friend named Ken with a photography studio. It was in the revitalized 1800's warehouse district of downtown Minneapolis. "Why don't the three of us get together? Ken is on the first floor, and the two floors above him are vacant. We could build out those two upper floors and have a full service entertainment company!" In the fall of 1984, we moved from 430 Oak Grove over to the brand new

American Artists multi-purpose Entertainment complex. It was a 5000 sq. ft. building in the city's newly formed arts district. We had a studio, along with film, video, photography, and choreography departments. Our one goal: to aid artists' in their development process.

Jesse Johnson was pretty much self-contained and he knew what he wanted; all I had to do was find him the right home for his writing and distribution of his recordings. He was a seasoned performer, singer, and guitar player — with a proven track record of hit records. A&M Records turned out to be the right home under the guidance of John McLain, A&R VP. After my first meeting with John he signed Jesse to A&M. Ron and Ken produced his music video and in less than a year Jesse and the newly formed American Artists earned a Gold record. With John's introduction Jesse produced and wrote songs for Janet Jackson's debut album, "Dream Street." We even participated in music for John Hughes, "The Breakfast Club" and "Pretty in Pink" earning Jesse and us two more gold albums. Jesse also wrote and produced Ta Mara and the Seen for A&M. The single, "Everybody Dance reached #3 on the R&B charts and #24 on the Billboard Hot 100 chart. The Phoenix was flying high again.

Through it all I kept thinking of Peter, the white Hendrix-like guitar-player-front man from Chameleon. I remembered Peter had striking-good looks. He was tall and hippie-like with long brown hair running well past his shoulders. He had the aura of David Bowie, and the rock chops of someone whose axe was an extension of his body. I had to find him; he'd be perfect for development in our newly formed complex — and I knew I could get him a record deal.

"Yeah, I'd love to meet with you, man." Peter said, with what sounded like a 60's acid-induced slur. "Looks like Chameleon is breaking up and I've been making original demos at home." "For the record, I thought you guys were great musicians, I just didn't hear any hits." I said. "My guess is the personal music you're creating is not teen or pop in any way. It's the kind of music that FM

AOR (album oriented rock) radio will eat up." "Yeah man, that's what I've always wanted to do — and the reason our keyboard player always threatened to punch my lights out. By the way, whatever happened between you and our agents who brought you out to hear us that night? I heard you guys broke up." I muttered something about a deep gash, and women's crotchless underwear.

Under Ron and Ken's guidance we shot an in-studio video of Peter and his new band. I sent out the video to the labels and invited them to fly in and hear Peter live in our new rehearsal space. The responses were enthusiastic and we moved to set up a showcase. Then, something unusual happened.

"I'm not sure I have the right number. Is this Owen?" Came the voice on the other end of the line. I could hear a strong accent but couldn't tell the origin. "Yes. How did you get my home number? Its unlisted." "Your office gave it to me. I'm the keyboard player in Chameleon and I'd like to come to your home and meet with you." "I live twenty-two miles out of town on lake Minnetonka. You sure you want to make the drive?"

The keyboard player arrived promptly at 8 p.m. as I was putting my son to bed. He produced a demo tape and we went down to the basement to listen. "You don't want to work with that guitar player from our band you want to work with me." He demanded. "I will beat that guitar player up if I get the chance!" "Whoa dude, before you do that let's have a listen to your tape." He slipped the tape into my cassette player and pressed play. What I heard was not my cup of tea. In fact, it was the opposite of my taste in music. It was instrumental: organy, horn-synthie, a little dramatic at times, but very light overall. I'm a funk, R&B, rock, Blues, hard rock, alt-Country, Country-rock guy.

"This shows a lot of promise and the drummer kicks ass." I meant it about the drummer. But honestly, the demo reminded me of when I used to go to the local roller-skating rink as a kid. If I'm not into the music, no matter how talented or successful the artist, I have to walk. I would not be a good manager for that act. "Thanks for making the drive, I'd like to hear more when you're ready." I said, lying through my teeth. "That's fine," he said. "Would you mind coming by my house next week? I'd like to play you more." I don't know why, but I agreed. There was a confidence and determination in his voice that I liked. And he was good looking with his long dark hair and mustache — reminded me of one of the singers in Three Dog Night. I just wished I loved his music.

The keyboard player's house was located in a blue-collar section of Minneapolis. It was an area for reserved more for physical, hard working Americans than long-haired musicians. He took me on a brief tour before playing me more songs. "And this is my special closet," he said, enthusiastically. He opened the door and I wanted it closed immediately. "Wow, that's great. Let's move on and hear more demos." I secretly prayed that he had no intention of using the items in the closet on me. He played me more demos and my reaction was the same: time to put on my skates.

The A&R folks came in from New York and Los Angeles to hear my latest "Jimi Hendrix" discovery. This would be the first showcase at our new facility in the historic warehouse district. Peter and his three-piece band played perfectly. Peter, again married to his guitar, sang and played to perfection. His rock solos were unique, gifted, and original as his fingers flew across the fret board. He never looked down at his hands!

After the showcase the comments were unanimous; "He's unbelievable." But there was a caveat to their praise. "It's just too bad that this is 1985. If this were 1967, there would be a bidding war to sign this guy." Fuck, they were right. In my love for his talent I'd never realized his sound was out of time for the current music scene. Funk, and Dance Music were all the rage. A new electronic invention called the synthesizer was taking over the airwaves. Groups like Wham!, Madonna, Tears For Fears, Ready for the World, and Prince were flying high. No one wanted to sit down, drop acid, and study guitar licks and serious lyrics — it was the time to put your arms in the air and jump around on the dance floor.

A few days later the keyboard player called again and asked for a meeting at my office. "I sent my music to a radio station on the east coast and they're playing it regularly." "Very cool." I responded, thinking this was one-time luck. "And I sent my music to the Olympics committee and they loved it!" That's perfect for them I thought. "And Private Music is interested in signing me to a record deal. Do you think you could help?" I knew Private Music — and its President, Ron Goldstein. He was a former Warner's guy. "Tell you what. My partner Ron is an attorney as well as a filmmaker. I'm sure he'll help you with the contract." This was a tough call for me. I loved the smell of a new record deal but I would not be a good manager, or anything else for this guy.

Ron helped the keyboard player with the deal and that was that. We then moved on and struck more label deals for artists at Capital, A&M, and even our own American Artists label through CBS/Columbia Records. Then, one day a year later it seemed as though the impossible happened.

I got a call at the office from my wife, "Turn on your TV at the office and watch Oprah!" We gathered in my office and I was dumbstruck. There was the keyboard player from Chameleon on Oprah — and he was with his new beau— Linda fucking Evans! We sat transfixed as they spoke of their true love for each other and he talked about his burgeoning worldwide career helped in part by Linda. And there they were for the world to see. Linda Evans — and her true love — Yanni!

The Hendrix-like artist faded into the woodwork and Yanni became an international star. It really hit home when my seventy five-year-old aunt called me. "Owen, I just saw this guy Yanni on a PBS special. He's magnificent, and so good-looking! And he lived in Minneapolis! Do you know him?" Even though I was stunned, I understood — you just can't call 'em all. A few weeks later my second son, Evan, was born and I was in heaven. The Phoenix was back y'all.

But Wait, There's More!

LATE NIGHT NEVER HAD IT SO GOOD

9 P.M., April 22nd 1992, Minneapolis, Minnesota — I was alone, and working late at Ktel International, the company made famous for late night advertising of compilation records and kitchen gadgets. Reeling from a divorce, and taking a much-needed break from managing artists, I took a position as VP of their owned music catalog division. My charge was to seek placements for their owned catalog of songs in film, TV, and commercials. The building that housed a hundred employees during the day was dark and empty — and so was I. With no family to go home to on a nightly basis the uninhabited offices and hallways offered both solace and purpose to my evenings — and an opportunity to progress quickly within the company. So when the phone lines lit up unexpectedly and exploded with hundreds of calls I was the only one around to answer the phone.

It was impossible to handle all the calls. One music retailer after another from across the nation was calling to find out if Ktel distributed an album by hip-hop artists O.C.U. (Organized Crime Unit) called, "Stronger than the Mafia." They wanted it now. The album had a track titled "Trigger Happy Police." The powerfully worded song was about taking revenge on the "pussy-ass police" who were shooting and beating black people in the streets of Chicago. When I asked a caller from New York what was going on he said, "Turn on your fucking television!" I ran back to my office and flipped on the tiny ten-inch screen. I couldn't believe what I was seeing; Los Angeles was in flames. The voice over kept repeating, "The four officers accused of beating Rodney King have just been acquitted, and rioters have taken to the streets of Los Angeles setting it ablaze."

Paradoxically, the tragedy of Rodney King and the city of Los Angeles could be instant gold for the Minneapolis based company — the distributor of O.C.U.'s album. The song was poised to become an anthem.

In December of 1991 Ktel signed O.C.U.'s label, Kapone Records for retail distribution. Once the deal was made the group, the label head, and their manager piled into a car and drove the five hundred miles from the Southside of Chicago to Minneapolis for a signing ceremony. Homicidal MC, Impact, Murder 1, Sudden Death, and DJ Tragic stood in the conference room and shook hands with Ktel's Chairman, Philip Kives, a self-made multi-millionaire who didn't know what rap music was and could care less. As he shook their hands he offered a simple, "Good luck, good luck to you." Homicidal MC looked over at me and said, "We drove seven hours through the snow to come to this white-ass city and all this motherfucker can say is good luck! Damn, that's some cold-ass shit."

Initially, the album was met with resistance due to its angry message and a sales staff that was more accustomed to selling "Girl Groups of the 60's" and slicer-dicers than "Proud to be a Gangster." But when the four policemen were acquitted of beating the shit out of Rodney King everyone in the nation wanted "Trigger Happy Police."

Sensing an opportunity to possibly sell hundreds of thousands of albums I frantically tried to reach Ktel's head of sales, the President, and even the Chairman at home. No one called back so I went home to my new one bedroom apartment. A few hours later the President called me after speaking with the Chairman. "I'm sorry Owen, he said, the sales staff is on reintroducing Veg-o-matics this week, and that's their charge. O.C.U. will have to wait until next week. Yep, Organized Crime Unit, and their hit anthem, "Trigger Happy Police" lost out to: "So easy to use it makes piles of julienne potatoes in seconds!"

* * * *

The first time I had a full on conversation with Philip Kives, Ktel's founder, Chairman and entrepreneurial multimillionaire, we went to a local delicatessen in Minneapolis for lunch. Philip lived in Winnipeg Canada where he held other businesses and a hotel, but would sometimes pop down unannounced to the International headquarters in Plymouth, Minnesota. He was a burly rusk of a man: tall and dark — with thick eyebrows and rugged good looks. It seemed to me that Philip would have made a better football player than a hawker of kitchen gadgets sold on television.

"The Lincoln delicatessen makes the best chicken soup in the entire Midwest!" I crowed. Turning pale, Philip gagged out, "I can't bear the sight or smell of chicken soup. Please, none for me! And I'd prefer if you didn't order it either." "Did you get food poisoning at one time?" I inquired, knowing that was usually the case. "No. I grew up on a farm in Saskatchewan, Canada. Back in the 30's we were so poor that we had no running water or electricity. To survive, we raised chickens. It was eggs for breakfast, chicken soup for lunch, and boiled chicken for dinner. On Friday nights my mother would bake a chicken for us at the neighbors. "Wow, I never would have guessed you grew up that poor." I said, growing nauseous at the thought of the chicken salad I was going to order.

"So you were Jewish farmers, eh?" I said, drawing him in with small talk. "Yeah, my parents fled persecution Eastern Europe. After a stop in Turkey they were given a dirt farm in Western Canada. We had nothin' else." Shedding some early entrepreneurial insight, Philip boasted that when he was growing up the locals would pay kids for gopher tails. "The gophers were giving the farmers a lot of trouble so they paid kids a penny a tail as proof that they killed them. I figured out a way to cut the tails in half so they couldn't tell the difference. I was makin' twenty-five cents a week while the other kids were makin' a dime." The waitress came to the table and we ordered corned beef — lean.

"I really got my start selling pots and pans door to door." Philip said, a stray bit of corned beef dangling from his mouth. I wondered if I should tell him. "They were the first generation of Teflon-like nonstick frying pans. I could make the sale so easy if I could get in the door and show a housewife how it worked — no butter or grease necessary and the eggs flew right out of the pan! Once the sale was made I had to move quickly on to another town. "How come?" I asked, thinking of the money he was making with these new magic pans. "Because after a few uses the Teflon flew out of the pan with the eggs."

"But my real education came from selling pots and pans at fairs and carnivals, and eventually the big time — on the boardwalk in Atlantic City. It was there that I learned how to separate lookers from buyers during the demonstrations." "How could you tell? "Well the first distraction was the children. They always ran up to the front to see what was going on, and the parents were happy to let them watch the show. But kids got in the way — I needed the parents up front." "So you chased them away?" "No, I told the children we had something special for them on the side of the stage. When they ran over there I had a guy give them a carrot. Then I could concentrate on the parents. I'd ask them to move in closer, start the demonstration, and get to the close." "And people bought right away?" "No, I'd just start saying thank you for your purchase, and repeat, thank you for your purchase. Pretty soon people would start looking around to see who was buying. If only one lady bought I'd say thank you to ten other people. Soon, people figured that if all these folks were buying they should too. Within a short time I was driving a Cadillac convertible."

Selling pots and pans door to door, at carnivals and on the boardwalk made Kives a good living but the real money was on television. "I had to figure a way to advertise the pans on television. Canadian TV was not nearly the cost of US television but, it didn't matter — I had no money." Philip said, as he ordered ice cream for desert and begged me not to tell his wife. "Eventually I started to sell pans directly to department stores. One of the biggest chains in Canada was Eaton's and I placed an order with them for seventy thousand dollars by promising them I would advertise my product on television and tag them in the commercial." "How could you afford the advertising?" "Simple, I took the order from Eaton's, showed it to a banker, and the bank lent me money on the spot." "Genius!" "I produced a cheap commercial only my hands, and the same sales techniques from the boardwalk. Viewers were asked to phone a number on the screen with their orders and Eaton's would deliver the pans right to their door. We sold thousands and thousands." And just like that Ktel, an acronym for Kieves Television was born. Ktel suddenly fit into the American lexicon and was right up there with another immediately recognizable product name: Kleenex.

I could see the parallels between Philip and myself. At eleven years old I had a carnival in my backyard. I came up with games, and stole candy and rounded up every old toy I ever owned to use as prizes. I remember marveling as kids plunked down a dime to play the games. Pretty soon I had thirty dollars in my pocket! A year later I built a radio station that had a three-block radius. I went door-to-door and asked for any neighborhood news that I could read on-air. Once the neighbors tuned in I came up with a rate card and sold them advertising. Within two months I had fifty bucks in my pocket. Then there was the time during sub zero weather when I took a hose and flooded my parent's backyard to make a skating rink. I charged the neighborhood kids a dime to skate, but all profits were lost when the charge for repairing the damaged lawn in the spring came to seven hundred dollars. In my early twenties I actually became a carnival barker at the Minnesota State Fair. I learned that Colonel Tom Parker, Elvis's famed manager, started out as a carnie guy as well. What we all had in common was the ability to know our audience, demonstrate the benefits of our product, and close the sale. It was marketing 101. Philip managed to turn gopher tails into millions by splitting them in half. Perhaps there's a lesson in that for all of us. I took those lessons and headed into advertising and the music business, eventually winding up with Prince. Philip took those lessons and headed straight into kitchen gadgets, like Veg-o-matic, The Fishin' Magician, and kitchen knives made from surgical steel. But then, Philip got into the music business and the results were just as dramatic.

In the late sixties and early seventies record labels didn't care much about hit records that had run their course. The music business was booming and the labels were on to their next hit. There simply was no need for a label to care about its "back catalog" of past hits. Philip's kitchen gadgets, now ubiquitously advertised on television and "guaranteed to make your life easier — fast" were booming too. So, when Philip heard about an album in the States that had "25 Country Hits by the Original Artists" he decided to take a flyer on the product and put it on television, just like the gadgets. The result: over a half a million units were sold. "25 Polka Hits" followed up "25 Country Hits" and sold another half a million units. The record labels now had a new revenue stream with their old hits, and Philip was on his way to become the pioneer of compilation albums, and a very wealthy man.

What followed were massive sellers like: "Music Machine," "Music Explosion," "Music Express," and "Hit Machine." The albums were all jam-packed with the hits of the day and North America ate it up. Within a very short time Ktel madness spread to Europe with offices in almost every major city. By the late seventies, early eighties Ktel was grossing north of one hundred eighty million dollars a year and was amassing more gold and platinum albums than most of the major labels.

As we left the delicatessen and headed back to the world headquarters I asked Philip how they could possibly fit so many hits on one vinyl album in those days. Most artist albums in those days had ten or maybe twelve cuts. "That was the easy part," Philip announced. "We used a cheap grade vinyl in the pressing process. It was very pliable, and spread out allowing for more time on each album. In addition, we would have an engineer cut a chorus out of a song here and there and fade the song early."

Yep, I guess Philip was still splitting gopher tails. Except this time it was vinyl albums.

I was fascinated with Philip. He was the only person I knew who could walk into a meeting and act like a bumpkin who just fell off a truck. Meeting attendees would pull me aside and ask, "Is he really the Chairman? He seems so dense." But on the way back in the car he'd recite everything that was said in the meeting — verbatim. During the meeting he had assessed the intent of every person in the room and had already decided if he was going to do business with them — or not. Philip was as dumb as the slyest fox you ever met. He was street smart, shrewd, and the cheapest human being I'd ever come across in business. Past employees said that he'd throw nickels around like they were manhole covers. This is a man who would rather cut off his own arm than fly first class: a man who lived modestly in a suburban home in Winnipeg — even though he had millions in the bank! I truly admired him.

The following are a few real-life stories that stood out during my time at the TV advertised powerhouse. In many cases I have chosen not to use the names of those involved — but the tales are true:

SHIRT HANGER CHRISTMAS:

One Christmas season I witnessed Philip Kives in action. Some guy invented a space saving hanger for shirts. Really, a very simple premise: instead of typically hanging shirts on the bar in your closet you would hang them on a parallel bar just below. Release one end of the bar and viola — the shirts would now be hanging vertically — a space saving dream! Philip had "his patent guy" in Minneapolis knock off the design by nuancing it a bit — thereby creating a new patent for the company. He advertised the "new miracle space saving invention" on television for the Christmas season. I watched as he put a million dollars in his pocket — in four weeks!

THE MIRACLE GOLF BALL FINDER:

One day this dude shows up at the headquarters claiming that he had used NASA technology to develop a golf ball finder. If true, this would be a groundbreaking discovery for golfers and net millions for the company. "Imagine never losing a golf ball again — no matter where it winds up," was his spiel. The head of the TV-advertised product department assembled the other department heads to witness this miraculous NASA discovery.We gathered in the conference room with genuine curiosity as the dude removed the finder from its velvet case. It was plastic, all black, and about as big as the old first portable cell phones. "This is how it works," he exclaimed as he pulled out a single collapsible silver antenna from the side of the device. Once the antenna was fully extended it swung freely around in a semi-circle. "The finder is able to sense the molecular structure of the golf ball." He said, as we gave out a collective, "Wow."

"Okay, who wants to go first?" The inventor said, producing a golf ball from his suit coat pocket. One of the department heads stepped forward. "Just toss the ball anywhere in the room and walk by it." The ball was thrown willy-nilly to a corner of the room. As the employee walked by the ball the antenna swung over and pointed directly at it! Technology at its finest — and millions for Ktel! One by one we tried it. We'd toss the ball to a corner of the room, along the side wall, under the conference room table — and, each time as we walked by the antenna would swing around and point at the ball!

The head of the product department got on the phone with Philip and they decided jump into this amazing product quickly, and in a big way. It was decided that a thirty second or a sixty second commercial would not do justice to a NASA miracle product. The golf ball finder warranted a half-hour infomercial filmed at a major golf course golf course. And to add maximum credibility, a top golf instructor would be paid to endorse the finder.

With the instructor in place, and the infomercial shot, they were ready to purchase the television media time. I don't know what hunch Philip's "patent guy" was playing, but at the last minute he wanted see the inner workings of the device before it was put on-air. I think he noticed the obvious; there was no place for a battery. In fact, there was no battery at all. The inventor was adamant that we not see the workings for fear that he would be, "Ripped off on his molecular patent and design." So when he left the building we all stood around as the patent guy took a hack saw and sawed the device in half. The black plastic was thick and tough, and hacksawing through it took quite some time. With the device now in two pieces we all leaned in to have a look at the "NASA" microchip technology. But there was nothing inside. It was just one big solid plastic piece. "Maybe we missed the electronics. Try sawing one of the pieces in half vertically," one of the media buyers said. Again, just four thick pieces of solid plastic lay before us.

"But then why did it work in the conference room?" We wanted to know. The patent guy said, "Lets take the other sample outdoors and I'll throw the golf ball in the bushes when you're not looking. Then give it a try." This time no one could find the ball. The antenna would swing this way and that way but it never located the ball. The head of sales figured it out. If you knew where the ball was your mind would adjust, and your hand would turn just so slightly as to allow the antenna to turn in the direction of the ball. If you didn't know where the ball was — you were fucked. It was a mental thing. The project was over. And with the threat of charges being filed the dude slipped quietly into the night — never to be seen again.

Until…

One day about a year later I happened to notice an article in the Minneapolis Star/Tribune. The headline read: "Southern Minnesota Police Department Scammed." The article went on to say that a man had scammed the Police Department for well over a hundred thousand dollars. He sold them devices using

"NASA technology" that could locate the molecular structure of marijuana hidden in school lockers. And as recently as 2009, the British press reported that as many as six thousand of the devices had been sold to Iraqi forces as bomb detectors. Some of the devices were sold for up to $40,000 each. The detectors, sold under the names GT-200 and Alpha 6, were exposed after they had failed to prevent a series of huge explosions as people passed through checkpoints in Iraq. Eventually, tests were conducted and it was found that the GT-200's ability to detect explosives was no better than random chance. All they had to do was call Ktel — we even had an "800" number.

Pig Vomit:

In 1993 when the President of Ktel ordered me to go to New York and sign the band Pig Vomit I reluctantly boarded the plane and headed east. Emotionally the journey was hard to take. Is this what happens to old music dudes I thought? One day you're working with the likes of The Rolling Stones, Stevie Wonder, and Elvis — then you're signing the biggest record deal in the history of the world for an eighteen-year-old genius — and now you're boarding a plane to visit Pig Vomit?

In all fairness, Pig Vomit was the prize of radio mogul Howard Stern during his time at K-ROCK in New York. The band appeared with him on his radio show, TV, and at his shows at Madison Square Gardens, and the Bitter End. In the President's mind the band represented a natural promotional and sales dream with the exposure that would be garnered from Howard's show.

Landing in NY I phoned the manager to set a meeting. Perhaps it was just my preconceived disdain for the project, but the voice on the other end sounded more like a three-card-monte street hustler than a manager of a band. His thick New York accent belted out, "Trust me. You're gonna love dis album, c'mon over now, I guarantee it! You're gonna make so much money." Since I came from the school of "let the music do the talking," I asked him to just have the album delivered to the hotel. "Okay, but I was gonna introduce you to the Vomit guys." The last thing I wanted to do was meet the Vomit guys.

The album arrived in a plain brown wrapper more suited for a take-out pastrami sandwich than a demo of an album. Popping it into my Walkman I let the music fly. The first song I heard was "Vagina," set to a "Rawhide" cowboy sounding music bed. The lyrics were something like, big or small I like them all. Huh? As a professional in the biz I was acutely aware of how to market and promote music. Airplay is key. Without it you're dead in the water. And who the fuck is going to play "Vagina"? Once you have your song in rotation on a few stations you can approach retail buyers and see if they'll take your product in and position it in their stores. But what retail chain was going to feature "Vagina" at the checkout counter? You'll also need to buy ads in local papers and tag the retailer. But what ad could we take out in print that would say "Vagina" on sale? Okay, I'll go to the next song, maybe we can get some action there. The song opened nicely enough like a sixties pop ballad, and then came the chorus, which was the title of the song: "Is it in yet?" Okay, maybe the next song will do the trick, it was titled, "Are you Ever Going to Come?" I scoured the track listing for anything promotable: "She Had Her Period" — nope, "Poor Old Fartin' Fool" — maybe I could license the song to a Tums commercial. Here's a winner, "Holy Shit, I Gotta' Pee!"

I phoned the "manager" who I now named, boss hog, and asked him how the hell we were going to promote this thing. Again came the thick New York accent, "How long youse been in dis business — 'bout ten minutes? Howard Stern is gonna mention it on his show and play the fuckin' shit out of it! It'll sell millions! You're trouble is you got no experience." "Okay, but can we get some assurance from Howard that he'll cooperate." "Howard don't put nuttin' like dat in writing, you crazy?" That's all I needed to hear. I jumped on the next flight and hightailed it back to Minneapolis.

"So you didn't tell the manager we were signing Pig Vomit, huh," the President wailed in anger. "No, I didn't, I said defiantly. You can't get airplay for the thing, it can't be promoted or advertised, and we can't get an assurance from Howard Stern or his staff that he'll get behind it." "Well, I'll just have to send someone else back to New York to do your job." I don't know what came over me, perhaps it was the insanity of it all, but somehow the demo cassette I was holding left my hands. It flew across the President's desk hitting him square in the chest. While he was still in shock I got up and walked back to my office. He followed me, and blocked the entrance to my office so I couldn't leave. He was red with fury. "If you ever do anything like that again I'll fire you on the spot," he said with full authority. I guess he couldn't fire me because a few weeks earlier I had done a deal that netted the company a million dollars. Philip would have never let me go because I brought in huge money for the company — and besides; Pig Vomit would have repulsed him.

The employee returned from New York triumphant. Although I never knew for sure, I heard he offered the Vomit crew a six-figure advance to close the deal. And I heard there was another promise to put six figures into marketing the release. But the marketing still fell on me — and I had a great promotional idea. Since vomit was the key word, I had our purchasing guy order hundreds of airline vomit bags. We printed the words, Pig Vomit on the outside of the bags and stuffed the promotional CDs into the bags. The bags were mailed out to every buyer at every retail chain in America. I ask you, where else would you put vomit? It was my own inside joke.

Despite the craziness, the folks at Ktel gave it their all to promote Pig Vomit. Pig Vomit's manager's hype that, "Howard Stern would promote the shit out of it," proved to be untrue at best. Howard mentioned the group and their album a couple of times on air but that was it.

A year later I was hired away by the Musicland/Sam Goody Group, also headquartered in Minneapolis. I was made Senior Vice President in charge of developing original music product for the fourteen hundred store chain. I didn't stick around for the final count on Pig Vomit sales but an employee called me anonymously to tell me that the company had taken a real bath on the project. The person also told me that some of the secretaries had gotten together and threatened to sue the company. They claimed harassment because they were forced to type the horrendous lyrics of the songs for the liner notes. I never heard the final outcome of the suit or even if it was real. Yep, pigs get slaughtered.

IF IT GOES UP — CHANCES ARE IT WILL COME CRASHING DOWN:

By the late nineties I was back in my own business again. For someone like me, corporate life sucked. I was too used to calling my own shots in my own businesses. I hated bosses; they just got in the way. When I first went to work for Ktel I made a bunch of deals without informing my boss (the President of the company). I didn't know someone had to approve my deals before I made them. When questioned, I would fire back with, "What the hell do you care?" "Because this is MY Company!" Came the response. Whoops. So after a two-year stint as SVP at Musicland/ Sam Goody I started a marketing consultancy company. Within a short time I was working out of my basement in Minneapolis with clients like Target, Best Buy, and Musicland. It was just the way I liked it: sitting in my basement — in underwear or sweats — and pulling down a six-figure salary with no employees.

"Hey Owen, you remember me?" I recognized the voice on the other end. It was someone I worked with at Ktel in the past. He was in the LA office, and I had busted him on something or another and got him in trouble. "I'm in Minneapolis, you want to have lunch?" "Ah, what is it regarding?" I said, ever so cautious. Was he seeking revenge? Was this a planned hit? These things happen in my business. "I'll tell you at lunch."

I picked a restaurant that would be crowded just in case there was going to be any funny business. As we sipped a glass of wine he told me that Philip had just named him the new President of Ktel. "And I'd like you to be my chief consultant." I was sure my gulp of wine was audible. "I'll pay you ten thousand dollars a month and you can keep your current clients." I was sure my second gulp was audible too. "What would you like me to do?" "Ktel is a great brand, almost like Kleenex. The company has been advertising music compilations on TV for over twenty-five years and you can't buy that kind of brand recognition." "Yeah,

Philip has done a great job." "And you've heard what is going on with the Internet — people are saying that soon music will be sold online." "So, where do I come in?"

In addition to hit records that Ktel licensed from the major labels the company also owned almost four thousand hit records. Well, almost hit records. There's a little known paragraph in most artist record deals. It refers to something known as re-records, a clause that says the artist cannot re-record their hit for anyone else for a period of five to seven years from date of release. After that, they are not only free to re-record their hit but they can also own that version. The folks at Ktel picked up on this fact, and sent artist after artist back into the studio to record the same version of their past hits. And because Ktel paid for the new version — they owned it. This was a blessing for artists with hits from the 50's, 60's, and 70's who were languishing with their label-owned hit records. For many artists and "one-hit-wonders," this meant their creative masterpiece just sat in the label's vaults while the label was on to its next discovery. Not everyone was lucky enough to be the Rolling Stones or The Beatles. Many of these rerecorded artists were either broke, reeling from a costly divorce, on the backside of a nasty drug or alcohol problem, or all the above. As long as the group still owned their name, and the original lead singer could still stand up, Ktel was there to record them under the Dominion label. Once the artist finished the recording Ktel would slap them on a compilation album, and send them off to retail. For me, this was very much the seedy underbelly of the business. My career was built on signing and developing new and original talent. But once I saw the revived careers and new monies paid to these old artists I relaxed — just a bit. Eventually, the major labels caught on to the scheme and would not allow their original recordings to be on the same compilations as Ktel's re-records. However, Ktel had discovered a whole new business and another viable asset — these new/old recordings could now be licensed into TV, films, and commercials. Who cares if it isn't the original recording when the music is under a scene in a movie, or soap commercial?

"So, your idea is to put the re-record catalog online?" "Yep, and eventually we'll put original records up with permission from the major labels. All you have to do is help me assemble the tracks with our A&R guy, and work with the CFO. I'll work with the tech department and our PR agency," He said, confident in his plan. I admired his chutzpah. "So what's the real angle?" "The real angle is that our stock price is sitting at around seven dollars a share, and has been for a long time. If the announcement that Ktel is embracing the Internet could drive up the stock price to ten or eleven dollars a share we win." "And I suppose that will make Philip happy? He's got tons of shares," "Yes, and he's given me quite a few shares too."

Under the new President's guidance we pulled off the mechanics of the venture and announced to the world that Ktel. com was now live. It was a clunky system that scarcely worked. But with Ktel's name recognition and the 1990's new magic word "dot com" the stock soon jumped to nine dollars a share! A few days later the stock jumped to twelve dollars a share! Mission accomplished. Everyone in the building ran around giving each other high-fives. An employee who had a bunch of shares sold and netted sixty thousand dollars. Others, who were not officers of the company sold too. It was a glorious time.

And when the stock climbed to twenty dollars a share we were shocked. Another week went by and the stock jumped again to thirty-five dollars a share, then forty-five, fifty, sixty, and eventually soared to over seventy dollars a share!

The employee who earlier had netted sixty thousand dollars realized that he could have been a millionaire had he held on. Every morning when he entered the building, the circles under his eyes grew visibly darker from lack of sleep. Eventually, he would come in the building and sit in his office with the door locked and the shades pulled. No longer able to function he disappeared. There was speculation that he had a breakdown.

Another long-standing employee held on and netted five million dollars. He was running around the building asking low-level employees if they knew the difference between a rich man and a wealthy man. "A wealthy man doesn't have to work another day in his life," he was overheard saying to his secretary. The new President was worried. Wall Street was watching, and if there were no Internet sales the whole thing would be seen as a stock manipulation. And that would invite shareholder lawsuits once the stock price came tumbling down.

The officers of the company who had to wait before they could sell eventually got out at around sixty dollars a share — just in time. Although I couldn't verify it I heard through the grapevine that the new President walked away with around eleven million dollars, and Philip netted around forty million dollars. Eventually the stock settled back down to seven dollars a share.

For reasons unknown to me the new President and Philip fell out, and Philip brought in a dude from New York to be the new, new head of the company. I was packing up my office when the new dude asked me to stay on as COO/General Manager. He was new to the record biz and needed my counsel — on a permanent basis. He offered me a huge salary to stay and I accepted. That's when one of the biggest challenges of my career happened.

"YOU WANT ME TO PUT MY WHAT, WHERE?":

I was sitting in my office on the phone when the new company head walked in. "You got a minute?" I signaled that I'd be off soon. Instead of leaving, he closed the door while I was chatting away. Turning around and facing the wall with his backside to me he proceeded to pull his pants down exposing his bare butt. I even caught a glimpse of the edge of his hanging balls.

Denial is a funny thing; it protects your brain from exploding with the reality of what you just experienced. That's great I thought. He feels comfortable enough with me that he can tuck his shirt in, in my presence. Guys do these things. I hung up the phone and we chatted briefly about something trivial before he left.

The following week as a marketing meeting ended he asked if he could walk with me back to my office. "Sure, what's up?" "I just want to ask you a couple of questions," he responded. He put his arm around me as we walked down the long hallway but he never said a word. We were just strolling like lovers on a Sunday afternoon — his arm around me. When we got to my office he turned around walked back to his office. Denial reappeared, and I remember thinking wow, he's a great guy, what a warm person.

A few days later another employee, our in-house attorney, came into to my office and closed the door. He seemed a little white in the face and quite agitated. "Owen, I don't know what's happening but as I was walking past our VP of sales office yesterday I saw the new head of the company in there with him. And his pants were pulled down! This could be a real dangerous situation if one of the female employees in the office saw it." "Yeah, he did the same thing to me a few weeks ago but I thought he was just tucking in his shirt," I said, as denial left the building and reality settled in. "We'll you're second in command Owen so just be aware of that."

The attorney was right, and I could imagine the courtroom scene with me as co-defendant being cross-examined. "When you learned of his behavior, Mr. Husney, what did you do to protect the other employees?" "Nothing." Smiling, the attorney for the plaintiffs turned to the judge and flatly states, "I rest my case your honor." After the guilty verdict we would be shipped off to prison where he would probably enjoy the affection of the inmates, while I would be traded for Marlboros. But if he was innocent, and I took action, I'd be accusing the Chairman's new apprentice of some crazy shit — putting me out of a job.

A few weeks went by and all was quiet. The President asked a few of us to take the afternoon off and play a round of golf with him. "Kind of a retreat," he said. On the 11th hole I hit my ball into a sand trap about fifty feet from the green. "What'll you give me if I hit it out of the trap and into the hole from here?" I kiddingly said to the new dude. "I'll let you put your wiener in my ass!" He responded without skipping a beat. I purposely hit the ball out of the trap about seventy yards beyond the green. After the game, a couple of stunned male employees confided in me that they also had witnessed him saying some overt sexual things to the secretaries. Gee, he's an equal opportunity offender I thought.

I phoned an attorney who told me that I first had to put him on notice. "Just walk into his office, close the door, and let him know." I wanted to be back in my basement office sitting in my PJs making six figures. "What do I say? Hi, how are you today? Could you please stop pulling your pants down and showing the employees your butthole and your balls? It distracts them from their doing their work." "You're the second in command Husney, your have to do it or be liable yourself. If that doesn't work, you have to bring it to the Chairman's attention and let him make a decision about what to do."

The next morning I walked into the his office and closed the door. Looking up from his paperwork he said, "You're closing the door? What's up, Owen?" "You got a sec?" I said. "For you Husney? Anything." I wondered if the "anything" included getting a hint of his backside again. "I have to give you the Minnesota talk," I said, manufacturing a story. I realize you're from New York City and they do things differently there, but this the Midwest. "Whaddya mean," he said earnestly. "Well, this area of the U.S. is kinda like the Bible belt — folks are a little more conservative and religious here compared to the coasts." "I'm listening," he said. "A few of the employees have come to me, and maybe they misunderstood, but they claim you've said and done some things around here that were inappropriate. "Whaddya mean?" "Look, let's just say that some your actions around the office would maybe fly in New York and Los Angeles, but they tend to cross the line here in good ol' Plymouth Minnesota." I was trying my best to lead him to water without making a direct accusation that might put me in trouble. The President looked up, and I saw the light bulb go off. His eyes opened wide and he said, "Okay, I get it. Now let's get back to work."

I returned to my office exuberant with my tactfulness. And from that moment on things got back to normal — for about two months.

The company head announced that we were going visit Trans World Entertainment Corporation in Albany NY. Trans World owned one of the largest chains of entertainment media retail stores in the United States. The company was responsible for a big chunk of Ktel's music business through its five hundred store chain. This meeting would be strategic. We were invited to present our new music releases for the upcoming year to the company's top buyers. Attendees would include the Pants Puller, our CFO, VP of Marketing, VP of Sales, and me. We flew into New York City in the morning and made the drive up to Albany in the President's car for the afternoon meeting.

The meeting was a resounding success. The next morning as our staff was loading their suitcases in the trunk they made an interesting discovery. In the trunk were a "very large" red dress, a makeup bag, and a "very large" pair of women's high heel shoes. They came running to me. "Owen, we're all pretty liberal-minded, but this is a little over the top. The president is well over six feet tall and the dress is for a very tall woman. How did these things magically show up? He knew we were putting our luggage back in the trunk this morning — did he do that on purpose? Did he forget? If we're wrong, where's the tall woman? Did he kill her? How do we look at him again without picturing him in that dress and shoes? You have to do something about it!" I opened the trunk and moved the dress, makeup, and shoes to the very back. "Just keep your mouths shut. Load up the fucking trunk and let's get the hell out of here." The staff was right. Whatever you want to do in your spare time is fine, but why do you have to put your spare time proclivities in our face? No one wants your butt, your comments, or your dresses front and center — this is a business. The ride back to NYC was silent. "Boy, everyone must be really tired. No one is saying a word!" The dude said, as he rattled of a list of company objectives for the New Year. But I already knew that the list of company objectivities would not include him.

The call to Philip was not an easy one. But Philip was a businessman who understood the consequences of disgruntled employees. He also understood the consequences of employee lawsuits. "Don't worry, Owen." He said, in a too familiar calm-cool inflection that meant immediate action was being taken. "He's going back home to New York for the holidays." "But he'll be back." I insisted. The dude went home for the holidays and no one ever saw him again. Ever.

WOULD YOU LIKE A LITTLE HEAD?:

The never-before-released Tupac album our distribution arm in New York took on was selling fast. It was on its way to become a gold album when we received a cease and desist order from Tupac's family. "You bootlegged the album from the family without permission, and if you continue to ship the album to retail you will be sued under the fullest extent of the law," read the complaint.

"I licensed the album from a guy in California who said he had the full permission of the family." Came the nervous reply from the head of our distribution in New York. "Well who the fuck is this guy?" When he told me the name I recognized it immediately. He was well known in the music business for being able to, "get things done." If you wanted a record played on a certain radio station, he got it done, if you needed a wrong to be righted, he got it done. "Did you give him money in advance to license the album"? "Yes I did." "So now we're fucked three ways," I said. "How so?" Tupac's family is pissed and they're coming after us, for sure we've lost our advance money, and if we go after the guy who brought us the album he's gonna, "do things to us." "I know, he's already threatened to "do things to me" after I told him he needed to correct the situation and give us our money back." "So where does that leave us?" I questioned. "Fucked." he replied. "This is a dangerous situation Owen." I knew that stopping the album and pulling it was not the problem. Keeping our head of distribution alive was the problem. "Well, I'm going to Los Angeles next week, maybe I can reason with him," I said. "Don't do it Owen." Came the anxious reply."

The dangerous lesson I learned from being beat on in school was that you could eventually kick the ass of the bully and make him go away. You just had to be dirtier than he was, fuck him over when he least expected it, and make sure he knew it was you who did it. There was a time in my band days when we played a gig in a small Wisconsin town that went horribly wrong. We had just finished playing a gig in Luck Wisconsin when a gang of farm boys wanted to take, "You fuckin' long hairs out to a field, string you up, and cut your fuckin' dicks off." Yep, we were out of luck in Luck Wisconsin. They held knives to our throats and told us to get in their car. I decided we should make a break for it and run for our band car. It worked, and we sped out of town with them chasing us to the Minnesota border. Once home, I phoned a local biker gang and told them the story. They raced back to the town, tore it up, and left a note from me telling them if they ever tried that again they'd be dead. When I was on the road managing bands I encountered many "connected" promoters, agents, and other "wise guys." But I had a reputation and a security force by then so they either embraced me or stayed away altogether. The idea was to never show fear. If you did, you'd be eaten alive. So when I called the dude who gave us the Tupac album: a man rumored to be a soldier in the Gambino crime family, a defendant who had successfully beat racketeering charges, a rumored loan shark who purportedly charged 5% a week — and asked for a meeting with him, I knew what I was doing — sort of.

"Ya, we need to talk." Came the dry, cold response on the other end of the line. Your guy in New York has a bad attitude and that's not good for him." He railed. "You familiar with the San Fernando Valley?" "A bit," I replied, not wanting him to know what I did, or did not know. He gave me the address and said, "Just look for a shopping center."

The "shopping center" turned out to be a stupid strip mall in the north Valley. Like so many others there was a Seven-Eleven, a nail salon, and a "keys made on the spot" kiosk in the center of the parking lot. Following his directions I went to the middle of the center and looked for the stairway that lead upstairs. I held my nose as I ascended; it was creepy and dirty and the railing was sticky to the touch. Once at the top there was only one door with no markings so I opened it and walked straight through.

The office was gorgeous. It was a huge open expanse with people sitting at computers doing who knows what. There were floor to ceiling windows with breathtaking views of the North Valley hills. Just then, a voice shot out from the employees. "Hey Owen. Its David!" I recognized him. In the seventies he was a promotion man for Warner Bros. "Hey everyone, this is the guy who discovered and managed Prince!" He exclaimed. Okay, at least someone will be able to cover for me when the shooting starts I thought. A tall, dapper guy in a dark suit approached me and said, "He'll be ready for you in a bit and then I'll take you into his office." The place was starkly void of any women. It was like a boys club, but I seriously doubted they were planning a golf outing for the afternoon. "He'll see you now." Came a voice from the dapper suit.

I walked through the double mahogany doors and straight into Don Corleone's office. The place was straight out of central casting: rich mahogany beams spread across the great expanse of the ceiling, the walls were covered floor to ceiling with dark carved wood with built in bookcases, thick Persian rugs with deep reds and blues covered the floors, and to the left of his hand carved mahogany desk was a complete bar, stocked to the max with expensive liquors — all reflected in the in the mirror behind them. The wood blinds that covered the windows were pulled shut, and multiple lamps with green glass shades provided lighting. The man himself, unlike dapper suit dude, was dressed casually; he wore a black un-tucked shirt with thin white vertical stripes. It was unbuttoned half way down, exposing a silver chain and a few strands of grayish chest hair beneath. The one thing that struck me however was that he was wearing a really shoddy rug on his head that was slightly off kilter. To keep from staring at it I had to remind myself that I was sitting above a Seven-Eleven in a strip mall.

"So, David tells me you're the man who discovered and managed Prince," came an East Coast accent that I didn't quite recognize. "That's what they tell me, but I don't believe everything I hear." I said, deflecting the seriousness of the moment. "He's funny." The man said to the dapper dude. And then he reached behind his desk and produced a large jar from a cabinet. Placing the jar on his desk he said, "This is what happens when people fuck with me." The jar was filled with a cloudy liquid and I strained to see what was inside. I made out what looked like a few strands of hair floating in the substance and then — a nose and eyes; holy shit it was a human head! The guy had a fucking shrunken head in a jar! I pictured the future, with someone else sitting in the same chair as me looking at my head in that jar. "Yep, he tried to kill me in Vietnam, but I taught him a lesson and now we just kinda hang out together." "He's a decorated soldier." Said dapper dude.

"I understand we have a little problem with your guy in New York," the man said. "Yeah, that's why I'm here. With all due respect I'd like to see if we could unravel this situation." "There will be no unraveling," he shot back. To get out you'll have to give me something." "Like what?" I said, thinking of my first-born.

And then it hit me. Would you like to hear something?" I said, continuing the conversation. "Naw, let's get this taken care of." I reached into my briefcase and pulled out a CD of very early Prince demos. "No one has ever heard these before — they were his earliest demos. I was thinking we could release these together through your label. It would be historic." "I'm interested, let's hear 'em." I played him a couple of the early Chris Moon demos — ones that I did not own and had no rights to. "You get me these for release and don't worry about your situation in New York." We shook hands, and I left knowing I'd just made a promise I couldn't keep to a guy who would have had no problem putting my head in a jar.

I figured that I'd get a hold of Chris back in Minneapolis and see if we could cut a deal to release the early songs. It had been at least fifteen years since I'd last spoken with him. But when I tried to reach him I found out that he moved away and left no forwarding contact info. At that point I started wondering just how long it took shrink a head. Do you have to boil it first? And how long do you have to boil it for?

I returned to the safety of Minneapolis wondering if it would just be better to send the dude the master recordings and let him release them illegally. At that point, Chris Moon, as the real owner of the masters, would be forced sue the dude. After that, I would be free to visit Chris's head in the jar. But then, a stroke of pure luck:

The dude in Los Angeles was arrested at a shopping center in Beverly Hills. According to the complaint he was loaning money and charging as much as 5% a week in interest. When borrowers didn't pay up he, and/or his henchmen beat the shit out of them. He pleaded guilty to extortion and was shipped off to prison. Ye sir, our guy in New York, Chris Moon, and I all dodged a bullet — literally. When law enforcement also claimed that he was a soldier in the Gambino crime family he said, "I'm a soldier, all right — a decorated veteran of the Vietnam War, and a recipient of The Purple Heart." He was telling the truth — I saw the proof.

I didn't stay with Ktel for long after this last episode. A few months later I met with a man who owned a large home shopping television network. My idea was to sell Ktel music product on-air like the jewelry, perfume, and other household products already being sold successfully. I met with the Chairman of the network and we hit it off immediately. After the third meeting he made me an offer I couldn't refuse. As I was leaving his office he said, "Owen, if you walk out of Ktel I'll write you a check for a half a million dollars and we'll go into business together." I returned to the Ktel headquarters and resigned immediately.

...But Wait, There's More! — and that's another story for another day.

Bob Keane

Did Bobby Fuller of the Bobby Fuller Four fight the law?
Did the law win?

In 2003 I got a call from a guy named Bob Keane, owner of Del-Fi records. "Is this Husney?" He belched. I'd heard of Bob but never met him. "Yes, this is Husney." And right away I was wondering why I had just used my last name too. "Heard you sell record labels. Come over tomorrow and we'll talk. I'm down on Melrose." "Sure, how do I get there?" "Just fucking go four blocks past La Cienega on Melrose, turn left, and immediately turn right into the alley. Park directly behind the blue-grey Mercedes. You can't miss it. It's a 1983 four door. The rear bumper is tilted to the right. Some asshole hit me from behind about six months ago. Gonna sue that son of a bitch when I get around to it. See you at 10 a.m. sharp. And remember Husney, you can only get in to my office from the alley door."

And that was the beginning. I didn't know then, that within 24 hours, I'd also be wandering into the midst of an unsolved murder.

By the year 2000, I decided that the world of running music companies and managing rock stars was no longer for me. I was tired. Tired of traveling and weary from answering the countless emails and "must talk" phone calls from employees, agents, and lawyers over the span of my almost forty years in the business. I was especially tired of listening to the endless narcissistic needs and rants of entitled celebrities who would call me at four in the morning asking why the sun wasn't up. It was time for a change.

There's another end of the business most people don't know about that involves catalogs. No, not Pottery Barn or Victoria's Secret but music catalogs; the accumulation of hit recordings called "Masters," that are owned by record labels. All record labels, large or small, own almost all the hit record Masters we grew up with and still listen to today.

By 2003 most of the old timers who were once the young mavericks that built the business desperately needed to sell their little independent labels. The industry had changed dramatically for them during the late nineties with the emergence of the Internet and its crippling effect on retail stores, so vital to their existence. Most of these label owners, now in their seventies and eighties, were once true pioneers in the music business but were now unable to keep up with the digital future or even comprehend it. To them it meant the end of the only livelihood they knew and they were forced to sell or go down with their ship. And, that's where I came in. My business was to facilitate the sale of their small but important record label Masters to the larger record label behemoths who were always ready, jaws open, to gobble them up. There was good money to be made acting as a real estate agent between those who wanted to sell and those who wanted to buy. I realized that this end of the business was less creative and glitzy but at least the hit records didn't call me at four in the morning asking why the sun wasn't up.

The next day after that fateful call I took the short eight minute drive from my house in the swimming pool speckled, celebrity-filled hills above Sunset Boulevard down to the endless blocks of black t-shirt, piercing, and tattoo shops on Melrose avenue.

Parking as I'd been ordered, I made my way to the dingy back wall of the tired, one-level office building, that I assumed had a gorgeous California faux front that I would never see. I passed through what looked like a ghetto back door. The screen was rusted and sprinkled with torn holes that looked like someone had fired buckshot through it at close range. It was off its hinges and closing it was a task, as it scraped along the uneven ground with an annoying screech. I entered the building and realized there was only one way to go, down. As I descended the faintly lit uneven stairs a grim wave of panic came over me. I imagined the whole thing was somehow a creepy setup and I would wind up like that scene in Pulp Fiction, captured, tied up in a basement, and used for sex games by men wearing full-head black masks and nothing else.

Then, emerging from the shadows at the bottom of the stairs someone said, "Down here, Husney," and a dim light was flipped on so I could partially see the basement. "Down here and around the corner to the right," a voice added, as I watched a huge silhouette disappear into the darkness and turn the corner.

At the bottom of the creaky, stairs I took a right and walked past leaning shelves of musty-smelling, water-stained and damaged cardboard boxes of old vinyl 45's and albums. They were mixed with newer boxes of CDs brandishing the names of acts and artists I had never heard of. All of the boxes screamed the name DEL-FI RECORDS in bright red 1950's block letters. Bob appeared from the shadows in what I presumed was his office, looking oddly like Orson Welles in the bloated years. Bob was tall and round. His blue and green California-floral shirt was at least one size too small, and even un-tucked it failed to hide his stark-white emerging belly. His pants were of the old-man-jeans variety: faded, loose and baggy, with a weak attempt at an ironed crease down the middle of each leg. Most surprising were his shoes. They were spotless white low rise tennis shoes that at first I assumed were brand new but upon close examination I realized they had been wiped clean countless times.

Bob's office was a dungeon of 1960's retro kitsch. In one corner was a box of those old desktop promotional tear-off calendars your dad used to get free from the Shell Station, but Bob's cheerfully proclaimed, "Happy New Year 1964 from your friends at Del-Fi Records." The walls featured yellowed and curling posters of Sam Cooke and Frank Zappa. On one wall there was a large thumbtacked poster of Ritchie Valens. He was playing a guitar with the words 'La Bamba' coming from his mouth in a cartoon bubble. A poster of Barry White looked down at us from its crusted perch behind Bob's desk. I wondered about the small fortune all this kitsch would get on eBay. Most of the acts were either has-beens or dead. The poster that really caught my eye however, was "The Bobby Fuller Four." It's headline read, "Tonight only hear The Bobby Fuller Four perform their #1 hit, I Fought the Law! Catch them at the Long Beach Arena! 8PM." I was curious. I remembered that Bobby Fuller died suddenly six months into an incredible career in the early sixties. As we circled his brown ragtag desk cluttered with useless pieces of paper, I asked Bob point blank how Bobby died

"I don't know how he died." Bob grumbled. "Let's get down to business."

"But I heard he was killed…" "Sit down, Husney," Bob bellowed as he slowly and carefully placed his large frame into his tattered office chair. "I told you, I don't know how he fucking died."

"But there's only a handful of people who could have done it." I insisted.

"That was 1964 almost forty years ago, forget about it. Are you here to sell my record label or conduct a goddamn investigation for the LAPD?" I took the hint.

"Okay, sorry. Let's go over the acts on your roster." I said, pulling papers out of my briefcase and feeling like I had naively waded into an alligator infested swamp.

"You know, I don't think you get it Husney, Bob snapped, they've been trying to pin that murder on me since the night it happened."

"Um, I uh, I thought you wanted to get down to business?"

"Shut up and listen." Bob said, as the rising purple veins in his neck began to bulge through his sagging skin. " I'm 86 years old. I've owned Del-Fi Records since 1959. It's been my whole fucking life, get it? Now I'm at the end." Then he leaned in so close, that I could see the white stubble of unshaved hairs on his upper lip reaching for the willy-nilly wild ones springing forth from his bulbous nose. "You guys fucking kill me. I signed 17-year-old Ritchie Valens and gave him a #1 hit record with La Bamba. I signed and discovered Sam Cooke, Barry White and Frank Zappa. I invented the Los Angeles surf sound but all anyone wants to know about is the Bobby Fuller Four. How did

Bobby die? Who killed him? It's all a bunch of B.S." Bob said, as his right hand nervously pushed through a thick head of perfectly white hair.

"I'm really sorry, I didn't mean to, I just… It's just such an intriguing story," I said.

"You're just like the rest of 'em. Hoping I'll tell you the truth. Maybe I'll let it slip if you keep questioning me, huh?" Bob said, flashing me a sarcastic wink.

"Well, I did sign a non-disclosure with you via fax this morning." I said.

"What the fuck does that mean?" Bob said.

"It means that I can't divulge any proprietary information with regard to you or your company. I'm selling your company for you, remember?"

Bob leaned in again and I could smell a faint hint of last night's alcohol. Or was it today's?

For someone who didn't want to talk Bob rattled on. "I should never have pinched "I Fought the Law" from one of Buddy Holly's Crickets. I gave it to Bobby. He didn't deserve it. It was a damn gift." Bob said. "Bobby drove up to LA from West Texas with his brother — a couple of real rednecks. He walks into my office. Says he wants to be a star. I told him to go back to Texas and pitch hay from the back of a truck. Right then and there he starts singing an original song. Then his brother Randy chimes in with crazy harmonies."

"Any good?" I said.

"It was shit. But Bobby was good looking".

"Really?" I said, thrilled that Bob was opening up more.

"Yeah, he had those bad-boy good looks. You know, thick dark eyebrows with a mustache and goatee. He was lean. And that long hair. Kinda swept back. He was just a good lookin' kid so I gave him that song. Told him to learn it and come back the next day."

"So you saw something in him?" I asked.

"Nah, I did it mostly to get him out of my office."

Bob continued. "The next day Bobby comes back with his brother and they sing 'I Fought the Law.' Knocked me off my fucking feet. The son of a bitch nailed it."

For the first time since I'd arrived I actually noticed a slight proud gleam in old Bob's tired blue eyes. "I put him in the studio the next day. Within three weeks I had pressed up the 45 and paid-off a disc jockey at KHJ to play it.

"I know it was a top 5 hit nationally. How long did it take to get there?" I said. I was trying to keep the floodgates open.

"Two fucking months and we had a monster hit." Bob said, the faint gleam now turning into a slight smile. "Four months later Bobby Fuller's is the toast of Hollywood, hanging out with the rat pack and the Kennedy's, and partying on the Sunset Strip. Then, we couldn't keep up with the orders for the single, the manufacturer wanted payment in advance, and my partner was afraid we were going to lose money." Just then I noticed a look of concern on his face for something that happened forty years earlier.

"I didn't know you had a partner. Del Fi Records was always Bob Keane." I said.

"He was a silent partner who funded the label." Bob said, cutting me short. "More coffee?" Bob was barely able to lift his ailing body out of the chair and walk the ten steps across the tiny chaotic office to the coffeemaker that looked like it was from a 1950's Maxwell House commercial.

He slowly turned towards me. "Bobby got too big too quick. Hollywood is a funny place. When you make it you need to know who to stay away from. Bobby never had time to figure it out. The poor son of a bitch started hanging around with some mob boss's call-girl girlfriend."

"That would do it." I said.

"I thought so too. But no one kills you for fucking a prostitute. Maybe rough you up a little." He paused and shot me a look. "Having fun Husney? Want more?" Bob said as he shuffled back to his battered desk.

"I ain't goin' anywhere am I?" I said, starting to sound like a tough-guy myself.

"One day Bobby brings this dirty wild-eyed hippie around to my office. The hippie whips out a guitar and starts singing some lame shit. I told Bobby to get the asshole out of my office. Bobby looks me square in the face and says, "You'll be sorry. He's gonna be big. I swear. Just remember his name. Charlie Manson." Bob said, with no expression whatsoever.

"Holy shit, so Manson killed him?"

"Nah, I never believed it." Bob said. "Bobby also managed to piss off the LA Police Department. He was doing that LSD crap with Timothy Leary in Malibu. Got caught. Told the police that he was a star and would make fools out of them in the press if they arrested him."

"So he fought the law and the law won?" I said.

"Funny guy, you." Bob snapped back. "Bobby was living with his mother at the time in an apartment over on Sycamore. He gets a call at midnight and takes off in his mother's brand new Oldsmobile — still wearing his bathrobe. The next morning I get a call that he's dead, still parked in front of his apartment. The police said he killed himself by drinking a glass of gasoline."

"That would do it." I said.

"Thought so too but the coroner said it's impossible to drink gasoline. You throw it right up."

"So now its 2003, the case is unsolved, and everybody still thinks I killed Bobby because I was closest to him. But I had no motive. I'm just a goddamn clarinet-player who started a record label."

"I get it." I said. "So what's your best guess?" Bob reached out and touched my arm. It was the first shred of warmth I felt since the beginning of our meeting. "I'm gonna tell you a little secret," he said almost whispering. "I've got cancer. Doc says I've got a little more than a year to live. That's why I'm selling my life's work. After I sell I go home and die."

"I'm so sorry." I whispered back.

"So you want my best guess?" Bob said, looking right past me to a yellowed Frank Zappa poster thumbtacked on the wall behind me. "I didn't know my finance partner was connected." Bob said, pushing his nose to the side. "I didn't know it at the time but he took insurance policies out on all our acts. Bobby was a huge success but we were losing money trying to press up 45's, record a full album, and pay all the promotion and marketing costs in advance. Next thing I know Bobby's dead and we collected a shit-load of money on the policy. But now everyone's dead so who gives a fuck?"

As I listened, I realized that Bob never seemed to feel any remorse nor did he convey any feeling of sadness for poor Bobby as he told me his story. Sure, a ton of time had passed since the incident but here was a nice young ambitious kid from Texas struck down only months into achieving his wildest dreams. Another Hollywood dreamer had left behind a brother and mother, both dependent upon him. And to this day no one knows why, how, or who murdered him.

Two months after my meeting with Bob Keane I found the right buyer, Warner Bros Records. They wanted the Del-Fi catalog. In order to eliminate any competition they were willing to pay well over our asking price to get it. I excitedly called Bob and told him the good news.

"Yeah? Well fuck 'em. I ain't sellin'," Bob said and hung up.

Knowing that I was about to lose a large amount of money on this transaction I immediately called Bob back and asked him to go to breakfast at Hugo's in Hollywood the next morning. "I'll pick you up." I promised.

During breakfast I never mentioned his negative reaction to the good news but as I dropped Bob back at his Melrose alley office I asked him about his sudden turn-around on selling.

As he reached for the door handle Bob turned to me, "What am I supposed to do Husney?" he said with tears forming in those tough old eyes, "Sell, go home, and die?" I watched as Bob slowly made his way to the torn screen door of his office. I heard it scrape against the concrete as he disappeared downstairs.

I raced up the hill back to my office and phoned Scott Pascucci, President of Warner's catalog division. "Scott, Bob turned down the offer but I have an idea."

"What?" Scott said incredulous. "The offer wasn't good enough for him?"

"I don't think that's it," I said.

"Good because there's no more money for him"

"As part of the deal could you offer Bob a cubicle at the label for a year? He could work on the Del-Fi history for a retrospective CD release package. Plus, Bob knows where all the hidden gems are that are still on the old recording tapes," I said biting my nails to the quick.

"OK, you got it but that's it," Scott said.

I called Bob back. "What is it this time Husney?" he said, a little more than annoyed.

"As part of your sale of the label you start work at Warner Bros Records on Monday."

All Bob said was, "Done. Good work, Husney."

Bob went to work at Warner Bros, paid off most of his debts, and died a little over a year later in 2005. Bobby Fuller's death remains a mystery to this day. It is still listed as an open cold case by the Los Angeles Police Department. I never knew if Bob told me the truth about what happened to Bobby Fuller but whatever the truth was, it's buried with old Bob.

Demons and Dreams
My Rain Fur Rent Story

JUST WHEN I THOUGHT MY LIFE
WOULD BE SMOOTH SAILING.

JANUARY 2004:

I moved from the Hollywood Hills to the ocean so I could get back to the water and my love of sailing. The days of managing artists and running companies for angry Chairmen with disgruntled employees were over. It was time to simplify.

My home-office was in a new complex at the water's edge in Marina del Rey with all windows on the water. It was only a forty-minute drive, but a world away from the bustle of LA. My backyard went from a sometimes-smoggy view of the city, to boats pulling in and out of the world's largest man-made harbor.

The one drawback was my ability to focus. If the shutters in front of my desk were open, I wanted to be outside playing at the water's edge — or meeting the "California Girls" who'd stroll along the walkways. So, during work hours the shutters were closed. The one exception was noontime. That's when I'd take the walkway two blocks north to the Mermaid, a tiny outdoor sandwich shop next to Mother's Beach. To say life was good was an understatement.

I joined the Marina del Rey single sailors club, and through a calamity of "Woody Allen" errors became its Commodore. The longstanding Commodore retired and two established members were nominated. But a woman who liked me threw my name into the hat. I didn't mind because it was a joke and I'd be a distant third. The day before the election one nominee dropped out citing personal differences with the club. On the day of the election the woman running against me dropped out due to health problems. So, three months into my move to the Marina I was Commodore Owen.

I lost my sailboat in a divorce so being Commodore was a dream. One of my duties was to assign members to boats for weekend sails. The boats were beautiful, ranging in length from 30-ft sloops to 55-ft wooden schooners. Most had one bedroom and a head, but some had living rooms, bedrooms, and gorgeous staterooms. As Commodore Owen, I could jump on some of the finest sailing crafts in the world and sail the Pacific.

The night of my first meeting as Commodore a fight broke out between two male members. One of them threw a glass of red wine at the other. He missed him by an inch but sprayed him with deep red wine ruining his white shirt. The other dude charged him. Hollering ensued, and a complete brawl broke out among the members. Then, without notice, all the lights went out in the large meeting room — plunging us into darkness. Everyone stopped cold and fumbled to the exits. After a few minutes the lights came back on and a matronly woman walked into the room with a tight-lipped grin. "That was a damn good trick," I said. "Where'd you learn that?" "I'm a kindergarten teacher," she said. Lessons learned.

Despite the meeting incident, life at the ocean was fucking great. I was living my independent dream, dating California girls, and doing as I pleased. That is until one spring afternoon when there was a knock on my door.

"How did you get in the building," I asked, shouting through the door. "I'm sorry, Mr. Husney, my name is Beau," came a low male voice from the other side. "I walked in with someone and found your name on the directory. I hope you don't mind." "I do mind. This is a security building for a reason. What do you want?" "I'm an engineer in a recording studio in Hollywood and I think you should hear this group I recorded. I have a CD for you." "So you drove all the out to the Marina to tell me this?

Sorry dude, I'm not managing anymore. Just leave the CD at my door and I'll call you," I said, with no intention of calling him.

Once he left I popped the CD in the player for the usual ten second listening. Most demos I'd listened to during my career didn't even make it beyond five seconds. I noticed the name of the group on the envelope: Rain Fur Rent. Funny, they misspelled their own name.

The lone acoustic guitar opening grabbed my attention with its proficiency and tonality. But then, what sounded like an electric violin came in layered over the top. Okay, you get another ten seconds. And then the drums, bass, and vocals came in. The dude who was singing knew what the fuck he was doing. His voice had both the reminiscent wail of Robert Plant, and the more contemporary texture of Chris Cornell. There was no bullshit here. And the drummer kicked ass even on this mid-tempo track. Their sound was organic and original — not derivative. Four minutes had gone by, and if I busted my ass I could make it down to parking lot and grab the guy who left the CD. Good thing I run three miles a day I thought as I caught up with him pulling out of the lot.

Beau sat on my deck watching an orange sun sink over the Pacific. It lingered on the horizon before surrendering to the sea. Lighted boats pulled into the darkened harbor. I sat inside transfixed listening to the rest of the songs on the demo. Rain Fur Rent had all the textural imperfections of the significant indie bands of the 90's. In the 80's, most pop music had become synth oriented: clean, crisp, and corporate. And then there were those hair bands. By the 90's the pendulum had swung back. Flannel shirts replaced slick outfits, and gritty vocals and guitars made a return. But by 2004, the contemporary rock groups that were popular had all but destroyed the genre by releasing soulless re-manufactured crap.

I didn't want to like Rain Fur Rent because I'd convinced myself I was out of the biz. But the music was pulling me in, one song at a time, until there were no more excuses — and no escape.

I asked Beau some well-rehearsed questions: "Where are they from? Does one person write the songs? Is there a manager? When can I meet them?" And the most important question, "Who have they signed their life away to?" Most artists have signed over management to some local knucklehead, signed to some bogus record label, or worse by the time I hear them. Untangling sucks, is expensive, and not worth the effort. "They're free and clear." Beau said.

"Who's the lead singer Beau?" "His name is Travis." "Where's he from?" "Amarillo, Texas." I liked the sound of that. "What do you know about him?" "His mom is a country-blues singer and his dad is a professional guitar player." Even better, I thought. "He told me he ran away from home at seventeen and wound up sleeping on stranger's couches. He started busking on the streets of central California for pocket change." Fucking perfect I thought. "Where do they live?" "Atascadero." "Huh?" "It's about halfway between LA and San Francisco." "What the hell is up there?" "I guess it's a few minutes away from San Luis Obispo, a huge college town. They play between there and San Francisco."

The vibe of the band was also reminiscent of the great late sixties — early seventies bands. Rain Fur Rent would be right at home playing with The Doors. How could something so real fall in my lap? "The dude on drums is kick-ass," I said, feelin' the vibe. "It's not a dude, she's a girl. Her name is Sarah." "All right Beau, go home. I want to hear them perform live wherever they are." After he left, I looked at the name of the band written in Sharpie on the CD. It confirmed, "Rain Fur Rent." Okay, this is intentional, but why?

I phoned my sailing buddy Ken to come along and hear the band. We headed east out of the Marina towards West Hollywood. Turning right off Sunset Blvd. we pulled into the Viper Room parking lot. The club, once owned by Johnny Depp, is painted all black inside and out. It was famous for infamous drug overdoses of Hollywood stars. These days, it was home to baby bands looking for possible recognition in an impossible business. The club had become one of the nefarious pay-to-play venues along Sunset. Bands, eager to showcase their talent, are asked to buy several hundred dollars in tickets for the night they perform. If they bought the tickets they were allowed to be one of fifteen bands rotated throughout the evening. They'd sell the tickets to their fans, friends, parents, and grandparents. They do it hopping to play in front of a label exec that might discover them. If they sold all the tickets they broke even. If not, they were out the money — but what the hell, it's showbiz and getting noticed is half the game. Even though we were on the list, Ken and I opted to buy tickets and support the cause.

We stood through an excruciating hour of music by well-intentioned posers when a voice out of nowhere announced that Rain Fur Rent was next. Bands must change over at lightning speed — no sound check, and barely enough time to tune up. The curtains were pulled tight on the tiny rounded stage, but through a crack I could see an open door in the back of the stage. The previous band's gear was being tossed out on to the street while a stage manager was yelling; "If you take too long to set up there will be consequences!"

Rain Fur Rent loaded-in and set up in record time. They knew the drill. In what seemed like a minute the curtains opened and the band walked out and took their positions: Tyson on violin, Grant on Bass, Sarah on drums, and Ryan on pedal steel. I prayed under my breath they'd be the real deal. Maybe I just wanted to prove to myself that I still "had it".

Travis walked out and people cheered. The crowd had seen a thousand bands that night but they knew who he was. And Travis looked the part: thin, shoulder length brown hair, not tall, with serious tats on his arms and, I assume, everywhere else. He had the rock look — a goatee braced against high cheekbones and finished with a serious attitude.

Someone counted down and the band broke in to "Compared to What?" One of my favorite original tracks on the demo. Travis had it. Apart from his rock and roll good looks Travis had the trappings of a true performer: a natural stage presence that demanded attention. He wasn't asking you to like him; he was giving himself to you. If you liked him, there was an immediate bond. If you didn't, well, too fucking bad for you. By the end of the first verse I knew I could still spot true talent. Okay, so this was about me.

As I listened, I was transported to a time in my life when hearing a new group was life moving; like the first time I heard John Mayall's *Blues Breakers*, or Cream, or Miles Davis, or Hendrix, or Muddy Waters, or Sly and the Family Stone or the Prince demos. The last time I heard something that moved me was Nirvana. After that, everything was derivative, or stupid. But Rain Fur Rent brought that "I'm home" quality back. Even though Travis's voice would be at home in a metal band there was something that worked brilliantly against a solid rhythm section, an electric violin, and a pedal steel guitar.

I had a trick from my days when I'd show up to hear newbie groups play live. I'd listen half way through the first song and then turn around and watch the audience. I turned around, and saw the entire Viper Room audience moving their heads up and down in unison to the beat of the music. Okay, time to meet the band.

I felt an immediate connection to Travis. We chatted outside the club while he downed the last smoky nub of a cigarette before tossing it onto Sunset Blvd. He was smart, shy, and wary of me. Almost every artist I've met was wary of me at first. It's a self-protective device. If they like me it means they could open themselves up to being hurt, burned, or both. And lord knows they've had enough of that in their lifetime. Once they find out my roots were in a rock band the ice melts. A good dose of my sarcastic humor lets them know I don't take myself too seriously. And, I have a track record. But was this attachment I felt a friend thing, or a true believer thing? As we chatted a fan approached us. "Man, you guys were great! And how cool is it that your dad came to see you."

We got back in the car and Ken said, "If you'd like an investor in this project, I'm in." "Are you sure? This is an all risk business." "I'm sure." Like me, Ken is smart enough to understand risk, but open enough to sense possibilities. And possibilities are where success lives. What we didn't know was that sinister forces were also at play.

"So, why Rain Fur Rent?" I said, noticing the same misspelling on the management contract. "Tyson spoke up, "We were Rain For Rent, but when we got popular on the Central Coast a sprinkler company sent us a cease and desist letter." "And Rain For Rent was the name of their company?" I guessed. "Yeah, they make industrial sprinklers for farm fields. So now we're Rain Fur Rent." I was now the official manager of Rain Fur Rent.

If we were going to do this right it was important for the band to all live under one roof. So, with Ken's investment, the band, sans Sarah, moved into a female super-fan's house in the North San Fernando Valley. The super-fan was divorced, believed in the band a thousand percent, and the rent kept her and the band in the house. A win-win. Rain Fur Rent set up shop in the Valley ranch-style home, dividing up rooms with curtains, and setting up a small recording studio. They partied and stocked the house with so much booze and other shit I nicknamed it the "Doors House." Little did I know how well stocked that house was.

After dinner, I'd fly down the 405 to the Doors House, light up a joint with Travis, and listen to song after song he had written and recorded on a small device. Although I knew all the band members contributed to the songs I sensed that Travis was the primary writer. It was astounding the amount of material he had composed. Psychedelic, Metal, orchestral, and heartfelt ballads all flew out of the speakers with a rich, relatable style.

"Is there a particular band or singer you admire?" "Yeah, Blind Melon." "Right, they were the early 90's band that had big success. Then, at the top of their game the lead singer, Shannon Hoon, died from an overdose. I loved their single, "No Rain." As Trav lit up another cigarette I asked him where he had been all my life — and why aren't these songs out already? "You're a music publisher's dream," I beamed. "I have my demons," was his simple response. I should have paid more attention to that response.

We re-recorded three of the band's demos in a state of the art studio. Armed with a short bio and presentation piece I met with super-power-music-lawyer, Gary Stiffelman. Gary sat back in his chair, listened to the three songs, and said, "Do they live here?" Bingo! That's always the million-dollar question. If someone doesn't like the songs they'll say anything to get you out of their office. If they like the group they want to know where the group lives. Without hesitation, Gary picked up the phone and called three major labels on the spot. He set meetings with all three.

The following week the band met in the conference room at Gary's office. He wanted spell out his fees and what was expected of the group. Travis sat quietly and asked a couple of questions. Gary then produced a simple letter of understanding and the group signed it. He was in action mode, so was I, and so was the group. On the way out of the meeting one of the group members approached me, "Whew, that was a close one." "What do you mean?" "Travis disappeared three days ago and we couldn't find him." "He was off writing somewhere," I said, sinking into denial. I phoned Travis the next day. "So, we're on our way," I said staying confident. "What did you think of Gary and that office of his?" "Owen, I haven't met Gary yet."

The Doors house took on a new relevancy for me. Questions flooded my mind; as manager, is it my job to monitor adults? Doesn't great creativity come from tortured souls? Do I lay down the law? Am I a counselor? Who am I to judge — wasn't I a drug-induced hippie musician once? As long as great music is flowing is it my job to interrupt whatever process it takes for creation? I know people need to manage their own lives. I also know some people self medicate, others self-sabotage, and many times it's a complicated combo. In the 60's and 70's using was almost a contractual prerequisite in the biz, but this is 2004 — do I want this in my life? But then, who cares? People are willing to invest their time, money, and belief in Rain Fur Rent because their writing and performing are great.

In a random event Atlantic Records A&R, Kevin Carvel, showed up to hear another band one night at a small club on Ventura Blvd. RFR went on first. When they finished he walked right up and handed me his card. "I think we should meet tomorrow or the next day at my office." Meanwhile other labels were lining up thanks to Gary's efforts, my contacts, and a shiny new demo from the group. Epic Records, Geffen Records, RCA, Velvet Hammer, Sony, Interscope, and Warner Bros all wanted to meet the band and hear them perform live. It was happening! Then, an A&R guy called from my old alma mater — Warner Bros. He wanted to meet as soon as possible. The meeting was a real wake up call.

The Warner Bros record's headquarters in Burbank is called the "Ski lodge" because of its sweeping redwood wood design and garden courts. There was a time in the 70's when I could walk into the building, say hi to the receptionist, and visit anyone in his or her office. This time I had to wait in the lobby for forty-five minutes while watching unknown faces come and go. "Right this way, Mr. Husney. He can see you now." I walked past the hundreds of gold and platinum albums lining the walls — some of them due to my efforts. The building carried so many memories from the old days it was like bumping into an old girlfriend — twenty-nine years later — and we were both a little worse for the wear.

"So we heard Rain Fur Rent's demo and we're quite impressed." The A&R dude said. "And we know of your history in this building. Good work, Owen." "Yeah, I'm super impressed with the band and Travis's song writing ability and voice," I added. The A&R dude continued, "So, a few questions. Is the band performing regularly?" "Yeah, they play up and down the Sunset strip, have a great following along the central coast, the college town of San Luis Obispo, and in San Francisco." "No, I mean do they have a following in clubs everywhere west of the

Mississippi? Have they sold thousands of CDs out of the trunk of their car? And do they have a huge MySpace following?" I was stunned. "What do you mean?" I said. "This is how we sign acts these days, Owen." Boy, was I old school.

"What happened to labels developing artists? Isn't that your job? Look, if I was selling thirty thousand CDs out of the trunk of my car, and the group was playing everywhere west of the Mississippi, and selling merch, why the fuck would I need you?"

The A&R dude looked befuddled and a little sad. "That's not the way the business is done these days," he said, with a touch of arrogance. I let loose, "Maybe I seem old school, but isn't it supposed to be about the music? You guys want everything handed to you on a silver platter these days. And now the accountants are running the business? That's why the music sucks. Prince had never been on the road when WB signed him. They believed in him and went to work. Thanks but no thanks." With that I got up and left the building, never to return. My Warner Bros dream was over.

The entire music business model had gone through a seismic shift since my heyday. This was 2004, and record sales were plummeting. New adversaries like file sharing, competition with DVDs, and video games were sucking money out of the music biz. And "corporate rock," was turning hard rock fans off altogether. I'm running around with RFR and a band called Nickelback is running up the charts. The experience taught me I had to take RFR in another Label direction that was more indie/ grass roots oriented. Their vibe was more attune to 90's bands like Alice in Chains, Blind Melon, or perhaps some of the Seattle based bands. It crossed my mind that Travis may have been born ten years too late.

Travis opened the door wide. "Hey man," thanks for driving out to the Doors house." "It's meetin' time." I said. "I don't like meetings. They bore me," Travis said, while smudging his cigarette into a filthy ashtray on the doorstep. "Nothing too deep. I want to discuss label direction." I said. As Travis turned to enter the house I noticed he had a black eye. "Hey man, what's that?" When he turned towards the light I noticed another large bruise on his left cheek. "Looks like you had a fight with a car door." I said, half joking. "Naw, one of the band members punched me out." "Huh?" Travis deflected. "Don't worry. It gets pretty intense with all of us living and rehearsing here." I shot back, "Oh, yeah, what else is going on here? I didn't fall off the bumpkin truck yesterday." "You know, we have our demons." I didn't know if those demons were smoked, ingested, shot, or snorted. I didn't care. I managed many bands in my lifetime, and though I'd seen major arguments I never saw black eyes and pounded faces. And besides, whoever punched Travis punched the front man, lead singer, and writer for the group. Where was the fucking sense in that?

The hastily installed string of bulbs barely illuminated our faces as we all sat at a large table in the backyard of the Doors House. Because of the recent events the band meeting took on a different tone. "I came out here to speak with you about taking our label pursuit to a more indie direction. However, from what I've seen, I have to say, whoever punched Travis, warranted or not, is an idiot. Travis is the face of Rain Fur Rent and therefore the money. If I've learned one thing from being around bands all my life it's that you NEVER fucking punch the money. Got it! You NEVER punch the fucking money. Managers may be babysitters but they're not drug counselors. Except for Sarah, y'all are destroying your dreams with your demons. This is an opportunity that most bands would kill for. And one more thing, people are investing their money, time, and belief in RFR. So when you sabotage yourselves, you're also sabotaging the lives of others. Clean up your shit! The band members blamed each other and an argument broke out. It seemed like it would soon escalate to an all out brawl. As the shouting grew louder the backyard lights went out plunging everyone into darkness. The arguing ended and the lights went back on. "That's an interesting trick

Owen. Where'd you learn that?" "From a kindergarten teacher,"
I replied. And with that I walked out the door.

I returned to my house fuming. I picked up a vase and
heaved it into the wall so hard it shattered into a million pieces.
While picking the splintered chards out of the carpet I noticed
the light flashing on my answering machine across the room.
"Hello Owen, this is Epic records assistant to the Vice President
of A&R. We'd like to fly Rain Fur Rent to New York to perform live for the Chairman of the Sony Music Label Group. I'll
get back to you tomorrow with the dates." I played the message
again and let it sink in, "The Chairman of the Sony Music Label
Group." This is the stuff dreams are made of. Okay, so the real
Doors, and most other bands started using after they made big I
rationalized. Isn't it still all about the music? And besides I felt a
real affinity for Travis. He was a true artist. Or, maybe he was like
a son. Either way, I was in denial.

It felt great to be back in biz organizing flights, bartering for
equipment rental, arranging hotels, and dealing with Sony to get
money out of them for my act. Two weeks later, we were on a
flight to NYC ready to show the world what RFR could do.

The next morning I woke the group up bright and early. This
was a big day and they needed to be ready for the 3 p.m. sound
check. Two vans picked us up and drove us to an old brick building on the lower East Side. We loaded the gear into the clunky
freight elevator and it took us up to the sixth floor. The showcase room was large, with brick walls and windows overlooking
the river. The sound check went off without a hitch and RFR
sounded as if they were on their fifth world tour, not like a band
hoping to get signed. Rain Fur Rent had arrived!

That night, the room was filled with Sony execs. There must
have been fifty people there to hear RFR — a band I "discov
ered" — after I was out of the management business. Sony provided food and drinks for the event. It was a gratifying moment
in my life — a life that had pretty much seen it all. The band
was ready to go on but where was the Chairman? Someone

approached me and said the band needed to wait until he arrived. One thing I've learned along the way is that when a band is ready to go they need to go on. The adrenaline rush is so important to overcoming fear. The wait was excruciating and I was a nervous father, ah manager. After forty-five minutes a discernable hush came over the room. The doors opened, the seas parted, and the king entered. It seemed like everyone was waiting for him to take his place before sitting down. RFR played their hearts out, the room exploded in applause, and the king left. "That was exceptional!" A Sony rep said. "We'd like to invite you to a special dinner as soon as you load out. Everyone loves the band!" Fuck yeah, I thought! We're on our way.

The restaurant was one of those expensive, trendy places in Midtown Manhattan: high ceilings, noisy crowds, and a menu high on kale. There were maybe twenty of us gathered around the table and the drinks were flowing. Travis was at the head of the table and I could sense he was uncomfortable. After twenty minutes he excused himself to go to the men's room.

"Where's Travis?" Said the A&R guy from Sony. I gave the manager answer, "He went to the men's room and should be right back." "Yeah, we've been looking for him. I want to tell him how much we enjoyed the band." I ran all over the two floors of the restaurant but Travis was nowhere to be found. A guy, who had never been in New York, with little to no money in his pocket, had left everyone behind and just walked out on to the streets. When I asked the band if he said anything they responded in unison, "That's Travis." Most musicians would kill to be in this position. And most managers would commit multiple murders to be in this position. Even if Sony weren't the right home for RFR, I would use my skills to put the group in a bidding war with a label that was right for them. So "where's Travis" had to be found — and New York is a big fucking city.

Exasperated, I returned to the hotel and knocked on Travis's door. The door opened and I breathed a sigh of relief. But the dude at the door wasn't Travis. By all appearances he looked like a homeless urchin. "Where's Travis?" I howled. "He's right there on the floor." The homeless dude slurred. They both looked like the demons were kicking in. I stayed in that room for hours until the homeless — whatever he was — dude left. Exhausted, I returned to my room.

At what point do you stop banging your head into the wall? Travis is smart and intuitive. I knew he was turned off by the corporate record label behemoth with its king at the helm. I even agreed with him. However, his extreme reaction of walking out on the very people who believed in him enough to fly his ass out to New York was dangerous, even lethal to his career. The music business is a small world and I knew word would spread like wildfire. It may be all about the music, but it can't be all about the pain. Still, I had one last idea up my sleeve.

I remembered a friend at RCA Records in New York who worked in A&R. He loved music that was real and not manu factured. For sure, he would understand RFR. "Hey Owen, haven't heard from you in a long time. You still managing?" "Well, Yeah, I thought I had left that behind, but I was pulled out of retirement by the group. I'd like to send you a song and get your feedback. Everyone in LA is chasing the group." "What kind of deal are you looking for?" He said. "I need a label that believes in the old school way of building an act — you know, grassroots stuff: colleges, clubs, and targeted marketing. This is an organic act, and I need someone who understands them. It can be done for little money. They already have a following in Los Angeles, on the Central Coast and San Francisco. Can you help?" "Have to say I'm intrigued, send me the demo."

The RCA guy got back within minutes of hearing RFR's demo. "I'll be in LA next week. If they are as good live as what I heard on the demo they'd be perfect for the new indic-incubator arm of our label. We start off small, and develop the act city by city. If they show growth and break through we "kick them upstairs" to our major label distribution and promotion. The group will have all the personal attention they need since we're only selecting a few acts for this plan. These guys sound like the perfect candidates." What I heard was a dream come true. "Sounds perfect, and I know the group will go for the concept. They're working on new songs right now so the only place you can hear them live is during rehearsal at The Doors House." Whoops, did I just say that?

The RCA guy came out to LA and listened to Rain Fur Rent rehearse at The Doors House. "They're the real deal Owen." Came the phone call once the he was back in New York. I'd like to set up a showcase for the group in LA and have the Senior Vice President of BMG/RCA fly out and hear them. If he gives the okay we'll make you an offer."

RCA rented a large rehearsal space in Hollywood and I filled it with a hundred guests. RFR went on for a half hour and dazzled. Travis and the band pulled it off with the natural ability of a band on their seventh album and walked off the stage in triumph. The Sr. VP of BMG/RCA approached me and said, "Let's go welcome Travis and the band to the label!" I was so proud: I was proud for my artist, I was a proud papa cheering for my son at the school play, and I was proud of myself for staying with it and delivering the band their dream. The Sr. VP and I walked around the rehearsal space to deliver the message but Travis was nowhere to be found.

As we walked outside Travis showed up from the alley behind the rehearsal space — cigarette in hand. I breathed a sigh of relief. He approached us, and the Sr. VP put out his hand to welcome him to the label. Travis took a long drag off his cigarette, held it, and then blew the smoke in the guy's face. "No one listens to music on your label," he said, rocking back and forth. "It's all about indie music labels these days!" I knew what happened. Travis went into the alley and caught a demon. And like in the movie The Exorcist, the demon was now doing the talking. I stepped on his foot as hard as I could, trying to drive the demon out. "Sorry guys, I'm not putting RCA's money into that." The big dude then turned on his heels, and walked off into the

Hollywood night. The band's dreams up in smoke like the last of Travis's cigarette. Rain Fur Rent was over.

Year's later…

"Hey Owen, I've got an idea for Travis," Kevin Carvel said. Kevin was the Atlantic A&R guy who heard RFR at a club early on. "You know what happened, I said." "Yeah, and I heard you put the wrath of God into him. Do you still talk to him?" "I may be crazy but I still believe in him. What's up?" "I remember you telling me he was a huge fan of the group Blind Melon." I interrupted Kevin, "Right, and the group who had massive success in the 90's when the lead singer, Shannon Hoon OD'd. Thanks for reminding me. I was sure that was going happen to us." "Well, the two major members of that group, Chris and Brad, have a studio now and are successfully producing acts. It would be a natural for them to produce Travis." "Okay, I'll call Travis, let's go meet them."

The three of us pulled into the parking lot of the studio in North Hollywood. Like most studios it was innocuous, even grungy on the outside. Once inside, it was a clean, professional studio meant for hard work. Chris and Brad came out and chatted with us in the lobby. Then, they asked Travis if he'd like to come into the studio and sing and play a song or two. I could tell Travis was home. He was at ease; he was with people he admired musically and professionally. After playing a couple of original songs it was obvious the Blind Melon guys felt the same way. Then they asked Travis if he knew any Blind Melon songs. Without hesitation he broke into a Blind Melon song and the room fell silent. Travis brought us to a place where we all experienced an uncanny sense of déjà vu. He channeled Shannon Hoon. We all felt it.

"Are you that connected to our band? It's a little scary" One of the producers offered. And with that, Travis removed his t-shirt to reveal a large outlined drawing of Shannon Hoon tattooed on his back. Once again, the room fell silent. Wheels were turning.

Standing there, I knew that Chris and Brad never fully realized their dream with Blind Melon due to Shannon Hoon's death. And would Travis, his own dreams dashed, be the one to complete the Blind Melon dream? Chris and Brad decided to reform Blind Melon around Travis. Today, Blind Melon, with Travis as lead singer, continues to tour festivals around the United States and around the world. And I heard that Travis was also singing lead in a super-group with Robby Krieger from The Doors on guitar, Robert DeLeo from Stone Temple Pilots on bass, and Rami Jaffe from Foo Fighters on keyboards.

Even though I don't see Travis much I'm proud of him. He taught me that, as an artist, finding your true home is as important as the air you breathe. It leaves less space for demons to reside. As Prince once taught me, "Music soothes the savage beast."

The moment was bittersweet for all of us: Travis, Chris and Brad, the labels, and me. For me, it was the realization that there had been a seismic shift in the music business since the last time I'd managed an artist. I was still potent at getting new acts in the door, but artist development at the labels was out the window. Being talented wasn't good enough — you had to bring an audience and built-in sales with you. The labels, in a panic over illegal file sharing and loss of revenues, were busy killing the new technology rather than embracing the future. Travis was home with the help Blind Melon, but performing their hits from the past came at the expense of his own writing. And Brad and Chris wanted to step back in time because their dream had been snatched away. We were all refugees from the great age of popular music.

As for me — I returned to my home at the ocean and jumped back into my dream — and onto a sailboat.

California Daydreamin'

"You can't go home again. But you can go back for 36 minutes/35 seconds and drag 300 people with you."

PART I: FEBRUARY 2015

There's a window above my office desk, its blinds shuttered so I can focus. The blind's thin brown slats are warped, their outer edges sun-bleached from shielding the desert heat. Warped blinds are a small price to pay for the warm winters in Los Angeles; I know, I'm from Minneapolis, Minnesota.

Beneath the wounded blinds is my desk, a proud guardian of secrets. It has just enough room for a Mac, two speakers, and a table lamp. The lamp's skewed shade coats the desktop in a wash of red twilight. On the desk's surface is a functioning stew of chaos: privileged legal docs from record labels, multi-page royalty reports freed from their clasps, and bits of low tech Post-it notes. They lay hither and there — topped with a crumple of restaurant receipts as garnish. Brown-stained rings from the bottom of coffee cups appear on the surface of unopened envelopes. There are so many rings on one envelope; it's like a felled tree revealing its age. I count the rings; it has been waiting nine days to be opened. Procrastination? No, just my rebellious way of saying, "Don't fuck with me today, I've got things to do." My desk is where numbers whisper their truths before others are allowed to scream the lies; where the realization of an artists past creative dream is reflected in today's tears of certainty. The items on my desk remind me that although music has the power to unite people, it's the business side that can tug and pull them apart. And like an old-timer in the biz once advised me, "Hey schmuck, it's not called show art, it's not called show friends, it's called show business — goddammit!"

Today, as usual, I'm steeped in paper pandemonium. Before me lay myriad spreadsheets, confidential contracts, and listings of private financial assets. This time it's the Bobby Darin Estate. Bobby Darin, once married to film star Sandra Dee, was a serious musical prodigy before his untimely death at age thirty-seven in 1973. Upon his death the estate went to their son, Dodd. By 2015, Dodd, a handsome facial mash up of his movie star mother and crooner father came to me to valuate the family legacy. Many clients come to me in hopes of understanding the worth of their inherited assets. They like to kick the tires to see what their property is worth in the marketplace. I can usually size up their intention after five minutes and jettison them in less time. I don't care how fucking big their showbiz parents were. But in this case it doesn't matter. I am a huge fan of Bobby Darin. He was part of the fabric of my life growing up. And because I am a musician I know what most others don't; Bobby Darin was not only a monster showman, but he also wrote many of his hits.

Bobby's catalog of creative works includes writing and record royalties from Bobby's first hit record, "Splish-Splash" in 1958, to "Dream Lover," Mack the Knife," Beyond The Sea," "If I Were a Carpenter," and countless other hit recordings. My bleary-eyed task is to strategically assemble and categorize the last five years of the estate's income streams from writing, recording, performing, and acting before presentation to potential suitors.

After hours of intense concentration the numbers begin to swirl — my vision reduced to a burning squint. In need of a break, I yank the blinds open with a click. Outside, the deep blue California sky stretches onward to a rugged mountain scape. The mountain is dotted on either side by reaching palms, and a solitary sky-bound seagull. I can hear the distant hum of a lawnmower. Instant relief; I love winter in Los Angeles.

Why did I move to Los Angeles from Minneapolis, Minnesota? Well, primarily for the music business. But truth be told, I also fled the bone-chilling cold. For many folks, the Minnesota winter is like a joyful Currier and Ives painting — sleighs of laughing bundled-up children being pulled through the lily-white snow by prancing horses; fathers waving as they carry freshly cut wood to keep home fires burning.

But for me, the anxiety of the looming bitter cold would appear by September, and full-on panic would set in by the end of October. In November, dead leaves falling to the brown ground, leaving black trees naked against grey skies was enough to send me screaming into the night. And by December, full on depression would set in as freezing temps brought the snow and ice — everything in my world reduced to monochromatic pointlessness.

Minnesota is a truly wonderful place to live, but I'm a sailor, not a skier. So, at age forty-five I did the math. I figured conservatively that if I lived to age seventy-five I'd only have thirty summers left in my life. But if I made the move to Los Angeles I'd have ninety summers to enjoy the Pacific Ocean! The decision was easy — get the fuck out. But like my blinds, the endless Shangri La summer in Los Angeles is a bit warped too; pictures can be deceiving.

No "Splish-Splash" here, California is in the throes of its worst drought in history and things are getting scary. They tell us it's conceivable that we might run completely out of water.

The State has recycled some catchy sayings for bathroom activities — "Sing shorter songs," and "If it's yellow let it mellow, if it's brown flush it down." The elites of Beverly Hills who continue to water their lawns in defiance of the ban are labeled as; "self absorbed assholes," while those with yellowing lawns in the suburbs of the San Fernando Valley are hailed as heroes. The city has urged people to turn in violators, pitting neighbor against neighbor; the fines are steep. Artificial turf is all the rage. And in the back of everyone's mind is the nagging fear that the cheerful, blue sky will do us all in.

I close my eyes and daydream that storm clouds are building. The clouds transform from innocent white puffs to grey-black billows and begin to whirl — bringing darkness to midday. The crack of distant thunder grows louder as flashes of electricity draw closer. I hear the first pregnant droplets strike my window with a ping and a pang; then, the expectant clouds deliver with a roar.

I imagine the neon signs in Hollywood's coffee shops and souvenir joints resonating as red and yellow splotches in the rain slick streets and star-studded sidewalks — sun seeking tourists scrambling for shelter. In the hills, high above Sunset Boulevard the sweet fragrance of tropical eucalyptus and night-blooming jasmine, released by the downpour, are free to permeate in LA's steamy hills and canyons. Atop the hill, I imagine a lone woman glaring out from a floor to ceiling window — the insidious fog interrupting her million-dollar view. Down below, the un-captured water that cleansed the grime and sins from my city of angles feeds uselessly into the LA River as it meanders past the prosperous and the penniless. In its final gesture, the river will deposit its unholy muddle into the open arms of the Pacific Ocean — dissipating forever, like so many Hollywood dreams.

Awake from my stupor, I find myself reflecting back to summers in Minneapolis. Why the sudden nostalgia? Was I now like Hubert Humphrey? — "He was always a Minnesotan, and always a son of the prairie. There was something in this land and its lakes and, especially its people, that fed the springs of love, the strains of ideas, and the torrents of enthusiasm". This is all true. But going deeper, I recall that Minneapolis was home to warm summer rains, where everything the winter sought to destroy awakens with an explosion of lush-green.

This February day, however, is just another dehydrated day in LA, and I have to deal with it. And besides, the Minnesota lush—green lasts for about three months before everything slips back into the abyss of frozen toes. Now, somewhat reconstituted, I close the misshapen blinds with a clack — and get back to work.

What I don't know is that within a few hours a simple email will force me to jump into life's rear view mirror and take a wild musical trajectory back in time. It will take me back to my hometown, and back to an understanding of the very core of my childhood.

PART II: YEP, LATER IN THE DAY

Back at my desk I'm pouring through the results of Darin's remarkable writing, performing, and acting career. Stark numbers have a tendency to reveal human brilliance. What stands out is that Darin managed to make the impossible transition from girl-swooning teen idol, to respected crooner, to serious folk artist, and even, after changing his name to Bob Darin, to an activist singer/songwriter. He floated seamlessly in and out of these personas with the ease of a musical triathlete. In my book he was a genius of invention and reinvention.

When "Splish Splash" hit in 1958 Pop music was so new that the artists were actually creating this new genre at the same time the business moguls were inventing and scheming the business side.

For the artists, there were no rules to creativity; they were free to explore the boundaries of their talent. Pop radio would play all genres of music — Pop, Rock, Country, Blues, and Soul, as long as the kids called in and requested it. Yeah, there was payola to get records played but if the kids couldn't dance to it, cop a feel to it, or cry to it — it was gone. Not so in today's pre-programmed, copycat world I think.

With the exception of Bobby Darin, few pop performers back in the day actually wrote and performed their own music. From the mid fifties to the early sixties there were those who wrote the music, those who performed the music, and the connivers who owned the music. For Darin, and a host of others, the Brill Building in New York was where it all came together under one roof — writers, performers, and owners. And for those who owned the music there were definitely no rules — it was truly the Wild West. Unfortunately, there were many gunfights at the OK Corral. Many unaware artists were left wounded on the battlefield — some mortally. It would be a few more years before the creative folks realized that there really were two words to, "show business" and begin take charge of their career.

I started playing guitar in the early sixties. Back then, I was free to explore too. There were no rules either. Just try your best to make great music and forget about what genre or what age group the song would appeal to. Practicing ceaselessly in my parent's basement I learned how to glide between the sounds of Folk music, Surf music, and the old Blues masters. And right behind me is the last vestige of that time.

My 50 year-old Fender Stratocaster has been cradled in its perch for so long I can't remember the last time I played it. Its once shiny black body is now dulled, nicked, and dented to the wood; it's neck worn dark from my fingers racing up and down the fret board. There was a time in my life when a guitar never left my hands. Back in my Minneapolis band days in the 60's there were countless times when I would suddenly awake at four in the morning, my guitar splayed across my chest like a first date who had accidentally stayed the night. Now, my relationship with my Strat is more like running into a past love in a neighborhood bar. Crying in our beer, we recall the good times; "We made some beautiful music together, didn't we babe?"

Since that time I have managed music, promoted music, and bought and sold music. But I haven't made or performed music in nearly 50 years. I am a musician who has evolved into a music businessman. Managing artists, running record labels, and brokering the sale of music catalogs has only kept me close to the music. In my soul of souls I am a musician but as a true artist, music has left the building — a sad thought.

The pictures on my office walls are framed relics from a past century. And they offer me a bit of solace: A letter from Dick Clark, a proof sheet of Prince's first test shots, a letter I wrote to Warner Bros telling them to ONLY use the name Prince — no last name, and no "The" before Prince. There's Kenny Rogers and me signing some deal, and an historic picture from a party I threw at Canter's Deli for the famed Brill Building songwriters.

But it's the pictures from when I was a musician that stand out to me: there's a black and white poster of our band from 1965 that screams, "Teen Dance! Ages 17 to 19 ONLY — The High Spirits — Hear their Top Ten hit recording, "Turn On Your Love Light" — Get your tickets! Only 5 days left!!!! Antioch Town Hall, Kansas City." There we are: six cute little guys, smiles all around, donned in seersucker suits, me with a guitar resting on my shoulder. We're all standing in a circle around a painted drumhead that cheerfully announces, "The High Spirits" in block lettering. I call that picture B.D. — before drugs. Next to it is a large black and white poster from 1967. This time "The High Spirits," is spelled out in twisted curls of psychedelic lettering. The band members are now dressed in ankle-length paisley robes and flowing scarfs, our faces half-shadowed, and our hair creeping past our shoulders. I'm leaning back in a contorted pose wailing on the guitar. I call that poster, A.D. — after drugs.

There is even a vinyl bootleg album of our band on the wall. The cover is a grainy black and white picture of us performing on stage somewhere in 1966. In front of the stage kids are staring up at us, others are dancing up a storm. I purchased the bootleg in the 90's at Tower Records on Sunset; so proud that my band had achieved enough notoriety that a thief wanted to rip us off.

And in the very middle, scotch taped to the wall, is a tattered and yellowed piece of paper with a quote from Albert Einstein that I've had with me as long as I can remember. It reads, "Great Spirits Have always encountered violent opposition from mediocre minds." — My Mantra.

An email pops up on my screen with a sharp ding. It's a reminder to save the date for my 50th high school reunion back in Minnesota. They wanted to know everything about me: Was I still alive? And if so, what I was doing? Where did I live? How many kids do I have? What's your wife's name? I was surprised they didn't ask if my prostate was enlarged, and if so, did I have trouble urinating. "Log on to our website and tell us!" But how could it be fifty fucking years?

Logging on to the 50th reunion website my band's song, "Turn on Your Love Light" came up and began to play! They didn't forget! Back then we had a very large regional hit with "Love Light." It was originally a blues/R&B hit by Bobby "Blue" Bland. Our cover was a white boy, garage-band version. It reached #3 on both stations in our hometown and spread to nineteen other major U.S. cities.

My high school identified heavily with the band. Three of our band members went to the school. 1965 was also a unique watershed year for graduates on the cusp of saying farewell to their childhood innocence. Rock and Roll was scarcely ten years old and growing exponentially by the minute. Drugs, rebellion of 1950's values, and the sexual revolution were just evolving. Viet Nam would soon kill or maim many of us. And the raw, bluesy, free-spirited music of our school band served as a gateway into a budding counter-culture revolution.

I never partied with my classmates at my all night graduation party. Instead, my band played it as a gig. After that party we left out on a local tour, then a much larger regional tour, and my life changed forever. We had a fairly successful record, our own small bus, a little money in our pockets, and groupies. To be certain, we were junior rock stars.

Alone in my office a nostalgic wave from back in the day swept over me with a sickening surge. How is it that the freedom of touring, playing on stage, and recording is reserved for the young? For me, the ship of rebellion and non-conformity, filtered through music, had sailed away years ago.

And then it hit me. Why not put the band back together and play the reunion? I immediately shot back a post on the reunion message board:

"Hello reunion committee — the last time The High Spirits played at SLP high school was for our all-night graduation party — almost 50 years ago...any interest if I could put the original members back together to play at the 50th reunion? Please let me know: Owen Husney."

The next morning the "OMG's" started coming in from the reunion committee. Rollie Troup, the person assigned to do music for the reunion asked me to contact the other band members and see if they were game. She was all for it. I attended grade school with Rollie so that meant I'd known her over sixty-three years. But I hadn't seen her in a half-century. Holy shit.

"Is everyone still alive?" she asked in the email. "Yup, all here. And nothing's really changed." I responded. "OMG!" Came the reply.

But that wasn't exactly accurate. Something had changed. Or better put, somebody had changed. And that would be the only glitch to the reunion. Cliff Siegel, aka "Little Cliffie Stone," was our gutsy, bad-ass lead singer in the band. He had attitude and sunglasses. His less than medium height, trim build, and a front man's snarky command of the stage gave us and the audiences reason enough to rebel. He never jumped around on stage; he'd swagger back and forth, working the ends of the stage with a coolness that commanded attention. But Cliff had transitioned to Lauren (same name as my wife) over a decade ago and was now fully a woman. When the hint of a reunion came up several years ago she didn't want to do it. "I don't want to get up on stage as a woman and sing like fucking Eric Burdon," she shot back. In disheartened retreat, I resigned myself to the fact that The High Spirits were over for good. And since Lauren was, is, and forever my best friend I respectfully never pushed it. But then again, I'm still a relentless music dog.

"Hi Lauren, it's O," I said, more than a little nervous on the call back to Minneapolis. "Dude, how are ya! How's Los Angeles?" "I'm great dudess, and you?" The call went on with another ten minutes of chitchat before I probed the question. "So, the St. Louis Park 50th reunion committee wants us to put the band back together and, uh, play next August. You up for it?" I said, bracing for the solar wind. "Listen, I really need you to hear me!" She said, sounding a tad more male than female now. "There has to be a stage. I'm not singing on the floor! All the original members have to agree to play — no subs. We have to rehearse long in advance; we can't sound like shit. They have to supply the gear, and that means a great sound system for me." A long pause, "O, you still there?" "Yeah, uh, I just wasn't expecting that answer after I asked you the last time. What changed?" "Well, to be honest, when I first transitioned it was important to me to be able to pass as female in public, which I did, and that felt good. But I still wasn't passing to myself. It's a process that's complicated and it takes time. Now, after a decade, people know me for who I am, I'm happy and comfortable with who I was meant to be. And we're still alive — so let's fuckin' rock!" And like that we were on.

I negotiated a deal with the reunion committee and gave them a list of our "demands" for the gig. The reunion would be at a Sheraton Hotel in the western suburbs of Minneapolis so we had the hall and our stage. There would be another band for the evening so we would show up with our instruments, plug into their amps, and play seven or eight songs. In exchange, we wouldn't charge the reunion committee for our performance or my travel expenses. They quickly agreed. Hell, I would have written them a check. But please, don't tell them.

My next call was to Jon Bream, the respected and long-standing music editor of the Minneapolis Star-Tribune. Jon had not only followed The High Spirits early on but had chronicled the rise of Prince from his earliest days with me to the present. I felt the whole 50th high school/High Spirits reunion thing would make for an interesting mention in press.

"It's worthy of a story," Jon said, hearing me out. "By the way, didn't your lead singer transition to a woman?" "Yes, but please, this isn't a Caitlyn Jenner piece, it's about a band getting together after fifty years and playing back at their high school 50th reunion." "I understand, I have a friend who transitioned — you have my word." I had given Jon lots of info that was "off the record" over the years and he never broke that promise so I trusted him with the story.

Now it was time to email all the other band members. I learned a few things over the years as a manager. One was to never call people and sell them on potential. Call with it all lined up and it's almost impossible for them to back out. Of course they all agreed. And then I thought, "Fuck, it's great to be back in rock n' roll!

The drought was still on as August rolled around. Outdoors the ground had gone from dry to downright crunchy. Some asshole in Beverley Hills made headlines by continuing to water the lawns on his estate and was paying $90,000 a month in fines but the city refused to reveal his name. Those of us who were letting it "mellow" were furious.

I had been practicing guitar since April. The "big gig" was at the end of the month in August. At first I thought it would be like getting back on a bike. It was, but more like riding a bike with two broken kneecaps. The rest of the band members, Lauren, Richard, Rick, Jay, and Doug still lived back in Minneapolis so they had been rehearsing together. To help, they would email me an MP3 of rehearsal and I would play along. Good method but not perfect. My sense of timing was off and I had a difficult time keeping up with the songs the band was sending me. Playing alone for your sofa is not like playing with a live rhythm section. And my fingers became fucking sore from relearning blues licks. Playing chords is no problem but bending strings and making them "cry" without callouses on your fingertips is another. Once your fingers start to bleed you're gettin' there. So that's the reason why blues players always look and sound so sad I thought. It's not the emotion of the music it's the fucking strings digging into their fingers!

"You only want to play eight or nine songs!" five heads on one body exclaimed in unison. "Yeah, I've been doing this a long time, so don't fuck with me" I shot back. "Every song we play after seven or eight just increases our chances of sounding like shit. Leave 'em on a high note and wanting more. That's how the fucking game is played," I said, with my old manager hat on. I knew from my management days that bands should never be democracies. Democracies just get bogged down in equal votes and favoritism. The bands that make it big are ruled by a talented jerk that believes they have the vision to call the shots.

We finally settled on:

"Baby Please Don't Go"
"I Believe" (original song, follow up to our "hit")
"Bright Lights Big City"/ "On Broadway" (Medley)
"Unchain My Heart"
"Midnight Hour"
"Around and Around"
"Runaway"
Turn On Your Love Light" (our "hit")
"Come On Up" (encore!)

The following Tuesday I was sailing on a plane headed back to my hometown of Minneapolis; my Texas Stratocaster in the luggage hold beneath me as I said goodbye to the scorched earth of Los Angeles. I was so happy to be on my musical way to the Midwest. Here I was, on tour again, if only for a night.

Two vodkas in I closed my eyes and allowed the hum of the plane to take over. There's a silent comfort in doing so despite the occasional outbursts of babies and other humans. I reflected on how I got "here." I wouldn't call it a journey as much as random events of dumb luck, stupidity, and life lessons learned.

Bringing It All Back Home

PART I — AUGUST 2015: REFLECTING
ON YOUR LIFE IS A BITCH

I was on my way back to Minneapolis to play at my 50th high school reunion. The last time I played at the high school was for my graduation all night party — exactly fifty years ago. Halfway through the flight back to Minneapolis I decided to make notes of some of my life experiences. I'd been telling stories from my life for more than thirty years: at business lunches, countless family events, and at dinners with friends. And people would always say, "You should write that down!" But isn't that what everyone says when they're being kind behind a backdrop of boredom?

It would be nice to think of only the good times, but they're enmeshed with the painful ones. It's like an Escher drawing with one emotion feeding into the other in an endless loop. When I thought of my first guitar I remembered the bully who wanted to smash it. When I looked into the mirror of my childhood I remembered the loneliness that seemed to follow a singular happy event. Should I dredge this stuff up? Would it be like pulling the scab off of an old wound — the renewed pain sending me flying back to a therapist's couch? Why would my experiences matter? I began scribbling notes on a legal pad.

Story after story swirled in my head as the plane touched down — then it hit me. Because my old band was playing at the 50th reunion of my high school, I wasn't just going back home; I was going back to 1965 — the year that brought me from pain to passion. While taxiing to the gate I wondered if the football guys were once again plotting my demise — fifty years later. Do 68 year olds still wear letter jackets and get into fistfights? Would my female classmates, who are probably grandmothers today, still appreciate our band's gritty sound; a sound that once awakened them from a carnal darkness? Had I unwittingly stepped into a time machine only to return to disappointment and pain?

I showed up at rehearsal the next day. Like in the old days were back in the basement. This time it was our drummer Doug's basement; a beautiful home a stone's throw from Paisley Park. Back in the day we rehearsed in the basement of my parent's tiny home because my mother was mostly deaf. Her only compliant was the constant, "Thumping." I hadn't seen most of my band mates for over twenty years. When we met up again we complimented each other, "Damn man, you still look the same!" But we knew we didn't. The person who didn't look quite the same was our lead singer Cliff who transitioned to Lauren. She looked the best of any of us. But none of that mattered today — because today was about the music.

Famed *Minneapolis Star-Tribune* Entertainment Editor, Jon Bream, was there too. And here he was back in the basement with the High Spirits! Would he really write about us? What if we sucked? I could see the headline, "Time for The High Spirits to put down their instruments and pick up the grandkids!" Maybe I shouldn't have asked him to stop by. After twenty minutes of chit chat it was time to pick up our instruments.

Lauren counted down, "One, two, three, four..." and we broke into, "Around & Around." The song, originally written and performed by Chuck Berry was covered early on by both the Rolling Stones and The Animals. Ours was a combo version of all three and we played it all the way through the first time. Holy shit, the magic that brought us together over fifty years ago was still there — we kicked ass! Where does magic come from, and where does it hide for almost fifty years? Is there a large warehouse in Omaha that stores artistic magic when not being used? And what happens to unclaimed magic? Is it sold to the highest bidder of a new generation? Well, The High Spirits reclaimed the magic that afternoon in Doug's basement as we reeled off one song after another. Jon brought along a photographer who snapped away as we journeyed back to 1965. Holy shit, this is a blast. We even talked about performing a few gigs a year for special events though we knew it would never happen. We wrapped up rehearsal with high-fives all around.

The next evening my wife and I arrived at the Sheraton Hotel in St. Louis Park. I was ready to kick ass for the reunion celebrants. A stern woman with a name tag was seated at a folding table outside the hall. She locked eyes with me and almost tripped over herself as she made her way over to us. There was urgency in her voice. "Do you know that people are crashing our sacred reunion? Word got out on Facebook and they're coming from all over the city! You need to do something." "What can I do?" I said. "You need to tell them they have to go home! This is OUR reunion!" Too bad, I thought. She doesn't realize she's dealing with an ex-manager. "Look, there's a reporter for the Star Tribune here, a film crew here, Bobby Z and Matt Fink from Prince's Revolution are here, and there's people from other high schools who's lives we touched some fifty years ago. We have a choice: kick 'em out now and cause a scene — in which case the band will pack up and go home — or give the St. Louis Park High School class of '65 the best fucking reunion anyone could ask for. It's up to you."

The High Spirits jumped on stage amid cheers from a standing room only crowd. Organizer Rollie Troup got up on stage and said, "The last time The High Spirits played the school was forty nine years ago at our graduation party. So ladies and gentlemen, The High Spirits!" Lauren was not on stage yet as cheers went up across the room. We broke into an instrumental opening of "Baby Please Don't Go" while rhythm guitar player Rick spoke up over the music, "Ladies and gentlemen, The High Spirits were the first band in the Twin Cities to have a lead singer as a designated front person. So now, I want to introduce to you the poster child for David Bowie's song, "Ch-ch-ch Changes, — the artist formerly known as little Clifford Stone — here's Lauren Siegal!" Lauren looked beautiful as she hit the stage. She was wearing a black top with a calf-length open shirt. Her white distressed jeans were tucked into knee-high red boots. I was jealous for a moment; if only I could wear makeup I'd look fifteen years younger too! Her long brown hair had several streaks of blonde on the right side that complemented her dangling earrings and silver strands of necklace. Her transition had served her well. And when Lauren got on stage she was all rock n' roll. Taking the mike from its stand she hollered out, "Are we gonna rock and fuckin' roll!! At once, a sea of baby boomers rushed the stage, smartphones in hand, filming and shooting pictures of The High Spirits as we broke into a hard-hitting version of, "Baby Please Don't Go." The place exploded. I spotted my wife Lauren (yes, Lauren too) in the crowd. She was raised in Los Angeles and was seven years old when our record broke. But there she was, iPhone in hand, snapping away with a big smile on her face.

The next morning, spread across the front page of the *Star-Tribune* entertainment section was the headline, "Rock 'n' roll high school: High Spirits shake up St. Louis Park's 50-year re-union." There was even a full picture of my son, Jordan, hugging Lauren Siegel.

The article continued — "No one is looking at the old photos on display in the hall. No one is grabbing a piece of the cake decorated with "50" in orange and black, the school colors. No one is even at the bar getting a drink.

Everyone at the St. Louis Park High School class of 1965 reunion is fixed on the band on stage at the Sheraton Minneapolis West.

Before you can say "there were 850 students in our class," the hotel ballroom's dance floor is jumping. Women dancing with women. Guys twirling gals around and around. These people are 68 years old!

By the time the High Spirits get to "Turn on Your Love Light," these Social Security types are standing on chairs to get a view of the band."

So you can go home if only for 36 minutes and 35 seconds.

PART II — 2016: THE UNIMAGINABLE

I returned home to drought driven Los Angeles with memories of Minneapolis, past and present, tied up in a neat bow. Now it was time to see if I could actually write down some of the pivotal moments from my life. The plane flights had given me just enough time to jot down the highlights. Then, I began to write in earnest. I learned that discipline is key. I tried writing the late night way: after Lauren went to bed I'd run down to my office and fire up the Mac. But within minutes I grew so tired I lay down on the couch in my office and slept. I tried the "Hemmingway:" after dinner; I poured a big martini and began to write — only to find myself facedown on my desk in a drooling stupor. I tried the Ken Kesey way: at four in the afternoon I smoked a big joint only to find myself looking up great comedy performances on YouTube and laughing my ass off. But then I found the key — get up at 6:30 a.m., grab a big coffee, and write until 9:00 or 10:00 a.m. Eventually the words flowed. And, as an added bonus, relentless rains came to my City of Angels forcing me to hang indoors. Chapter after chapter, hilarious and painful, began to flow.

I was almost finished with my memoir — and then — the unimaginable happened.

The Unimaginable

APRIL 21, 2016, 7:41 AM:

As usual, a cup of coffee accompanied me to my desk for the morning write. It was a short ride to my downstairs home office. I had decided in January that I would push my day job aside and finish my book. The caveat was that I had to practice strict discipline; that meant waking early and knocking out at least four hours a day — no matter what. Today, as every day, I sat at my desk in my socks and skivvies and hammered out a sentence that would probably be deleted sooner or later.

My cell rang and I noticed the familiar area code of St. Paul Minnesota — 651. Doesn't this idiot know it's freaking early in Los Angeles? "Hallo," I belted. "Is this Owen Husney?" The authority of his voice perplexed me. "Yeah, what can I do for ya?" "This is Craig Cheatham, Asst. News Director at KSTP-TV in the Twin Cities. Can we get a comment?" "About what?" "There was a body found at Paisley Park this morning." "So, why are you asking me?" I snarled, "Someone probably fell off the scaffolding on the sound stage. Call Prince's publicist if you want to know who it is." "Well, we think its Prince." A long beat ensued. "You want a comment from me, and you THINK its Prince? Why don't you call me when you fucking KNOW." I said, never even considering the possibility, and furious at his newshound insinuation. "Can I have your email, Mr. Husney?" Twenty minutes later a Chanhassen Minnesota Police report showed up on my screen. In part, it said:

"Carver County Sheriff Jim Olson reports that on April 21, 2016, at or about 9:43 am (CDT), Sheriff's deputies responded to a medical call at Paisley Park Studios in Chanhassen. First Responders attempted to provide lifesaving CPR, but were unable to revive the victim. He was pronounced dead at 10:07 am. He has been identified as Prince Rogers Nelson (57) of Chanhassen."

As I read the report everything in my periphery turned dark. Only the words on screen were visible — like light at the end of a long black tunnel. I read the words again, "He has been identified as Prince Rogers Nelson (57) of Chanhassen."

My cell rang again. "Mr. Husney? This is Craig Cheatham, KSTP. Did you get my email? I was wondering if you could give us a statement." I mumbled something about one of the greatest loses in the history of contemporary music, hung up, and went back into the tunnel as a single tear found it's way down my face.

I sent a text to Bobby Z with a single word: "Devastated."

Within seconds he texted me back: "Beyond devastated."

My wife Lauren called from her office and wanted to know if she should come home. I told her I thought I could handle it but I'd call if I needed her. Lauren is Director of Child and Adolescent Services for Our House, one of the leading non-profit grief support centers in the nation.

I conference called my sons in New York and told them the news. "I'm older than him. I was supposed to go first," was all I said. Then I broke down.

There was a loud knock at my front door. Still in my skivvies I opened the door slowly while standing behind it. Outside, was every major local, national, and international news service. Microphones were shoved in my face. They were shouting, "Mr. Husney can you give us a comment? Do you believe Prince's overdose was an accident or an opioid overdose? Did you know he was an addict?"

He overdosed? *Opioids?* Prince never had a glass of wine in front of me let alone opioids. I remembered being concerned though when his plane made an emergency landing the week before after a gig Atlanta. I even called back to friends in Minneapolis once I heard the news. "Something is fucking wrong I told them." "Naw, the papers here said he had the flu."

While the gaggle of reporters hovered outside my door I called my wife back. "There's twenty people standing outside by the pool looking for a comment, and I'm in shock. There are news trucks with those huge satellite antennas in the circle. I'm sure the neighbors think I murdered someone. The reporters want to know if Prince was a drug addict. How the fuck did they find me?! Why do they care about me?!" Lauren suggested I speak to the press. "It will help you through your shock." She was right.

But why were they interested in talking to me? Prince had accomplished near-miracles in his career since we were together. Certainly there were those close to him now who could offer insight to a curious public. Then I realized: as highly visible as Prince became once fame hit, his personal life was just as shrouded in secrecy. They presumed there must be clues to the "real" person hidden in his earliest beginnings — before the veneer of super-stardom.

I showered, and invited the press in one by one: CBS, NBC, ABC, BBC, German television, local television and so many more. I would not allow the interviews to veer into drugs, and I would not allow them to ask me about present day Prince, or what he was thinking. I would only talk about the young, beautiful, gifted kid who showed up at my door in Minneapolis one fall day in 1976 — and how he was able to impact the world through his music.

I said goodbye to the last reporter and collapsed in the chair in our bedroom. My cellphone rang and it was CNN. "We'd like to put you live on-air with Brooke Baldwin in five minutes." I told them I'd agree as long there would be no mention of drugs and I'd only discuss the time I was with him. Brooke conducted a very respectful interview. I hung up and my phone rang. "Owen, this is CNN again. Anderson Cooper heard your interview and would like to speak with you live on-air tonight. I agreed and hung up.

I did another fifteen interviews from the chair. I knew no one would understand it, but I saw it as my duty to get out ahead of the story and keep it to the gift Prince had given us all through his music. I was still protecting him — even though it was from my small vantage point, and almost forty years later.

I sat in the CNN green room with Van Jones, a man I had seen on television almost daily. We'd never met before. I was just some guy in the green room. But that didn't matter, I couldn't speak, and at the end of this day I didn't have the energy to introduce myself. Someone called my name and I was led to a small dark room with a TV camera and a monitor. I forgot that Anderson was in New York and I would be in one of those boxes on the screen. Within minutes Anderson's face appeared on the monitor and a red light showed on the camera.

"Owen Husney was Prince's first manager and he joins us now…"

After the interview I was waiting in the CNN lobby for the car to take me home. Van Jones walked past me and out the door. Our eyes met through the glass. He stopped, took a beat, and raised his hand in a gesture that said, "I know."

Closure

2016:

In May, Lauren and I were invited to attend a private memorial service for Prince at The Academy of Motion Pictures Arts and Sciences in Beverly Hills. Prince's former wives, Mayte Garcia and Manuela Testolini, hosted the memorial. Friends and family, Warner Bros execs, ex-band members, and a who's who from Larry King to Spike Lee showed up to say their tearful goodbyes. It was nice to hear and share stories with folks I hadn't seen in years.

I left feeling empty.

They were grieving the loss of an icon. I was grieving the young, vulnerable, eighteen year old who showed up at my house in Minneapolis one fall day in 1976. The teen with the intellect and drive of a man three times his age; the teen with a teddy bear smile that could change your way of thinking in a heartbeat — the teen with the courage of a lion and the talent to prove it.

I've had a reoccurring dream for the past forty years. The night after the memorial was no exception. It goes like this: Prince shows up at my doorstep. I invite him in and we laugh like the old days, and then he plays me a new song that blows me away. But I know it's just a dream. Usually I awake with a warm feeling, but this time I awake feeling cheated.

Maybe he would have been in his seventies, me in my eighties, and we'd bump into each other at some music awards event where he was being honored. Perhaps on one of my return trips to Minneapolis I'd wheel my walker into Paisley Park. He'd hear I was in the building and we'd chat while eating soft foods. But he was found dead — alone in an elevator in an empty building. It wasn't supposed to happen that way.

There could have been that one last time.

Healing: But Who Am I?

T he Revolution, Prince's iconic band from Purple Rain, announced almost immediately after Prince's death that they would tour. At first, I thought it a quick attempt at notoriety, but soon realized it was a necessary component to healing — for the fans, and those who worked alongside him. We all needed something, and nothing heals better than music.

Bobby Z invited Lauren and I to one of the Revolution rehearsals at S.I.R. in Los Angeles. When I entered the room we hugged, one by one. The band returned to the rehearsal stage and began to sketch out the songs that had catapulted them to ultra-fame. We planned on staying a half hour at most, but as they rolled through the set I was unable to move. Hearing the songs live — exactly as Prince would have wanted them to be played — was like a thousand therapists helping me through my shock.

The following August I was invited to come to Minneapolis and see the Revolution play at First Avenue — the famous club where Prince played often and where he filmed Purple Rain. My oldest son, Jordan, flew in from New York to join me.

The day before the concert we attended the Minnesota State Fair — something I hadn't done in over twenty years. We walked endlessly through the fairgrounds: the midway with its rides and barkers, the animal barns, and we strolled past booths selling everything edible on a stick. We walked into the horticultural building to view my cousin's annual ribbon-winning vegetables. On the way to my cousin's display I noticed something peculiar. On the walls were the winners of the yearly "seed art" competition. The one rule for the competition was simple: the different color seeds must be authentic seeds used by farmers in Minnesota. To be honest, the artwork was beautiful. The seeds are arranged and affixed to paper to form an art piece that is supposed to reflect something truly Minnesotan: a landscape, a rural setting, and perhaps, a past founding father. But this year the dominant seed-art pieces were all Prince! Beautiful likenesses, his iconic symbol, and gorgeous album cover representations adorned the walls. My first impulse was to laugh. But then I realized that the entire state of Minnesota was mourning Prince. From its largest cities, to the furthest stretches of its hinterland, Prince made Minnesotans proud. He never left the state, he was theirs, and now he was gone. Oddly, standing there I felt more comfortable and at peace than at any time since Prince's passing. I was home.

The following evening The Revolution took the stage at First Avenue and played their hearts out. A packed venue moved in unison to one celebrated hit after the next. I saw a thousand faces from my past: all reminders of my birthplace, and the city that shaped me. The healing had begun.

* * * *

A few months later I was asked to return to Minneapolis. My office in the building at 430 Oak Grove was receiving an historical plaque. The building, now an upscale apartment complex, was home to my Ad Company, and the very office where Chris Moon first played me the demo he and Prince recorded. Later, it would become American Artists Management, and the home where Prince, Andre, and Bobby Z would jam late into the night as my humble tape machine recorded all for posterity. It was one of the places in the city that was being honored as ground zero to the "Minneapolis Sound." Andre Cymone rightfully joined me for the presentation. Together, we signed the wall outside my office door where the plaque would be enshrined. Once again, my life had come full circle.

After the installation I got in my car and drove to every location that was meaningful to my life: The big home where I lived as a child, the tiny apartment we had to move to, the small house we settled in where my band was born. I drove past St. Louis Park high school (watching out for bullies in letter jackets), the Marigold Ballroom, now a Hyatt Hotel, the Minneapolis

Armory, the Minneapolis auditorium, and all the apartments and homes I lived in along the way. I drove past the first apartment we rented for Prince after we signed him to a management contract, and the second home we rented for him on France Avenue.

I knocked on the door at 4248 Linden Hills Blvd. The surprised occupants wanted to know who I was, and why I was there. I explained that it was the home where my former wife, Britt, and I lived when I first met Prince. The owners were fans, and stunned to know that he had hung out there. I showed them the "Whitman" photo of Prince and my dog sitting on their living room floor. We sat in the den, and I told them this was the room where Prince and I watched "Roots" together. I showed them another photo of Prince playing piano in their dining room. I left them speechless.

* * * *

That night, I headed west on 394 back to my hotel in Minnetonka. As I watched the darkening sun fade into the horizon I began to think about what my stories and experiences really meant. In the scheme of things does anyone really care what I have to say? It was a tough thought that had never occurred to me before — and to be honest, the notion frightened me.

Within seconds the answer came clearly into view.

With all my passionate adventures and musical encounters on the way to discovering Prince and others — and with all the "Famous People Who've Met Me" along the way — it shouldn't matter who cares: I was really a man on a journey to discover himself.